FORUM BOOKS

General Editor Martin E. Marty

Science and Religion

New Perspectives on the Dialogue

edited by

Ian G. Barbour

SCM PRESS LTD
LONDON

SBN 334 01550 2
© Ian G. Barbour 1968
First British edition 1968
published by SCM Press Ltd
56 Bloomsbury Street London WC1
Typeset in the United States of America
and printed in Great Britain by
Fletcher & Son Ltd
Norwich

CONTENTS

FORUM BOOKS

The editors of this series recognize the need for books of a convenient size on religion and related topics. Laymen and clergymen, students and the interested general reader can use *Forum Books* for personal study, or as a basis for group discussion. At a time when religious institutions are experiencing dramatic change, when religious ideas are being debated with new intensity, and when religious elements in culture are being called into question, the books in the series gather together examples of important writings which reproduce both historical and contemporary reflections on these subjects. Each editor has taken pains to provide helpful background comment as a context for the readings, but for the most part the selections speak for themselves with clarity and force.

MARTIN E. MARTY, *General Editor*
Divinity School
University of Chicago

Note to the British Edition

Some of the books cited in American
editions have separate British editions.
A list of these, with acknowledgements,
will be found on page 324

PREFACE

The purpose of this book is to encourage discussion, not to present a systematic set of answers. We have deliberately restricted attention to a few problems, and sought a variety of viewpoints concerning each. In Chapter 1 the various schools of thought represented in the volume are outlined; it serves as an introduction to the contributors, and views them in the context of contemporary writing about science and religion. Chapters 2 and 3 summarize recent thought among Roman Catholic and biblical scholars.

The problem of Part Two is the relation between religion and *the methods of science*. Is the scientific method the only path to knowledge? Are theology and science similar enterprises (as Coulson and Schilling argue) or are they radically different (as Evans suggests)? Such questions about the relation of religion to *science as a way of knowing* are more basic than problems arising from particular scientific theories. Many persons today find that their religious beliefs are challenged not by any specific scientific discoveries but by the conviction that assertions in science can be proven while those in religion cannot. Science has been one of the influences on the "death of God" movement, as Ferré's essay indicates. Both Ferré and Evans provide careful philosophical analyses of the problem of verifying or evaluating theological statements. The central issue of Part Two, then, is the status of religious beliefs in an age of science.

Part Three deals with the scientific concept of *evolution* and its relation to the theological concept of *creation*. On the scientific side, the idea of evolutionary history is taken to include the astonomers' theories about *the origins of stars* (see chapter by Jones) and the biochemists' theories about *the origins of life* from complex nonliving molecules (see Schmitt's chapter), as well as the biologists' theories about *the origins of animal and human forms* (see Gilkey, Teilhard, and Birch). On the theological side, the central problem is God's relation to this evolutionary process. Can we speak of God's activity in nature if the sequence of events can be explained in terms of natural forces? What kind of claim does the doctrine of creation make, and does it have anything to do with the scientific account of origins?

In Part Four we are concerned not with science as a way of knowing, nor with science as a particular content of knowledge, but with science as a way of controlling and transforming the world—that is, with *applied science* or *technology*. Should the Christian be wary of material progress because it encourages man's self-sufficiency and diverts his interest from his eternal destiny; or should the applications of science be welcomed as a form of service to the neighbor in need, alleviating poverty and disease around the world? Should *automation* be viewed as a dehumanizing force in which the machine is enslaving man, or as a liberating force which increases productivity and frees man from routine toil? The final chapters examine briefly the theological implications of three new areas of scientific advance in which the future may see dramatic discoveries: (1) *electronic computers* rival human intelligence and suggest that the mind is essentially a machine; (2) *knowledge of genetics* may enable man to control his own evolutionary future, create a new race of men, or prefabricate a new species; (3) *the existence of intelligent life on other planets* has been under serious discussion.

How will such scientific discoveries affect the Christian understanding of man?

All the authors included come from the technologically advanced, predominantly Christian West; space limitations preclude discussion of the relations between science and religion in the newly developing nations whose backgrounds lie in other religious traditions. Within this limitation, a variety of viewpoints are represented. Four of the authors are Roman Catholics (McMullin, Schmitt, Teilhard, Clarke) and one is Eastern Orthodox (Dobzhansky), while the Protestants range from neo-orthodox views (Berkhof, Gilkey, Easton) to liberal perspectives (Schilling, Birch) and more radical proposals (Ferré, Cox). In terms of occupation, the group is about equally divided between theologians, philosophers, and scientists (Coulson, Schilling, Schmitt, Birch, Teilhard and Dobzhansky), though many of these men have had training and experience in more than one field. Of the selections included, five were written specifically for this volume (Barbour, Evans, Ferré, Jones, Easton); the remainder appeared originally in the books or journals indicated on the opening page of each chapter. I am grateful to Prof. John Compton of Vanderbilt University for his assistance in the preparation of the volume.

IAN G. BARBOUR

PART ONE: INTRODUCTION

I

SCIENCE AND RELIGION TODAY

Ian G. Barbour*

In this chapter some trends in recent thought on science and religion are surveyed to provide a context for subsequent chapters.[1] *Questions of method* are the primary concern here, but the problem of *evolution and creation* is also considered. This will provide an introduction to Parts Two and Three of the volume as well (Part Four, dealing with problems of ethics and applied science, is perhaps less in need of a systematic introduction). We will focus on Protestant thought, since Father McMullin surveys the Catholic scene in the next chapter.

I. THE "CONFLICTS" OF THE PAST

Because recent thought on science and religion involves a deliberate attempt *to avoid the mistakes of the past,* we must

* Ian Barbour is Chairman of the Religion Department and Professor of Physics at Carleton College. He was formerly Chairman of the Physics Department at Kalamazoo College. He holds a Ph.D. in physics from the University of Chicago and a B.D. in theology from Yale, and has written articles in both fields. His book Christianity and the Scientist (1960) deals with the role and motives of the scientist and the ethical problems arising from the applications of science. Issues in Science and Religion (1966) discusses the methods of science and the implications of particular scientific discoveries.

[1] A more detailed exposition and discussion of these trends is given in Ian G. Barbour, *Issues in Science and Religion* (Englewood Cliffs, N.J.: Prentice-Hall, 1966), chaps. 4, 5, 12, and 13.

start by summarizing some issues which were prominent in earlier centuries:[2] (1) scriptural literalism, (2) the God of the gaps, and (3) evolutionary naturalism.

1. Scriptural Literalism

The condemnation of Galileo by the Church was the product of many complex factors,[3] among which was the fact that both the biblical narrative and Aristotelian cosmology—which together had so deeply molded Western thought—assumed that the earth is the center of the universe. The conflict in Darwin's day again involved many issues,[4] including the further demotion of man's status by the discovery of his descent from animal life; but much of the controversy centered in a literal interpretation of Genesis and belief in the once-for-all creation of each species in its present form. Conservative Christians read the Bible as divinely dictated information on scientific as well as religious topics. The only way they knew to defend the dignity of man and the idea of divine purpose in the world was to reject evolution in the name of scriptural infallibility. In the heat of the conflict, the loudest voices were those advocating extreme positions: on the one hand, a scriptural literalism in which every word of the Bible was accepted as divinely revealed, and on the other an evolutionary naturalism and modernism in which the Bible was dismissed or virtually ignored.

Increasingly prominent, however, was a middle position which actually had stronger historical precedents. The medieval Church had allowed for "allegorical interpretation" and for various "levels of truth" in the biblical message. The Protestant

[2] An excellent history of theological responses to science is John Dillenberger, *Protestant Thought and Natural Science* (Garden City, N.Y.: Doubleday & Co., 1960).

[3] See Jerome J. Langford, O.P., *Galileo, Science and the Church* (New York: Desclee Company, 1966).

[4] See John C. Greene, *The Death of Adam* (Iowa City, Iowa: Iowa State University Press, 1959) and *Darwin and the Modern World-View* (Baton Rouge, La.: Louisiana State University Press, 1961).

Reformers (especially Luther) had seen the locus of authority not in the written book itself, but in the person of Christ to whom scripture witnessed. Moreover the historical and literary analysis of biblical documents had begun to call the infallibility of scripture into question long before Darwin. By the close of the nineteenth century, evolution and biblical scholarship were widely accepted in Protestant circles; efforts by fundamentalist groups to gain control of several of the major denominations in the 1920's were unsuccessful. But this did not mean that Protestantism rejected the importance of the Bible. We will note shortly that the central concept in neo-orthodoxy was *revelation,* understood not as the divine dictation of inerrant propositions but as God's self-disclosure in the life of Israel and the person of Christ. The authors in the present volume see in Genesis the images of a prescientific cosmology used to express abiding religious insights. Scriptural literalism is no longer a major issue between science and religion.

2. *The God of the Gaps*

Newton described the solar system as a set of masses obeying mechanical laws, but he held that God must intervene periodically to readjust the planets and keep them in orbit; a century later Laplace calculated that the planetary deviations would correct themselves. Scientists of the eighteenth century assumed that various useful organs, such as the eye, had been created in their present form by divine design; Darwin showed that adaptation could be the result of natural selection operating on random variations. The "God of the gaps," invoked to explain scientifically unexplained facts, retreated further as the gaps in human knowledge were closed; in each case divine intervention was no longer needed. God's special action as a cause producing effects on the same level as natural causes was replaced by *law-obeying natural causes* in each area of scientific advance.

There are, of course, many "gaps" still remaining today, since the scientific account of the history of the universe is far from complete. In their respective chapters below, Jones discusses current astronomical theories about the origin of stars, Schmitt analyzes the transition from matter to life, and Easton discusses the possibility that intelligent life has evolved on other planets. The Christian may be tempted to claim that in each of these cases there is a gap which can only be crossed by divine intervention. But past history has taught the dangers of bringing God in as a stopgap where the scientific explanation is incomplete.

The authors in this volume speak of God's activity in various ways without postulating "intervention." (1) In Thomistic and neo-orthodox thought (Schmitt, Gilkey), evolution is God's way of creating; the "primary causality" of God is said to operate *through rather than in violation of* the "secondary causality" of natural forces—of which a potentially complete account can be given at the scientific level. (2) In existentialism, God's activity occurs *in the realm of personal existence* not in the impersonal and mechanical realm of nature which the scientist describes. A similar viewpoint is evident among linguistic philosophers (Evans, Jones), who hold that the religious function of the doctrine of creation is the expression and evocation of *present attitudes toward the world,* rather than the assertion of claims about divine action in cosmological events of the past. (3) Birch and Teilhard, however, question the prevailing mechanistic picture of nature and portray God as *an immanent influence on the cosmic process.* They seem to assume new kinds of gap in the scientific account (Birch's "chance," Teilhard's "within of things"), but I shall suggest later that these differ in important respects from the gaps of past centuries. Thus the "God of the gaps" is rejected by most theologians as well as scientists today.

3. *Evolutionary Naturalism*

Philosophies which claimed support from science also contributed to the conflicts of the past. These were as varied as

T. H. Huxley's atheistic naturalism, Herbert Spencer's evolutionary agnosticism, Haeckel's atomistic materialism, and Nietzsche's justification of an ethic of power by appeal to the evolutionary struggle for survival. Others in the late nineteenth century tried to base a modified theism on evolution. To some of the "modernists" God was an impersonal cosmic force; for all of them, divine immanence virtually replaced transcendence. In effect they "deified" the evolutionary process, making it the means of grace and the source of progress. Human dignity, which had been threatened by man's animal ancestry, was restored by making man the forefront of an inevitable cosmic advance to yet higher levels. Both God and man may have been absorbed into nature, but in the mood of Victorian optimism nature itself seemed to be moving toward a glorious future.

Naturalism and modernism still have their adherents today, but it is now more evident that they must be defended *as philosophical viewpoints* rather than as conclusions from science. Thus when Julian Huxley or C. H. Waddington use the direction of evolution ("toward greater intelligence and co-operation") as a source of ethical norms, it is clear that their commitments are not scientifically verifiable. Philosophers today are cautious about the extension of specific scientific findings into over-all cosmic principles, metaphysical systems, or ethical norms. An argument between a theist and an exponent of naturalism need be viewed no longer as a conflict between religion and science, but rather as a confrontation between "alternative world-views." Naturalism is still a live option, but it is not an issue between science and religion as such.

By the same token, most contemporary authors are cautious about *attempts to use scientific findings as evidence for theism*. Such arguments have had a long and interesting history. From Newton to Paley, many scientists saw in the skillful design of the myriad features of animal life the hand of an intelligent designer. Such a *natural theology,* which was once used as a supplement to Christian beliefs, had all but replaced the latter in eighteenth-century Deism. This form of the argument from design was undermined by Darwin, who attributed the functional usefulness of particular organs to the long, slow process of variation and selection. After Darwin the argument was reformulated by applying the concept of design not to specific organs or organisms, but to the directionality of the whole evolutionary process. Design, it was said, is built into the laws and structures through which life and mind could emerge; purpose is evidenced by the order and creativity of nature and the coordination of different levels of existence whereby intelligence and personality could come into being.

This *reformulated argument from design* is occasionally presented today, but it is not central in current writing about science and religion. Catholic thought has had a long tradition of natural theology, but always as a preamble to revealed theology rather than as a self-sufficient basis for religious beliefs. Most contemporary Protestant theologians have little interest in natural theology, and most philosophers are dubious about deriving any far-reaching metaphysical conclusions— whether naturalistic or theistic—from scientific theories. The contributors to this volume are not trying to derive theology from science, but are asking instead how the God known in Christ and in religious experience is related to the processes of nature.

II. THREE WAYS OF ISOLATING SCIENCE AND RELIGION

We have seen that in past centuries scientific and religious questions were often confused. On the one hand, literalists treated the Bible as a textbook in science. On the other, well-meaning scientists and theologians invoked the "God of the gaps" to explain the scientifically unknown, while naturalists and modernists tried to base theology on the findings of science. It is not surprising that twentieth-century thinkers wanted to preserve the integrity of both science and religion, and took great pains to put up *No Trespassing* signs between them. They insisted that each field is autonomous and should attend to its own affairs without meddling in the other's domain. This absolute separation was motivated by concern, not just to avoid the unnecessary conflicts of the past, but to be faithful to the distinctive character of each enterprise. The dominant viewpoints of recent decades have stressed the independence of the two areas as watertight compartments of human thought—thereby eliminating any possible conflict, but also preventing any possible interaction. I shall summarize three movements which have contributed to this separation: (1) the neo-orthodox emphasis on *the distinctiveness of revelation;* (2) the existentialist insistence on *personal involvement* in religious questions; and (3) the claim of analytical philosophers that scientific and religious languages *serve unrelated functions* in human life.

1. *The Distinctiveness of God's Self-Revelation*

The dominant movement in Protestant thought between the two world wars was *neo-orthodoxy,* which sought to recover the Reformation emphasis on the centrality of Christ and the primacy of revelation, while fully accepting the results of modern biblical scholarship and scientific research. According to Karl Barth and his followers, God can be known *only as he has revealed himself* in Christ and is acknowledged in faith. No argument from the world, no attempted "natural theology," can reach the transcendent God who in his freedom has disclosed himself in history—and not, except very ambiguously, in nature. Thus Berkhof states in Chapter 3 below: "Nature in itself does not reveal God." Religious faith depends entirely on divine initiative, not on human discovery of the kind by which science advances. The scientist is free to carry out his work without interference from the theologian, and vice versa, since their methods and their subject matter are totally dissimilar.[5]

[5] A neo-orthodox view is given in W. A. Whitehouse, *Christian Faith and the Scientific Attitude* (New York: Philosophical Library, 1952).

The Bible must be taken seriously but not literally, according to neo-orthodoxy. Scripture is not itself revelation; it is a fallible human record witnessing to revelatory events. The locus of divine activity was not the dictation of a text, but the lives of men and communities—Israel, the prophets, the person of Christ, and those in the early Church and subsequent history who responded to him. The biblical writings express diverse interpretations of these events; we must acknowledge the human limitations of their authors and the cultural influences on their thought. Their opinions concerning scientific questions reflect the erroneous speculations of ancient times. We need not retain these primitive scientific ideas, which were so often the cause of past conflicts.

As an example of the neo-orthodox separation of religious from scientific questions, consider the presentation of the *doctrine of creation* given by Langdon Gilkey in Chapter 8 below and at greater length elsewhere.[6] He asserts that the religious meaning of creation is on a totally different level from all scientific theories about cosmic or biological evolution. Science deals with finite causal relationships within the temporal process. Religion deals with the meaning of our personal existence and the status and significance of the whole world-process. Thus the doctrine of creation is not really about temporal origins in the past, but about the *basic relationship between God and the world in the present.* In Genesis these religious insights were expressed as a myth of primeval beginnings, employing the imagery of a prescientific cosmology. But the two main *religious* affirmations, which we can still accept, are about the fundamental character of God and the world:

a. *God is sovereign, transcendent, and purposeful.* In the biblical view, God is self-sufficient and distinct from the world. The idea of creation stands as a barrier against any pantheism which would make him a part of the world or an impersonal cosmic force. He is not limited by materials that happened to be on

[6] Langdon Gilkey, *Maker of Heaven and Earth* (Garden City, N.Y.: Doubleday & Co., 1959).

hand, as in Greek or Oriental creation myths; creation "out of nothing" symbolizes the idea that *all* things owe their existence to God. Ontological dependence is a continuing relation between creature and creator, not a primeval event "at the beginning." Moreover the belief that God has purposes in world history has led to the conviction that time is significant and directional, rather than cyclical as in the outlook of most ancient cultures.

b. The world is orderly and essentially good. Of every created thing in the Genesis story it is said: "And behold, it was very good." Judaism and early Christianity held an affirmative attitude toward the world, though this was modified by later trends toward otherworldliness and life-denial. Against any dualistic belief that matter is inherently evil, the biblical outlook holds that material existence was intended by God. The body, for example, is not something to be depreciated or escaped from, though it may be misused to the detriment of human fulfillment. Historians have maintained that this biblical view of the goodness of the created order, coupled with the Greek view of the rationality of the cosmos, contributed to the rise of science in the West; such belief in the dependability of nature had to precede the attempt to study its regularities.

These assertions about God and the world are said to be the distinctive *theological* content of the idea of creation. The religious meaning can be separated from the ancient cosmology in which it was expressed. Similarly Adam is understood not as a historical individual but as a symbol of Everyman in his movement from innocence to responsibility, sin, anxiety, and guilt. The locus of evil is assigned to man's will and freedom—not his body or intellect, nor society or external necessity. Everyman's sin is compounded of prideful egocentricity and disobedience to God. Genesis 3 is taken as a mythical representation of human nature, just as Genesis 1 and 2 are taken as a mythical representation of the basic relationship between the world and God. Such insights are said to have nothing to do with scientific accounts of origins.

Is there then any connection at all between the doctrine of creation and the findings of astronomy or biology about the evolution of stars or men? On the neo-orthodox reading, the scientific details are of no theological interest, for they describe only the operation of *secondary causality*. God acts by *primary causality,* which is an activity on a completely different level and not an intervention among the gaps between physical forces. God creates through evolutionary laws which he has ordained, and he governs through and with natural causes, not in violation of them. Gilkey writes in his contribution: "Divine causality works through the finite; in regard to origins, God works through all the secondary causes that have played their part in the development of life on earth." Catholic writings in the Thomistic tradition have similarly spoken of God as the ground of the whole temporal order, who conserves it in being.[7] Schmitt states below that "God continually creates the world," and McMullin writes, "His creation and conservation are one and the same, timeless and all-wise. There are no last moment additions to his plan: everything is allowed for in the original blueprint." Theological assertions are here on a totally different level from scientific assertions.

2. *Religious Involvement vs. Scientific Objectivity*

Another movement which has contributed to the sharp separation of the spheres of science and religion in the twentieth century is *existentialism.* Here the contrast is based on the dichotomy between the realm of *personal selfhood,* which can be known only in subjective involvement, and the realm of *impersonal objects,* which is known in the objective detachment of the scientist. Common to all existentialist writings—whether atheistic or theistic—is the conviction that we can know authentic human existence only by being personally involved as unique

[7] An excellent study from a neo-Thomist perspective has been written by an Anglican, E. L. Mascall, *Christian Theology and Natural Science* (New York: Ronald Press, 1956).

individuals making free decisions. The meaning of man's life is found only in commitment and action, never in the spectatorial, rationalistic attitude of the scientist searching for abstract general concepts or universal laws.

The detached analysis and manipulative control of impersonal objects in science has been called an *I-It* relationship. *I-Thou* relationships, by contrast, occur when there is total participation of the whole self, directness and immediacy of apprehension, and concern for another person as an end in himself. Such encounter occurs in the reciprocal interaction and openness of true dialogue, and in the awareness, sensitivity, and availability of genuine love. Man's confrontation with God always has the immediacy and involvement of an *I-Thou* relationship. Karl Heim portrays two contrasting dimensions of existence which he calls "spaces": the nonobjective "ego-space" inaccessible to science and the "world-space" which the scientist can investigate.[8]

Rudolph Bultmann's version of Christian existentialism has had considerable influence since the Second World War. He maintains that God's activity cannot be described in the language of space and time as if it were on the same plane as natural occurrences. Moreover, he asserts, nature is known today to be a completely closed system of cause-and-effect laws. The Bible sometimes uses "objective" language to speak of God's acts, but we can retain the original experiential meaning of such passages by translating them into *the language of man's self-understanding,* his hopes and fears, choices and actions. One must ask of any biblical assertion: What does it say about my personal existence and my relationship to God? The Christian message always refers to *new possibilities for my life*— decision, rebirth, the realization of my true being; it never refers to observable occurrences in the external world apart from my involvement. Religious faith brings a new self-understanding amid the anxieties and hopes of personal life—without conflict-

[8] Karl Heim, *Christian Faith and Natural Science* (New York: Harper & Row, 1953).

ing with the scientific assumption that the world is law-abiding.

The doctrine of creation, as Bultmann interprets it, is not a statement about the origin of the universe, but a personal confession that *"the Lord is my Creator."* It is not a description of purported past actions of God in space and time, but an acknowledgment of present dependence on God and a confession "that I understand myself to be a creature which owes its existence to God."[9] In gratitude I accept my life as a gift. Here Bultmann has applied his thesis that all theological formulations must be statements about the transformation of man's life by *a new understanding of personal existence*. Such affirmations have no connection with scientific theories about external events in the impersonal order of nature which could be described neutrally without the personal involvement of the individual. There is no "God of the gaps" here, because God acts in the realm of selfhood, not in the realm of nature.

While existentialism as such is not represented in the present volume, its influence on neo-orthodoxy is evident. For example, Gilkey argues that religious questions are always "existential," and he quotes Bultmann on the meaning of creation. Moreover the linguistic analysts, to whom we now turn, have by a somewhat different route reached rather similar conclusions—for example, the contrast of personal involvement in religion with objective detachment in science as portrayed in the chapter by Evans.

3. *Science and Religion as Unrelated Languages*

In addition to the neo-orthodox emphasis on revelation and the existentialist emphasis on personal involvement, a third development has contributed to the sharp differentiation of science from religion: the school of *linguistic analysis* which is predominant among philosophers in England and America today. A generation ago, many philosophers endorsed logical

[9] Rudolph Bultmann, *Jesus Christ and Mythology* (New York: Charles Scribner's Sons, 1958), p. 69.

positivism, which looked on scientific statements as the norm for all discourse and dismissed any statement not subject to empirical verification as "meaningless." Since World War II, however, it has been increasingly recognized that differing types of language serve differing functions not reducible to each other. Each area of discourse—artistic, moral, scientific, religious, and so forth—reflects a distinctive interest and fulfills a distinctive purpose in human life. Science and religion are both legitimate enterprises, but they do totally different jobs.

Scientific language, according to these philosophers, is used primarily for prediction and control. A theory is a useful tool for summarizing data, correlating regularities in observable phenomena, and producing technological applications. Science asks carefully delimited questions of a specific and technical kind. Its conclusions must be testable by observations. We must not expect it to do jobs for which it was not designed, such as providing an over-all world-view, a philosophy of life, a metaphysical system, or a set of ethical norms. The scientist is no wiser than anyone else when he steps out of his laboratory and speculates beyond his strictly scientific work.

Toulmin, for example, insists that evolution is a biological theory, not a cosmic process.[10] It has neither theistic nor naturalistic implications; nor can it serve as the basis of ethics. It leads neither to natural theology nor to evolutionary naturalism. Thus Toulmin criticizes Julian Huxley for elevating Evolution (with a capital E) into a universal principle, which is no longer functioning as a biological theory. Many scientists today share Toulmin's caution about making sweeping claims for their discoveries or extrapolating their theories into cosmic philosophies. Science, in this view, can neither provide support for religion nor threaten it so long as each sticks to its proper task.

The distinctive function of *religious language,* linguistic philosophers tell us, is to recommend a way of life, to elicit a set of

[10] Stephen Toulmin, "Contemporary Scientific Mythology," in Alasdair MacIntyre, ed., *Metaphysical Beliefs* (London: SCM Press, 1957).

attitudes, to acknowledge and encourage allegiance to particular moral principles. Religious statements also propose a characteristic self-understanding, expressing and engendering certain attitudes toward human existence as well as commitments to patterns of action. Other statements express and evoke worship, and are used in the context of the worshiping community; or they may grow out of and perhaps lead to personal religious experience. Much of the recent philosophical discussion has dwelt on such functions of religious language as ethical dedication, self-commitment, and existential life-orientation.[11]

Donald Evans' chapter below distinguishes science and religion by the way their languages are used. He argues that a person's use of religious language is self-involving, whereas the use of scientific language is not. Moreover religious language is not testable by observations. He has given elsewhere a detailed linguistic analysis of the doctrine of creation.[12] Evans reads the creation story as *a parable suggesting attitudes toward the world*. Most parables are not narratives of events which actually happened; their whole point is to commend certain attitudes. We should act *as if* the world were a creation; for though the Genesis story is not factual, we have it on divine authority that the attitudes it proposes are indeed appropriate. The biblical images lead to responses which are fitting. Evans insists that there is no core of propositional truth and no actual historical events of which the parable is an interpretation. There are no neutral facts here which could be asserted without self-involvement, no primeval events which might be related to scientific accounts. The functions served by religious language about creation are quite unlike those of hypotheses about origins in astronomy or biology; the doctrine must be completely dissociated from all scientific and cosmological questions.

[11] See for example Ian Ramsey, *Religious Language* (London: SCM Press, 1957) or T. R. Miles, *Religion and the Scientific Outlook* (London: George Allen & Unwin, 1959).

[12] Donald D. Evans, *The Logic of Self-Involvement* (London: SCM Press, 1963).

Evans' book spells out the *religious attitudes* which the idea of creation expresses: "In the biblical context, if I say 'God is my Creator' I acknowledge my status as God's obedient servant and possession, I acknowledge God's gift of existence, and I acknowledge God's self-commitment to me." Besides witnessing to our sense of creatureliness and dependence on God, the doctrine symbolizes our acceptance of the world as purposeful and our own existence as significant. To accept a parable is to adopt the attitude it endorses, which in this case means looking on the world and our own lives as a gift. In this rendition, the doctrine of creation is primarily *a way of looking at the world*. A similar viewpoint is found in Owen Jones' contribution below, though he gives greater stress to the role of the doctrine in interpreting as well as in responding to the world. "To see the world *as a creation*," he suggests, is to interpret it as the purposive self-expression of a person. It is to accept it *as if* it were the product of divine intention. This involves a particular way of looking at the world today, not a claim about scientific events "at the beginning of time."[13]

In summary, the combined effect of these three movements— neo-orthodoxy, existentialism, and language analysis—has been *to isolate science and religion* from each other. The distinctive features of religion—namely revelation, personal involvement, and endorsement of a way of life—are held to be absent from science. There can be no significant dialogue if there are no common interests and no points of contact between the fields. As an example, we have shown that in each case the doctrine of creation is said to have nothing to do with evolution or astronomy. All three movements discourage the construction of any general picture of reality and abandon the search for inclusive metaphysical categories. Science and religion are left each to its own specialized job, each to accomplish its own purposes in its own way. There can be no conflict between them; but neither can there be fruitful communication.

[13] See also Miles, *op. cit.*, p. 165 f.

III. SOME AREAS OF RECENT DIALOGUE

To avoid the conflicts of the past, and to defend the distinctive characteristics of both science and religion, most twentieth-century authors have stressed the contrasts in method and the independence of content outlined above. But throughout this period there were some writers who saw *similarities in method* and *possibilities for fruitful interaction* between the two fields. Among these were exponents of theological liberalism who avoided the extremes of nineteenth-century modernism but shared its concern for the intelligibility of religious beliefs and the coherence of all knowledge. There was an increasing recognition that the radical isolation of science and religion had bypassed rather than solved some important problems, such as the cognitive status of religious beliefs and the relation between God and the processes of nature. In the last few years there have been new currents of thought among philosophers, including challenges to the positivistic interpretation of science and renewed interest in metaphysical questions. Theologians have expressed the need for a "theology of nature"—not along the lines of the older "natural theology," but rather as a perspective on nature in the framework of a theology derived from other sources. Some of these trends are summarized under three headings: (1) methodological parallels, (2) evolutionary theologies, and (3) the prospects for dialogue.

1. *Methodological Parallels*

The contrast between the methods of the two fields has been questioned from both sides. Let us first note some recent *challenges to the positivist interpretation of science*. It has been pointed out that the actual practice of scientists is a much more human enterprise than the logician's idealized account had recognized. Hanson has argued that there are no completely uninterpreted facts which could be described in a supposedly objective observation-language.[14] Even the simplest data are "theory-laden," reported in a language which already incorporates theoretical concepts. Again, Kuhn has shown how the "received tradition" of a given scientific community influences the concepts through which it sees and describes the world and even defines the sorts of questions that may legitimately be asked and the kinds of solution that are to be sought.[15] The accepted standard examples ("paradigms") of past research will control the direction of scientific inquiry. Kuhn indicates that a change of paradigms produces far-reaching effects, yet the choice between competing paradigms is not determined by any systematic rules. Other authors have insisted that scientific theories are never given to us directly by the data; they are mental constructs produced by creative imagination, not by precise observation alone.

Both positivists and existentialists had accepted a dichotomy between the realm of personal involvement and the realm of objective detachment. By contrast, Polanyi devotes a major volume to *the personal role of the knower in science*.[16] The scientist, he suggests, must exercise personal judgment in the assessment of evidence—for example, in the decision whether an unexplained discrepancy disproves a theory or can be set aside as an anomaly or attributed to chance variation. Like a judge weighing ambiguous evidence or a doctor making a difficult diagnosis, the scientist is given no simple set of rules to follow; in all three cases it is commitment to universality, not an alleged impersonal detachment, that protects decisions from pure subjectivity. Polanyi also suggests that intellectual beauty, symmetry, and simplicity, as well as "empirical agreement," influence the scientist's choice among competing theories. There is, then, no absolute dichotomy of "objectivity" in science and

[14] N. R. Hanson, *Patterns of Discovery* (Cambridge, Eng.: The University Press, 1961).

[15] Thomas S. Kuhn, *The Structure of Scientific Revolutions* (Chicago: University of Chicago Press, 1962).

[16] Michael Polanyi, *Personal Knowledge* (Chicago: University of Chicago Press, 1958).

"subjectivity" in religion, but only varying degrees and types of personal involvement and dedication to truth in various fields. Polanyi maintains that science requires moral commitments not unlike those in religion.

In his contribution to the present volume, C. A. Coulson holds that *the methods of science and religion have much in common*. On the one hand, science has its presuppositions, such as the orderliness and intelligibility of the universe; moreover, the moral attitudes required by science are similar to the virtues enjoined by religion, including humility, cooperation, universality, and integrity. Science advances by creative imagination, not by any mere collecting of facts. Conversely, religious inquiry should involve critical reflection on experience not unlike that which goes on in science.[17] The unity of nature and the harmony of its laws support belief in a cosmic mind; above all, man's religious experience points to a personal God. Coulson defends two propositions often found in Protestant liberalism: (1) a consistent and comprehensive world-view should be based on the rational interpretation of the totality of human experience, and (2) man's religious and moral experience are the primary basis for religious beliefs. If religion, like science, is the human interpretation of experience, then the gulf between the methods of the two fields has been narrowed from both sides.[18] Attitudes in religious inquiry are not altogether dissimilar from those in science.

Harold Schilling has explored in detail a number of *parallels between the two fields*.[19] He is impressed by the corporate character of all inquiry and discusses the dynamics of both the scientific and the religious community. He articulates the im-

[17] See also C. A. Coulson, *Science and Christian Belief* (Chapel Hill, N.C.: University of North Carolina Press, 1955).

[18] An interpretation of both biological evolution and religious experience in the framework of liberal theology is set forth in Charles E. Raven, *Natural Religion and Christian Theology* (Cambridge, Eng.: The University Press, 1953), Vol. 2.

[19] Harold K. Schilling, *Science and Religion* (New York: Charles Scribner's Sons, 1962).

plicit assumptions of science (e. g., faith in the dependability of nature) and analyzes the loyalties and commitments mediated by the community of scientists. He finds that both scientists and theologians today recognize the partial and limited character of their undertakings. In the selection reprinted here, Schilling delineates in both fields a threefold structure: experience, theoretical interpretation, and practical application. He explicitly states that he is not trying to derive theology from science or even to justify theology by analogies with science. He is attempting rather to describe and compare the methods of the two enterprises, and finds that there are *parallels*—that is, real *similarities* which yet allow for *differences*. Perhaps Coulson and Schilling devote insufficient attention to the differences (such as those brought out in Evans' chapter), but the similarities are surely present and had been ignored in most of the earlier literature.

2. *Evolutionary Theologies*

Turning now from dialogue about method to dialogue about content, we find evolution prominent among the scientific discoveries in whose theological implications there is renewed interest. Consider first some of the themes of Whitehead's *process philosophy* which are reflected in Charles Birch's recent book[20] and his article reprinted here; very similar ideas were expressed by the Jesuit paleontologist, Teilhard de Chardin:

a. Nature as dynamic process. The world is a process of becoming, always changing and developing, radically temporal in character. It is an incomplete cosmos still coming into being. Birch criticizes the prevalent deterministic and mechanistic view of nature, and affirms the presence of chance and indeterminacy. There is novelty, spontaneity, and risk in the history of nature. Process thought is also critical of reductionism (the assumption that the behavior of any system can be exhaustively

[20] L. Charles Birch, *Nature and God* (Philadelphia: Westminster Press, 1965).

B

explained by the laws governing the behavior of its component parts). It defends organismic categories that refer to higher-level activities; an organism is an integral whole with a hierarchy of levels of organization. The world is a web of mutually interconnected events—"a universal interweaving" as Teilhard puts it—a single continuous process across space and time.

b. Continuity of the levels of reality. Teilhard states that each level (matter, life, thought, society) has its roots in earlier levels and represents the flowering of what was potentially present all along.[21] The higher is already in the lower in rudimentary form. There is no sharp line between the nonliving and the living; life is incipient in matter. Teilhard attaches great importance to the "within of things" which finally developed into consciousness. In a similar vein, Birch (following White-head) considers even low-level organisms as centers of experience, though he attributes consciousness only to higher animals. He looks on "matter" and "mind" not as two entities or substances, but as different patterns of events in systems having many levels of organization; among simple organisms the patterns of "mentality" are almost negligible. But in principle man is continuous with the rest of nature (rather than essentially discontinuous, as neo-orthodoxy and existentialism assume). Birch shows, for example, that mentality and culture have their precursors in the animal kingdom. Because of this continuity, man can be taken as a clue for interpreting nature, Teilhard asserts. Our own consciousness is the one instance in which we know reality from within, and it provides at least a remote analogy for imagining the experience of lower forms of life.

c. The directionality of evolution. Birch interprets the past as a slow development toward increasing freedom and awareness, but it has been a costly trial-and-error experiment. Evolution, he suggests, resembles a long and risky travail, not a simple and

---

[21] Pierre Teilhard de Chardin, *The Phenomenon of Man* (New York: Harper & Row, 1959). Among the secondary works in English, volumes by Claude Tresmontant, Charles Raven, Olivier Rabut, Henri de Lubac, and Christopher Mooney are particularly valuable.

direct ascent. It involves both chance and order; it is a creative process whereby the improbable becomes probable but not inevitable. Teilhard also mentions "chance" and the "groping" progress of evolution, but makes out a clearer directionality toward complexity and consciousness—a "favored axis" as he calls it in the article reprinted here. The universe is "personalizing," and in its further social development personality will be enhanced and not submerged.

In contrast to neo-orthodoxy, Birch holds that these characteristics of the evolutionary process *are relevant to our understanding of God's relation to the world.* He is not proposing a natural theology; he is asking how the God known in the experience of forgiveness and grace is to be understood as Creator, and he proposes that the theologian must take evolutionary ideas about man and nature into account. He argues that creation is a slow and incomplete process, and that God respects the freedom of his creatures. He calls this "a God of persuasion rather than coercion" who shares in the suffering of the world. Costly love, of which the cross is the supreme expression, is woven into the fabric of all existence. As in Whitehead's writing, God is not viewed as omnipotent and unchanging, but as reciprocally interacting with the world. He is never the sole cause of an event, but he does influence events. The power of love is always its ability to evoke a response while respecting the integrity of the other. God elicits the self-creation of individual entities, thereby allowing for freedom and novelty as well as order and structure.

In Whiteheadian thought, the idea of creation takes the form of *continuing creativity.*[22] Every event is looked on as the outcome of three factors: lawful past causes, God's influence, and the emerging entity's own action toward the future. Human experience is used as the clue for understanding the experience of all entities, though Whitehead recognizes that for

[22] For a recent discussion, see John B. Cobb, *A Christian Natural Theology: Based on the Thought of Alfred North Whitehead* (Philadelphia: Westminster Press, 1965).

low levels of existence the opportunity for novelty is vanishingly small. But in general more than one alternative is left open, and there are plural potentialities to which the creature itself must respond. To be sure, God is here limited in his power to act; but we must remember that the orderly structures of the world are also part of his purposes. In presenting alternative potentialities to the world, God is source of novelty as well as order, but the action of existing entities is always necessary for novelty to be realized. Thus God acts along with other causes; we can never extricate his action from the complex of natural processes through which he works. Yet God makes a difference in events —not just in our attitude toward events as the existentialists and language analysts propose. God continues to be a source of order and novelty, but this function is not associated with a primeval beginning; it occurs throughout time, which may be infinite and without "beginning."

Let us consider finally the theological side of Teilhard's writing. Some interpreters have read *The Phenomenon of Man* as a contribution to *natural theology,* an argument from evolution to God. His own preface to the book seems to support such a conclusion. Perhaps Teilhard's desire to communicate with his scientific colleagues led him to seek justification from science for convictions at least partially derived from other sources. I would submit that his writing can most appropriately be viewed as *a synthesis* of scientific ideas *with* religious ideas derived primarily from historical revelation and religious experience. In the Epilogue of the book he confesses, concerning his idea of God, that "doubtless I should never have ventured to envisage the latter or formulate the hypothesis rationally if, in my consciousness as a believer, I had not found not only its speculative model but also its living reality." His other writings make clear how deeply he was molded by his Christian heritage and by his own experience.

In the essay reprinted here, Teilhard first traces the direction of evolution from matter through life and thought to society. At this point he states: "Further than this we cannot see and our argument must cease—except, as I have now to show, in the case of the Christian, who, drawing upon an added source of knowledge may advance yet another step." He then outlines a vision of the Church as the fulfillment of the "human social organism." He speaks of a new evolutionary impulse in man, "born of the psychic combination of two kinds of faith—in the transcendent action of a personal God and the innate perfectibility of a world in progress." Teilhard, it appears, was attempting a synthesis of science and Christian thought, and was indebted to both.

If Teilhard's ideas do represent such a synthesis, we would expect that *his concept of God* was modified by evolutionary ideas, even if it was not derived from evolution alone. Teilhard, like Whitehead, held that God is actively involved in an incomplete world—in this respect resembling the living God of the Bible more than Aristotle's Unmoved Mover or Aquinas' Unchanging Absolute. God fulfills himself in creating the world. God's immanence is strongly emphasized (by Teilhard the Christian mystic as well as Teilhard the evolutionary monist); but the accusation of pantheism is unfounded, for transcendence is not neglected. He maintains that the Christian understanding of God's action in the world must reflect the new understanding of nature, which only recently has been known to be dynamic rather than static. Teilhard regrettably did not say much about the mode of God's activity and its relation to natural selection or the "within of things"; he was not trained as a philosopher, and the task of systematic philosophical elaboration remains for others to carry on. Several recent Catholic thinkers have used a number of his ideas within a more fully developed metaphysics, attempting to correct problematic or ambiguous aspects of his thought.[23]

[23] E. g., Andrew Van Melsen, *Evolution and Philosophy* (Pittsburgh, Pa.: Duquesne University Press, 1965); Peter Schoonenberg, *God's World in the Making* (Pittsburgh, Pa.: Duquesne University Press, 1964).

3. *The Prospects for Dialogue*

Can these proposals for dialogue manage to avoid the mistakes that have produced the conflicts of the past, such as the "God of the gaps" and the modernist attenuation of the gospel? Can they, in addition, do justice to the distinctive characteristics of religion and of science, on which neo-orthodoxy, existentialism, and language analysis have rightly insisted? Is it possible to move from "isolation" to "dialogue" without renewing the conflicts? I shall list what I take to be some of the key issues in the subsequent chapters, and suggest some conclusions about them.

a. What is the place of nature in theology? The twentieth-century protest against *natural theology* seems justified. To the Christian community, Christ is the central event in which God is revealed, as neo-orthodoxy insists. Personal involvement is indeed a prerequisite of religious understanding, as existentialism claims. Worship and self-commitment are the distinctive functions of religious language, as linguistic analysts recognized. Arguments from nature can never replace historical revelation and religious experience as the starting points of theology. God is known as Redeemer before he is known as Creator. Yet I would submit that within Christian thought *a theology of nature* has an important though secondary place. If Christianity is radically interiorized or reduced to personal attitudes, the natural order is left devoid of meaning. To neo-orthodoxy, nature is the unredeemed setting for man's redemption. To existentialism, nature is the impersonal stage for the drama of personal existence. What was God doing, then, in the long stretches of time before man appeared? Is God related only to human existence? Can we so sharply separate man and his history from nature, now that we are aware of the continuity of life? Can the theologian explicate the doctrines of creation and providence, which refer to nature, without some analysis of the structure of nature? In short, can we have a theology of nature which avoids the limitations of natural theology?

b. Should we seek a unified world-view? There are dangers, of course, that any attempted synthesis of science and religion will distort one field or the other by imposing alien categories and threatening its integrity. But I would argue that *we cannot remain content with a plurality of unrelated languages.* "Complementary languages" are, after all, languages about a single world. Moreover, religious language does make cognitive claims in addition to evoking distinctive attitudes; the attitudes are deemed appropriate only because reality is assumed to have a particular character. Without *religious beliefs* there would be no religious attitudes. Existentialism and language analysis make such drastic reductions in the truth-claims of religion that it tends to become a subjective and private affair. I would maintain that both science and theology use language "realistically," and neither will settle for "useful fictions." As Schilling suggests, there are parallels in their methods, including a similar interaction of experience and interpretation in both fields. Thus we must seek *a coherent interpretation of all experience.* Such concern for the intelligibility and coherence of existence is also supported by the biblical conviction that God is Lord of all that is—and of man's total life rather than of some separate "religious" sphere. Can such coherence be achieved without violating the integrity of either field? Behind this lies the even more basic methodological question discussed with particular clarity in the essays by Ferré and Evans: are religious beliefs subject to *evaluation* and *testing,* even if not to *verification* in the strictly positivist sense?

c. Is metaphysics a bridge between science and religion? Traditionally, metaphysics has been the branch of philosophy devoted to the elaboration of a coherent and comprehensive set of categories in terms of which every element in experience can be interpreted. It sought an inclusive conceptual scheme to represent the most general characteristics of events. With the growth of logical positivism and language analysis, metaphysics was largely ignored, though there seems to be a recent revival of interest in many of the classical metaphysical problems (such as the questions of mind and body, freedom and determinism, purpose and mechanism). I would maintain that every philosopher, scientist, and theologian assumes an implicit metaphysics and uses metaphysical categories whether he intends to or not. To be sure, Christianity should not be equated with any one metaphysical system or forced to fit a neat and final synthesis which claims to encompass all reality. Our immediate goal should be neither isolation, at one extreme, nor closed synthesis at the other, but rather dialogue about metaphysical assumptions and their coherence. Let us also admit the tentative and partial character of any synthesis attempted; the most that can be hoped is that it will illuminate a wider range of data more adequately than any of the alternatives examined.

d. Is the idea of God's creativity in nature a reversion to the "God of the gaps"? The existentialist solves the problem by assigning nature to the scientist and confining religion to man's inward life; he holds that any reference to God as acting violates the scientific assumption that complete explanations of events can in principle be given in terms of natural forces. Another solution, endorsed by neo-orthodoxy and neo-Thomism, allows for a "gapless" account of scientific *secondary causes,* while affirming God's *primary causality* at a totally different level. God's role was to design the laws through which evolution could automatically occur; as in Deism, God then has no continuing active relationship to the world. (He may "sustain the world in being," but this is a general and uniform action, undiscriminating toward any particular events.) By contrast, *process philosophy* seems to posit many infinitesimal gaps in the natural order instead of the few big ones around which past conflicts centered. Whitehead and his followers have opposed both reductionism and determinism; they point to indeterminacy at various levels, from the quantum atom and evolutionary mutation to human freedom. But the "gaps" they invoke are unlike those formerly posited, for scientific laws are now acknowledged to be selective, abstractive, and often statistical. Moreover, for Whitehead an entity's response to God is always its own activity, not a change imposed by an omnipotent intervention. Thus God's contribution cannot be separated out as an external intrusion filling a gap, though God does have a specific role in the unfolding of events. Can such a scheme allow for both a world ruled by law and a God who acts?

e. *Does evolution have implications for our understanding of God?* Tradition pictured a static world created initially in its present form; in the century after Newton, the image of watch and watchmaker seemed appropriate. What image of God is called for if the world resembles a developing organism more than a machine? Both Teilhard and Birch represent *God as participant* in a dynamic world process, though not as simply part of the process itself. Can this emphasis on divine immanence be maintained without losing (as the modernists did) the biblical understanding of God's sovereignty and transcendence? Granted that *continuing creation* is a biblical concept, can divine creativity in nature be presented in a way which is consistent with both the biblical view of God and the evolutionary view of nature? The reader must form his own conclusions on these issues as he confronts the arguments of Part Two and Part Three below.

2

SCIENCE AND THE CATHOLIC TRADITION

Ernan McMullin*

It is a striking fact, and one often commented on, that the underlying attitude of the average Catholic toward the whole enterprise of theoretic science is usually assumed to be one of hostility. He is the inheritor of a sad tradition of misunderstanding and misjudgment in this matter, one which goes back more than three centuries to the period in which physical science, as we know it today, was just beginning to take shape.

The Church's condemnation of Galileo marked—though the Church's spokesmen could not realize it—a moment of grave decision. Galileo had been eloquently (if not always convincingly) contending for the freedom of the "new science" from theological control. In his forthright *Letter to Castelli*, he

* Father McMullin is Chairman of the Department of Philosophy at University of Notre Dame. He has had graduate training in physics, theology, and philosophy, specializing in the field of philosophy of science. He edited and contributed to The Concept of Matter (1963) and wrote a chapter in Science and Religion, edited by John C. Monsma (1962). The following article appeared in America, December 12, 1959, pp. 346–50. Reprinted with permission from America, The National Catholic Weekly Review, 106 W. 56th St., New York City.

argued that

the authority of the Sacred Scriptures has as its sole aim to convince men of those truths which are necessary for their salvation. . . . But that the same God who has endowed us with senses, reason and understanding should not wish us to use them and should desire to impart to us by another means knowledge which we have it in our power to acquire by their use—this is a thing which I do not think I am bound to believe.

He was on the right track, as it turned out, but the theologians were not going to be easily convinced of this. Their supervisory competence in matters physical had too long gone uncontested for them to take kindly to a man who warned them bluntly that "professors of theology should not arrogate to themselves the authority to decide on controversies in professions they have neither studied nor practiced." Forgetting the caution of Augustine, who had written that "the Holy Spirit did not desire that men should learn things [from the Bible] that are useful to no one for salvation," and ignoring the lesson of Aquinas, whose successful efforts to establish the autonomy of philosophy had met with vehement opposition from the Augustinian theologians of his day, the theologians declared that the theory that the earth moved was formally heretical. This was equivalent to outlawing the upstart new science of the "mathematicians"; it was, in fact, a declaration of war.

It is easy to find excuses for the theologians. The die-hard Aristotelians whom Galileo had confounded were the ones who actually initiated the campaign to have his novel views declared heretical. As the denunciation to the Holy Office phrased it, the Galileans "were treading under foot the entire philosophy of Aristotle, which had been of such service to scholastic theology." Strong measures of repression were therefore demanded by the beleaguered philosophers, who were, as Galileo wryly put it, "unable to withstand assault on their own." In addition, the theologians themselves had been growing increasingly sensitive about questions involving the interpretation of Scripture; the Protestant challenge had made them much less receptive to developments in the concept of inspiration than their predecessors had been. The Church's reaction to the 17th-century crisis was thus very different from her reaction to the very similar crisis in the mid-13th century, when Aristotle's novel views in physics and psychology seemed to threaten the intellectual foundations of Christendom. That Galileo failed in his attempt to provide a way for the Church to assimilate the new learning where Aquinas had succeeded, is not so much an indication of a difference between the two men (though Galileo with his scorching polemic and soaring vanity stirred up a fierceness of personal opposition that the serene Aquinas never had to contend with) or between their aims, as it is an indication of the failure of nerve that followed the Counter Reformation, a failure which all but paralyzed intellectual initiative in the Church for two centuries.

A SUSPICIOUSNESS TOWARD SCIENCE

Physical science had not originated in the East nor in the Arab world, even though mathematics and technology were already relatively advanced in these areas, but rather in the Christian West, whose belief in the orderliness and "creatureliness" of the universe encouraged a constructive and theoretical approach to the problems of nature. In the early growth of this science, bishops like Grosseteste, Albert of Saxony and Oresme, as well as priests like Albertus Magnus, Bradwardine and Buridan had played a decisive part. In Galileo's own day, the contributions to science of priests like Copernicus and Mersenne were known to all; indeed, Galileo's strongest support came from priest-friends—Foscarini, the Carmelite provincial; Castelli, the Benedictine professor of philosophy; Ciampoli, secretary to Urban VIII; Dini, archbishop of Fermo. But within a generation all this had changed. Reactionism set in, and the intellectual forces of the Church gradually withdrew from the fields of secular learning which they had dominated for so long, back to the seemingly secure fortifications of a tried and true traditionalism. For the next two hundred years scarcely a single theologian, philosopher or scientist of the caliber of a Cajetan or a Copernicus was to appear behind those fortifications. Their places were taken by the preacher and the casuist. During the time when the "modern" mind was being molded by intellectual giants like Newton, Leibnitz and Kant, the Church was voiceless and intellectually almost impotent; she could take no part in directing the flood of new ideas. The age of Newman and Mercier and Lemaître was still a long way off.

But this unhappy story reveals only one of the causes of the latent hostility between scientists and Christian theologians that sometimes, even today, breaks out into open warfare. In England, the national church at first greeted the new science rapturously, seeing in it a wonderful manner of discovering (in Robert Boyle's phrase) "the footsteps and impressions and perfections of the Creator," of scrutinizing "the vast library of creation" (John Ray). But a nagging doubt soon arose. Did not the new physics lead to a mechanistic world-view which was incompatible with belief in the Christian God? And so the Anglican apologists began to find themselves on the defensive against allegations that they were promoting atheism (Bishop Bentley's reproach against Newton); they set about writing treatises like *The Darkness of Atheism Dispelled by the Light of Nature* (Charleston) and *The Wisdom of God Manifested in the Works of Creation* (Boyle). These works tried to provide a rational basis for a belief in God which would be acceptable to scientists. They searched for "such principles as might work with considering men for the belief in a deity" (Newton in a letter to Bentley). But their natural religion, with its emphasis on physical law and design, took little account of the supernatural side of the Christian message; instead of shoring up Christianity, natural religion soon began to displace it. As a recent writer puts it, "although their absorption in natural religion and the external manifestations of divine power did not dispute or deny any specific Christian doctrine, it did more to undermine Christianity than any conclusion of natural science ever did" (Westfall).

In the century that followed, Anglican theology was buried in the deist landslide. The Watchmaker God of the Newtonian world-machine (who had to intervene in the universe to keep planetary systems stable) became less and less believable as time wore on and scientific explanation was seen to be total in its own order. We do not *need* the hypothesis of God in physics, as Laplace explained patiently to Napoleon. Neither do we need it in biology, as Darwin's century was soon to discover. The diversity of species, the marvelous intricacy of organisms, the adaptation of living beings to their environment—all these and many other striking facts about the living world which had formerly been thought to be explicable only in terms of special divine "interventions," now appeared as natural corollaries of the all-embracing scientific concept of evolution. But the Anglican Church felt that the time had come to make a stand (American Protestant groups like the Baptists were later to come to the same decision), and so they joined battle with the "atheist" defenders of the new theory—Huxley, Haeckel, Tyndall and the rest. History repeated itself—except that the Anglicans lacked the canonical sword Galileo's opponents had been able to wield—and the results were just as disastrous as before.

And so, both ways were tried. The Catholic Church, after an auspicious start, lost confidence and treated the new science with suspicion as a potential competitor of theology. This led for a time to the eclipse of science within the Church and to a near rupture of the harmonious, but always precarious balance between faith and natural reason which had prevailed since the time of Aquinas. The Anglican churchmen welcomed the new science as a helpmate of theology; but it ultimately proved a Trojan horse to them. Here, then, is the background we must keep in mind when we talk of the "conflict" between science and Christianity. It will be seen that the tension is due to two main factors—the past efforts of theologians to regiment science and to extend their competence considerably beyond its proper limits, and the growing "Caesarism" of science, which seems to explain everything and to make supernatural modes of thought appear hopelessly old-fashioned. The "Catholic" attitude toward science has been strongly affected by these factors. The peculiar combination of bad conscience and inferiority complex they can give rise to is vividly illustrated, for example, by the statements about science and scientists that one sometimes finds in certain sections of the Catholic press.

CAN THE GAP BE BRIDGED?

There is a real problem to be faced here. Science has unquestionably encouraged the spread of irreligion. Are we then to retreat from it, as some leading Protestant and Jewish thinkers seem to advocate? Are we to set science over against religion as an alien and hostile fact, or are we to incorporate it in our world-view as part of that total intelligibility which it is given to man alone to discover in God's universe? Does the advance of science pose a threat to the Christian's theological understanding of the universe?

To answer this last question, we must see something of what is meant by "explanation"—scientific, philosophical and theological. Each discipline proceeds in a different way to "explain" the same thing; each has, if you will, a different idea of what constitutes "explanation." For the scientist, the death of a dog will be "explained" in terms of a virus; for the philosopher, it will be "explained" in terms of matter and form; for the theologian, it will be "explained" as part of God's providence. Now the exponent of any one of these modes of explanation is quite liable to regard the other modes as being trivial or even spurious. For instance, the scientist may protest to the theologian: "Your statement that God is good is applicable to every contingency that can arise. Therefore, its truth cannot be tested and it explains nothing." Nor does it, in the scientific sense of the word, for science requires that an explanation be specific and thus, conceivably, falsifiable.

Of course, this objection will not be taken seriously by

anyone who has first grasped the difference between these quite diverse ideals of "explanation" and has then satisfied himself of the legitimacy of each. Furthermore, an analysis of the methods of procedure followed in these disciplines shows that each of the orders of explanation is autonomous and—in principle, at least—*complete* in its own domain. This means, for example, that there cannot ordinarily be any question of science happening on "something it can never explain." Science is capable of explaining any repeatable physical phenomenon, according to its *own* sense of the word "explain."

These points are understood much better today than they used to be. It was once assumed that each kind of being (a stone, a gnat, a star) was fashioned separately by God; this implied that the *only* explanation of why things are as they are is a theological one. The projection of a scientific framework back into the prehistory of our universe—in the theory of biological evolution, for example—indicates that the matter is much more complicated than this. We are beginning to see a continuous line of descent from the primitive nebula almost to man himself. Science has discovered the laws by which the stars evolved; we know why the earth is the sort of planet it is; we know a little, at least, of what brought about those genetic changes which produced more and more complicated animal nervous systems until finally one may have been sufficiently developed for God to infuse into it the breath of rationality, the human soul.

It is a majestic picture that science here presents to us, one after the heart of Augustine, who saw the whole plan of God's creation contained germinally in the original desolation. God is not "intervening" at every moment, as Platonic teleology and Aristotelian physics led medieval thinkers to assume. God is *transcendent;* He is no demiurge or watchmaker. His creation and conservation are one and the same, timeless and all-wise. There are no last-moment additions to His plan: everything is allowed for in the original blueprint.

SCIENCE, TOO, IS GOD'S

Science now begins to emerge as an essential component in our understanding of God's plan. Man is still the pivotal point in the universe. The scientist realizes better than most of us that the rationality on which science depends can be found only in a single creature, and that this creature alone has the incredible power of encompassing the universe in the sweep of his mind, of becoming "potentially all things," in Aquinas' happy phrase. The whole history of the world has led up to this creature. The Aristotelian of Galileo's *Dialog* objected to the vast empty spaces between planets and stars in Copernicus' model of the universe as "vain and superfluous," because they did not serve man. Galileo's spokesman tartly replied that it is not for *us* to say what is vain. Nowadays we can answer this objection even more effectively. No longer is man's key role as the "crown of the universe" to be insured by the crude device of making his dwelling its physical center. We can understand that enormous spaces are necessary if somewhere, by the ordinary laws of physics, planetary systems are to appear. We can appreciate the fantastic time-scale that is required if on one of those planets an incredibly improbable and complex grouping of atoms is to occur, and if a new kind of matter which will have the power of adaptation and development is to appear. We can realize that a profusion of living creatures must try their luck in the struggle for existence if some day one of them is to be found a suitable abode for an immortal spirit. The advance of science does *not* therefore involve any weakening of the plausibility of theological ways of thinking, if it be properly understood. On the contrary, it notably deepens our theological appreciation of the grandeur and nobility of God's plan for man and the universe.

It has often been said that Catholicism is lacking in a theology of the temporal order, that its otherworldliness and preoccupation with the absolute have made it dilatory in evolving a true humanism. That there is an element of truth in this allegation cannot be denied. Catholic thinkers, like Maritain, Thils, Dondeyne, Mouroux and Norris Clarke have been trying hard to remedy the fault. They have sought to validate proximate temporal ends for man. Among other things, they point out that advances in technology are liberating man more and more from his slavery to matter—to disease, hunger, climatic extremes, exhausting labor and so on. Man has tapped sources of untold energy. He is about to conquer the barriers of space. The range of his brain is being enormously extended by intricate electronic computers. He will soon be able to communicate almost instantaneously with any one of his fellows. His whole conception of work and of society is gradually being transformed. Three hundred years ago, science scarcely touched the daily life of man; the range of his mind and body, the energies at his disposition, even his means of communication were almost as physically limited as those of his primitive ancestors tens of thousands of years before. Today man's whole relation to the universe is changing at a pace that few have really grasped. Yet we are still only on the threshold of undreamed-of changes. Biology and psychology are at approximately the level of theoretical development that physics was in the time of Newton. What the next century will bring only God knows.

There are two points of view among Christians regarding this upheaval. One is that technology is a "bad thing," that it replaces God's image in creation by that of man, that it is a manifestation of the "original sin" of man's nature, a sign of his inordinate desire for knowledge and greed for power. This attitude (which is exemplified in the work of some few American Catholic writers, like Wilhelmsen and Carol Jackson) is partly Manichean, but is chiefly rooted in a "good-old-days" mentality which Catholicism somehow seems to foster among some of its adherents. The opposite view is that technology is man's way of obeying God's command to Adam to "dominate the earth"; it "transforms matter by imposing upon it traces, as it were, of rationality, of spirituality, even of humanity" (Thils). In remaking the universe in the image of man, science brings it nearer the image of Christ, too, thus helping it participate in its own way in the work of redemption (Dubarle, Teilhard de Chardin). It may even be (as D'Arcy, Malevez and others suggest) that in transforming the earth, science is preparing for that "glorified earth" on which the resurrection of the body is to take place and which will be entirely dominated by man.

Be this as it may, it is certain, at least, that the technological transformation of the world is in itself good. But it unquestionably poses man with the gravest challenge he has ever faced. The more man's capacities are magnified, the greater the dangers to which the weakness of his still human nature exposes him and his world. It is imperative, then, that man's spiritual growth match the increase of his physical potentialities. It is not merely that man needs new wisdom and new restraint as he gains command of nuclear and genetic forces. It is not just that the terrible new capacity he possesses for dominating his fellow man may turn his head and put an end to freedom on the earth. It is above all the fact of *knowledge,* the feeling of omnipotent reach, that can make the mind of man so swell with pride that it may set itself over against God.

In this growing crisis, the troubled scientist can find little solace in either of the great philosophical orientations which have, between them, dominated the intellectual arena for over three centuries. The tradition which stretches back from Nagel and Ayer through Mach and Hume to Locke and Hobbes, and which in its various manifestations has been labeled "empiricist," "phenomenalist" and "positivist," could never find room for the notion of a transcendent Creator. Within the limits of its own categories and starting-point, the most it could hope to achieve was either a rational affirmation of a limited God (the deism of the 18th century is an instructive example of where such an effort is bound to fail) or else an incompletely rational affirmation of a Creator. (The fideism of the later medieval nominalists or of many of the leading Protestant thinkers of today might here be quoted as examples.) On the other hand, the idealist tradition, represented in our own day by such great scientific figures as Einstein and Eddington, deifies the human mind, and therefore tends to accentuate rather than diminish the peril in which the scientist now finds himself. Existentialism may be regarded as an anguished attempt not so much to resolve as to underline this dilemma bequeathed to the modern world by Descartes. It recalls man to a sense of his own contingency, to wonder at the *fact* and not merely the modalities of his existence.

But this recall is not enough. If we refuse to move beyond the level of human frailty and fleetingness, the human condition becomes a horrid absurdity without a history or a meaning. It must be seen as demanding a total creative Cause as its existential ground. This requires acute metaphysical analysis of the kind in which Aristotle and Aquinas excelled and which contemporary thought is beginning to master again after many centuries of neglect. Here is where the realist metaphysical inheritance of the Christian can be of such immense service. Yet the very strength and complexity of this inheritance poses a great danger, too—the danger of treating the words of a master philosopher as things, of converting philosophy into history. Metaphysics more than any other part of philosophy requires an utter integrity, to which the memorizing of "theses" and the division of the history of philosophy into the "good guys" and the "bad guys," in the manner of a juvenile western, are altogether alien.

A KEY TO UNDERSTANDING NATURE

The passionate desire for understanding and comprehensiveness which distinguishes the true metaphysician can be seen in the best of contemporary Catholic thought—in the works of Maréchal, Maritain, Lonergan and de Raeymaeker. It is here (so it seems to me) that the scientist may find a way of relating man to nature and to his Creator. Man is seen as totally dependent upon God at every moment of his existence. Everything that he is or makes himself to be, the very fact that he is at all, all these find their ultimate ground in the Creator. Man accepts things as they are, tries to understand them and modify them. But the whole order of space and time, of man and materials, takes its being from One who stands alone, who conserves the world in being and does not merely modify it.

The scientific quest itself takes on its full significance only within this context of *creation,* of the universe as God's handiwork. This insight is probably the principal legacy that the Judeo-Christian tradition has bequeathed to philosophy, as Pieper and other historians of medieval philosophy have often stressed. Natural science is, then, in its own way a searching out of the intelligible imprint that the Creator has impressed upon His work. It is true that some have held that science tells us nothing of real structure; it is to be regarded, they say, simply as a convenient way of cataloguing phenomena. This was Bellarmine's contention against Galileo, and it echoed a distrust of the "mathematicians" which was common at that day among philosophers and theologians. It is the view of modern positivism, too—a view which, partly through the influence of Duhem, has tinged the whole of contemporary Catholic thinking on the nature of science. Though possessing a certain plausibility in the context of descriptive theories of motion, this view is utterly and demonstrably inadequate as an account of what science in general is doing. It makes the scientist either a collector of curiosities or a technologist.

Science, then, must be taken to disclose in some sense, however oblique, the hidden structures of the real. We can now begin to realize the true dignity of the scientist's vocation. It is he who is charged with interpreting the Book of Nature in which God reveals Himself no less surely—though much less clearly—than in the Bible. What the scientist finds is what God Himself has put there, the intelligible structures which are the proper objects of man's God-given intellect. Next to love of God and neighbor in the scale of values governing those spiritual activities which make us the "image of God" comes intellectual understanding. And foremost among the goals of that understanding is the scientific grasp of that created world to which God has fitted man's sensory powers. If we are to prepare for eternal life by the development, both natural and supernatural, of our faculties of intellect and will, it would seem that scientific understanding is among the highest of natural activities, one that every Christian should hold in the most profound esteem.

The struggle which convulses the world today can, in a certain sense, be regarded as a conflict between two competing theologies of science. One theology assigns to science a messianic role in bringing about the millennium here on earth; secularists of the West and Communists of the East agree in making scientific progress the supreme norm for man. Christianity, however, sees its millennium elsewhere, and declares that prayerful union with God is more important to human destiny than is scientific research. The scientific exploration of the universe, as our late Holy Father so often emphasized, is good, but it attains its full significance only when it reverently respects God's overlordship. It must be carried out with humility; there must be a real ascesis of knowledge, of the kind that the Incarnation not only dramatizes and symbolizes, but also makes possible for the individual Christian. The Word of God freely limited Himself by assuming our condition, and even gave Himself over to suffering and death for the love of men. The scientist who looks upon nature and sees in it the imprint of this same Word cannot fail to realize that his commitment to truth must involve an equal commitment to love, and that the discovery of truth must lead man to humility, not to pride.

3

SCIENCE AND THE
BIBLICAL WORLD-VIEW

Hendrikus Berkhof*

I. INTRODUCTION

Without any deliberate choice on his part, modern man has entered into a new experience and understanding of nature and of history. For many centuries there was a general tendency to consider subhuman nature as an entirely terrestrial static reality, this planet being conceived as the stage for the drama of human life. In European culture, history was thought of as covering a short period of but a few thousand years, and also as a somewhat static reality, within which Fall, Incarnation and Consummation were seen as three incidents, of which the second and the third aimed at the restoration of a supposedly perfect beginning.

* Hendrikus Berkhof is Professor of Systematic Theology at the University of Leiden in Holland. His theological writings have appeared in Dutch, German, and English, and reflect the neo-orthodox concern to take the Bible seriously but not literally. We include this selection as an example of renewed interest in the role of nature in biblical theology. It is the first part of a study document, "God in Nature and History," which Professor Berkhof prepared in 1965 at the invitation of the Division of Studies of the World Council of Churches, which circulated it in "Study Encounter, Vol. 1, No. 3" as a basis for discussion. The author and the World Council have graciously allowed us to print it here.

This world-view underwent a slow disintegration in the period succeeding the Renaissance. The process speeded up about 1850. Now, since 1950, the quick destruction of its last remnants has become manifest, as it has given way to a radically new and dynamic concept of nature and history.

For modern man nature is thus no longer a static, geocentric, limited entity, but a process in an almost infinite space and an almost endless time. The earth is a tiny satellite of a little star in one of the many galaxies discovered by terrestrial telescopes. The evolution of nature on this planet began about four billion years ago. That evolution went on through all kinds of events, in a chequered career, as matter, then life, and then conscious life came to be, through ever higher and more complex unities, characterized by a gradually increasing degree of freedom—until about 500,000 years ago the phenomenon of man emerged.

When man thinks of history, he thinks of a human sequel to the history of nature. *Homo sapiens,* with his unique capacity for self-consciousness, has been in process of development for many centuries of struggling for greater freedom, higher human-ity, and wider universality. He is bound to, and rooted in, the soil of subhuman nature, but his tending towards higher possibilities in the future is in full accord with the evolutionary force that has unconsciously guided the whole of creation from the very beginning. Man partakes in powers and processes that are full of risks as well as of promises. This is why he lives in fluctuating moods of optimism and pessimism, an ambiguity everywhere reflected in the expressions of modern culture.

The Christian Church is bewildered by this new experience and understanding. For centuries the Bible has been thought of as witnessing to a small geocentric and static world, governed by a wise and almighty God, whose main interest is to help man, the crown of his creation, to his eternal destiny. Now, however, man looks insignificant indeed against the background of the vast dimensions of time and space. He is emerging out of lower nature, and that seems to be governed by a grand, arbitrary and blind power. Has the God of the Bible still any relevance for this great new world-view?

Christendom, embarrassed by these facts and questions, has often given evasive answers to this new challenge. These answers have either denied the clear facts of science (fundamentalism) or the essentials of the Christian faith (liberalism, modernism), or else have tried to separate the realms of faith and of science, by limiting God's work to the inner life and to existential decision, and by denying his relation to the visible realities of nature and history (pietism, theological existentialism).

To label these answers as "evasive" is to admit an obligation to look for better answers, and to seek a new and better mutual relationship between the Christian message and the modern view of life and of the world. In trying to accept that obligation, this paper will start from the biblical side, aiming at a fresh understanding of what the Old and the New Testaments teach about God's active presence in nature and history.

II. THE GOD OF HISTORY AS THE GOD OF NATURE

The heart of Israel's faith, as set forth in the Old Testament, was that God has made Himself known in the events of history. This was a radically new idea and experience in the world of religions. For the primitive and ancient religions of the Middle East, God or the gods are revealed in nature. Nature is the external aspect of divine reality. God is as nature is—blessing and harming, ambiguous, capricious. And history is no more than a part of nature, partaking in the same divine natural reality, obeying the same laws as the seasons, the stars and the weather.

Through Moses, Israel encountered this God of history. She met Him at that great turning-point in her story when she was rescued from her life in Egypt, the "house of bondage." This new God was nameless. He called Himself "I am I." This meant a refusal to give a name by which He could be conjured. It meant at the same time a strong promise: you will experience My presence as you need it; "I shall be with you in the way in which I shall be with you." This God goes before his people through the desert, leading the way to the future, to the promised land. This does not mean that his way is always evident to the faithful. Mostly his guidance and purposes are hidden. "Thy footprints were unseen" (Ps. 77:19). Time and again, however, when his people in disobedience and distress need it, He speaks in judgment and in grace through the events of history. Then Israel sees anew, repentant and encouraged, her way ahead through history. And she knows that this same God in a hidden way is the Lord of all history, both of Israel's and also of that of all the nations.

History for Israel is no longer a part of nature. Unlike nature, it is directed towards a goal. This goal is higher and wider than Israel itself. It embraces all the nations. The history of Israel is the preparation for a universal history, for in Israel "all the families of the earth will be blessed" (Gen. 12:3).

In worshipping a God of history, Israel inevitably developed an attitude to history different from that of the religions of all other nations; but her attitude to nature was also different. For Israel, there is no direct encounter with God in the phenomena of nature. The divine wisdom is not to be found in them (Job 28). Therefore the old nature-feasts which Israel inherited from her neighbours, the feast of unleavened bread, the feast of the first-fruits and the feast of booths, were in the course of Israel's history turned into memorial feasts of God's historical deeds (Cf. Ex. 23:14–17 with Deut. 16:1–17). Nature is not so much the realm where God is revealed to man, as the realm in which man, created in God's image, has to realise God's purpose for his creation (Gen. 1:26–30). This does not imply that Israel had a negative attitude towards nature. On the contrary, she believed and confessed that the God of history is also the last secret of nature. God is one, and his creation is one. History and nature therefore are governed by the same will. When history is believed to be the realm of the covenant-God, and the way towards his kingdom, then nature also must serve Him and his goal. So the creation of nature is conceived of as the opening act of history. In the ancient religions, history is naturalized; in Israel nature is historicized. In her scriptures, particularly in the Psalms, nature plays a great role, but almost without exception in connection with God's acts in history and his covenant with Israel, to which nature also bears witness and responds (cf. Psalms 19, 29, 65, 67, 74, 75, 89, 96, 104, 136, 147 and 148). After God's character in his historical deeds is discovered, this character can also be discerned and these deeds seen prefigured in the processes of nature. The order of nature can now be interpreted as a prefiguration, on the one hand, and a confirmation, on the other, of God's steadfast truth and loyalty towards his people (cf. Is. 42:5 f., Jer. 31:35–37).

In the order of knowledge, history comes first; in the order of being, nature. The interrelation between man, history and nature is particularly clear in the opening chapters of Genesis. For the Yahwist (Gen. 2:4–25), nature in general and the Garden of Eden in particular are the stage-setting of human history, with its challenges and failures. In Gen. 1, the Priestly writer delineates creation as history, the opening phase of the history of mankind and of Israel. For him, therefore, nature cannot be an eternal process, but must have a beginning. This beginning is called creation. Creation is a unique deed and at the same time a continuing action, because the God who defeated the powers of chaos in the beginning is still fighting the powers of rebellion which resist his covenant-actions (cf. Is. 51:9 f.). Therefore history is the continuation of creation.

It is also clear that history cannot be an end in itself, but must have an end beyond itself. God's creative and redemptive work will not be complete until all the powers of darkness are definitely brought beneath the rule of the God who wants the whole earth to be full of the glory of his covenant. So creation is the beginning of a chain in which nature, history and consummation are inseparable links. This continuum can be seen in its true character and unity, however, only from the middle of God's revelatory deeds in history, whence both a backward and a forward look are possible.

A good illustration of this faith is Psalm 75. It starts with the praise of God's "wondrous deeds" in history. Then the poet hears God say that He maintains and continues in history the work which He began in creation: "it is I who keep steady the pillars of the earth," even "when the earth totters and all its inhabitants." This conviction fills the poet with boldness. He now turns to God's enemies and reminds them of God's sovereignty over history. "It is God who executes judgment, putting down one and lifting up another." The poet looks forward to the moment when "all the wicked of the earth" shall be defeated. Then the promise of creation, of the God who makes steady the pillars of his earth, will be completely fulfilled.

So Israel believed in the ultimate significance of her historical encounter with God; she believed that in this encounter the final reality was disclosed, and that this reality is the key to the understanding of all things, in nature and history, from creation to consummation.

III. CHRIST, THE MEDIATOR OF REDEMPTION AND CREATION

The New Testament testifies to the fact that a great new disclosure-event has taken place. God reveals Himself anew in the field of history, now not only through man, but in man, as man. This disclosure-event surpasses the events of the past for the following reasons:

a. The Christ-event is the turning-point of the covenant-relation. Jesus Christ is both the fulfilment of God's action in wrath and grace, and the true covenant-partner, who acts vicariously on behalf of his people, in his life, teaching and sacrifice.

b. In his resurrection and in the outpouring of his Spirit, the great eschatological future is anticipated. Consequent upon these events, the Church comes into being, and the message of the radical justification of the godless and of the renewal of life is proclaimed.

c. The finality of this event is shown in the wiping out of the boundaries between the Chosen People and the nations, and in the spreading of the Gospel and the growth of the Church over all the earth, as the foretaste of the Kingdom in accordance with the eschatological expectancy of the prophets.

This involves a complex relationship between the Christ-event and the preceding revelations, a relationship which can be set out only under several heads—parallelism, cohesion and confirmation, as well as renewal, deepening and surpassing, and at times even contradiction. It is important to see how the framework of the unity of creation, nature, history and consummation is maintained, and how at the same time this whole concept is deepened and elaborated through the experience of God's final action in history in Jesus Christ. The same order will here be taken as above, that of history, creation and consummation.

The deepest driving powers of *history* are revealed in the double event of cross and resurrection. The witnesses see history as the battlefield of God with the powers of guilt and destruction. They see his rescuing initiative, as well as human resistance and rebellion. They see how God seemingly yields to this rebellion, but in reality uses it and gears it to his redemptive purpose. They see how God overcomes the resistance and makes grace and life triumph over sin and death. From this centre and perspective the witnesses look back to the history of Israel, which they see as a continuous struggle between the covenant-God and his resistant people (Matt. 21:33-39, Acts 7:1-53, Rom. 7:7 ff.), and to the history of the nations, which they consider as essentially a-historical, governed by the patience of God (Acts 14:16, 17:30, Rom. 3:25 f.) but subjected to the consequences of Adam's sin (Rom. 5) and to "the elemental spirit of the universe" (Gal. 4:3). At the same time, the witnesses look forward and see future history, under the influence of the Gospel, as a continuous and increasingly wide and intense display of the mystery of the cross and resurrection, of the struggle between the powers of the Spirit and the powers of darkness, and of the final victory of Christ's kingdom (II Thess. 2, the Book of Revelation). New Testament scholars have pointed to the analogy and connection between the Passion-story and the eschatological passages (Mark 13, at the opening of the Passion-story) and to the parallels between christological and eschatological events (the darkening of the sun, appearance of the Son of Man, resurrection).

To take seriously the final events in Christ, must also mean that he is confessed as the ultimate secret of *creation*. The key to the understanding of history must at the same time be the key to the understanding of creation, since both are essentially one. This confession of Christ as the mediator of creation is found in a particularly articulated form in three traditions, in John 1, Col. 1 and Heb. 1. All these passages make use of expressions borrowed from the popular Hellenistic philosophy of their time (probably in its turn influenced by Jewish Wisdom-speculations) about an intermediary hypostasis between the Most High God and the created world. Traditional theology has interpreted these passages as describing the work of the pre-existent Logos, the second Person in the Trinity, whom it has sharply distinguished from the incarnate Logos, Jesus Christ, to whom it ascribed the work of salvation. None of these three passages, however, knows this distinction. Without interruption they pass from the work in creation to the work in history (cf. Col. 1:17 f. and Heb. 1:3). In John it is almost impossible to say where the one ends and the other begins. In all these passages both actions are ascribed to the same Person, called the Word (John), the Son (Hebrews), the Son of His Love (Colossians). Moreover in all these passages the main emphasis is on the historical work of the revelation of God's glory (John), of atonement and restoration (Colossians), and of purification for sins (Hebrews). Apparently this historical work is considered as the consequence and completion of his creative work. Compared with similar passages in Hellenistic philosophy, it is a striking fact that these authors cut off any speculation about the Logos-substance in creation and nature. They point to history as the only realm where the secret of creation is revealed and fulfilled. On the other hand, we must also say that what is revealed in history is no unrelated incident, but the realization of a condition which had been God's purpose from the very beginning. The historical Jesus of Nazareth is the key to the understanding of the meaning of the whole created world. One should notice the way in which Colossians plays with the word "first" (15, 17, 18; a play unfortunately obscured in various translations). Does this mean that the historical Jesus of Nazareth was pre-existent and present at the work of creation? At any rate this is nearer to the mind of our authors than to consider the Logos as the second Person of the Trinity, detaching creation from redemption and opening the door for speculation about a God beyond history—as happened in the theology of the Apologetes and of Origen, to such a degree that the preaching of historical revelation and redemption was pushed aside by cosmological metaphysics. We have no choice but to interpret these pronouncements either mythologically (the historical person of Jesus was pre-existent) or metaphorically (God created the world as the realm of his revelation and redemption in Jesus). I assume that the authors believed the first and by it meant the second. When mythical language lost its significance, these three confessions had to be understood metaphorically. God's creation of the first Adam was effected with the last Adam in view, and the latter had to complete creation and to rescue the world from its incompleteness and estrangement. Just as in the Old Testament creation is described in terms of the Exodus (God's deliverance from chaos, darkness and flood), so in the New Testament it is described as the first revelation of the mind of Christ, the new man, the true image of God.

.   .   .   .

IV. THE BIBLICAL AND THE MODERN WORLD-VIEW

It may now be seen that the distance between the biblical and the modern world-view is far smaller than is often supposed. It may even be said that the modern concept of the world and of life is much nearer to the Christian faith than the traditional static concept of nature and history, as outlined in the introductory section to this paper. This is so for the following reasons:

a. Creation is the first history, and nature is part of this pre-history. The word "generations" (*toledoth*) is used in Genesis not only for the succession of human generations, but also for the history of creation: "These are the generations of the heavens and the earth when they were created" (Gen. 2:4). Both Israel and modern science have a radically historicized conception of creation and nature.

b. Creation and nature are pre-history, directed towards man. Man is rooted in this pre-history. At the same time this history comes in man to a new decisive phase.

c. According to this, creation as the opening act of history is not complete. When we read that "God saw that it was (very) good" (Gen. 1), we should not understand the word "good" in the Greek sense of being perfect, but in the Hebrew sense of being fit and suitable for its function, for the goal it has to serve—in this case, for the history of God and man, for which it has to serve as a stage-setting.

d. Nature in itself does not reveal God. He reveals Himself in history through his words and deeds. Looking back from God's work in history, however, man can recognize also in his stage-setting work some traces of his being (e. g. his majesty, his power, his inscrutability).

e. The great creation-nature-history process has not yet come to an end. New developments are still to be expected. Living in a great historical process means looking constantly forward, believing in an open future.

Now the question arises: supposing all this to be true, why then did it remain hidden for so long? Why did the Church so strongly resist the historicizing of nature in modern evolutionary theories? Why was the Church, which by her preaching led the ancient world out of a naturalistic life-concept into God's history, so reluctant to draw the consequences of her own convictions? Why did she cling for so many centuries to a static, unhistorical concept of life?

The reason is that for centuries the Church in Western Europe not only preached the Christian message, but also saw it as her duty to preserve and to develop the Graeco-Roman scientific heritage. This was a heritage of static conceptions about nature and history. The Christian message was thus framed in a static world-concept, which was handed down with the same ecclesiastical authority. Since the Enlightenment, this concept has been attacked. Both attackers and defenders have seen the attack as an assault upon Christianity. This misunderstanding could easily arise and be maintained, because the attack often used mechanistic and deterministic categories unsuitable for the Christian faith. So, in the nineteenth century, one was urged to make an unnecessary choice between a static-Christian conception of creation and history and the modern idea of evolution. This situation lasted until the middle of this century, when the conviction gained ground on both sides that the alternative was a false one.

This does not mean, however, that the Christian faith can identify itself with the modern world-view. Science never reaches final results, nor—and this is more important—can it by its nature and limits give answers to the questions which it raises. It can describe a process in its phenomena, but cannot make any statements about the meaning or goal of the process. When scientists do sometimes make such statements, they then adopt the role of theologians or philosophers. The Church believes that only the encounter with God in history, centred in Jesus Christ, gives the answer to these questions. At the same time she is deeply indebted to modern science, because its approach and results have compelled her to re-examine her convictions and to free herself from traditions that are alien to her message. She should be far more grateful to God than she has been hitherto for the way in which He has used science to clarify and deepen the insights of her faith.

C

PART TWO: THE METHODS
OF SCIENCE AND RELIGION

4

THE SIMILARITY OF
SCIENCE AND RELIGION

*Charles A. Coulson**

Every schoolboy knows—or thinks he knows—that modern science has destroyed any serious claims by Christianity to provide an understanding of the world in which we live, and of the people who live in it; for many people science has taken the place of Christianity as the sure and safe ground on which to build a way of life. Certainly no education today will have any "bite" unless it can deal faithfully and intelligently with it. This is not to say that the schoolboy has got hold of things the right

* C. A. Coulson is Rouse Ball Professor of Mathematics at the University of Oxford. In addition to his publications in mathematics and theoretical physics, he has written extensively on science and religion, including Science and Christian Belief (1955). The selection below is an essay on "The Natural Sciences" in a symposium entitled An Approach to Christian Education (1956) edited by Rupert E. Davies and reprinted here by permission of the Epworth Press, London (section headings have been added). In the role of presuppositions and "the personal element" in science he sees significant parallels with religion; as indicated in Chapter 1 above, such methodological similarities constitute one of the "areas of recent dialogue" among those concerned to relate the two fields. Given originally as a talk to schoolteachers, it is somewhat popular in presentation and will serve to present without technical language some of the issues of method which are our concern in Part Two.

way round (for in fact, as I shall show in a few minutes, he has actually grasped the stick by the wrong end); nor is it to agree that anyone really does build his way of life on scientific principles (the Communists are the only large body of people to make this claim explicitly and officially, and few claims are more preposterous, as we shall see later). But this conviction about science lies deep in the unconscious thinking of the ordinary man, who sees all round him the exciting and varied products of a technology that provides for almost every physical and mental need, and who concludes that the scientific mode of thought and experiment out of which this technology grew is large enough, and solid enough, to be a chief foundation for his life. Those of us who are professional scientists know only too well that, willy-nilly, we are the High Priests of the New Order. We may not like it, but we can do very little about it—a situation which suggests pretty strongly that a Christian philosophy of the natural sciences is much needed.

CONTEMPORARY SCIENTIFIC HUMANISM

It is most important to know on what this conviction of "Everyman" rests. It is not easy to crystallize it simply, but once we have got past the unhappy tendency to gape and be mesmerized by the sheer magnificence of scientific achievement, we can perhaps state his case as follows. Science makes claims about the nature of reality; its very success in understanding and predicting the behaviour of the universe buttresses these claims and gives them validity. The claims of science are different from, and superior to, the claims made by religion because, unlike religion, science makes no presuppositions in its enquiry, and is based on hard and unchallengeable facts. The laws which embody these facts, and which we call scientific laws, have shown themselves capable of almost unlimited extension, so that we may reasonably look for the time when every aspect of a man's experience is covered by them. They possess permanence and truth because they are irrevocable and unalterable. They possess universality because they are accessible to anyone with the necessary mental training. Their comprehensiveness, their vigour, their obvious power will eventually drive away all other systems of belief, which will come to be recognized as myths out of which man must grow; and though we cannot at this moment predict the nature of the changes that will come over man's ethics and his way of thinking as science grows, we can at least be sure that any old-fashioned system of thought, or vested interest, such as religion or capitalism, which impedes the progressive development of a complete science of man, must be cast out, just as, in older days, the Christian religion itself was useful for casting out the demons of uncivilized and illiterate savages.

We could summarize all this in some words by a former president of the Carnegie Endowment for International Peace: "The greatest event in the world today is not the awakening of Asia nor the rise of communism—vast and portentous as those events are. It is the advent of a new way of living, due to science, a change in the conditions of work and the structure of society which began not so very long ago in the West and is now reaching out over all mankind."

It is important to realize that in this summary of the scientific case we have passed far beyond mere technology. We may begin there, because that is about as far as the man in the street could state his beliefs; but his unrecognized convictions go much deeper. He knows that science grows, even though he may have no personal knowledge of any of it; and he knows that scientific controversy almost always issues in universal agreement, frequently very quickly. It is not surprising then that science becomes the ground of that hope, which all men cherish, that their highest ideals will be realized on earth. Professor Waddington, one of the most outspoken of the leaders in this great movement, puts the "scientific attitude" very pungently: "At the present time only science has the vigour and the authority of achievement, to make these highest human values captivate men's hearts and minds, and restore faith to them." Science is the great cohesive force in modern society, and because of its very splendour and excellence it outmodes any other rival interpretation of man's life.

It is quite clear that if all this were true, there could be no Christian philosophy of education in science; for that would be an intolerable restriction on science. But in fact it is not all true; and my chief concern here must be to show just how far it is true and how far it is false. A proper recognition of the true status of science, once it had been obtained, would soon show itself in the teaching of science, and in our struggle to find a correct and satisfying relationship between scientific knowledge and religious knowledge.

But first a little history. This so-called conflict is in no sense a legacy of the past, unless by the past we mean the last one hundred and fifty years. We ought to keep on reminding ourselves that, as scholars like Professor Butterfield have shown, science was literally cradled in the Christian faith; it is indeed a child of Christian thought. A few illustrations will make this clear. When modern science was beginning, in the seventeenth century, its leaders were almost all devout and convinced Christians. Isaac Newton in physics, John Ray in biology, Robert Boyle in chemistry, Kepler in astronomy—these are a small selection from the great names that could be mentioned. Two bishops were among the original members of the Royal Society—the most distinguished of all scientific societies—and one of them actually proposed Newton for membership. Any doubt about the function of the Royal Society is soon dispelled when we recall that in their second charter the Fellows were commanded to direct their studies "to the Glory of God the Creator, and the benefit of the human race." Nearly two hundred years later, in 1831, when the British Association was being founded for the advancement of science, a similar obligation was accepted. The historian of that first meeting in York, after paying tribute to the Church "without whose aid the Association would never have been founded," states as the reason for this interest, that "true religion and true science ever lead to the same great end, manifesting and exalting the glory and goodness of the great object of our common worship." Perhaps this is why its first two Presidents were clergymen. Even in 1860, in that stormy meeting at Oxford where Bishop Wilberforce so unwisely attacked Darwin's theory of natural selection, the first public support for the theory itself came from a Dean of the Church, at a time when other biologists like Owen were ridiculing it. It is a plain fact of history that this is true, just as it is a plain fact also that in the Middle Ages, centuries before men knew how to discover scientific laws, Christians were hankering after them, convinced that the rationality of God would be in doubt until it could be vindicated in an understood "order and constancy of Nature." What a strange irony that these very laws later became a stumbling-block, and their autonomy seemed to make of God nothing more than an hypothesis for which man had no further need!

It is now time to go back to that hypothetical statement of the claims of modern science, and to see how far its various elements do correctly reflect the temper and tradition of the subject. The argument rested on three main assertions: (1) that science started with no presuppositions, whereas religion was overloaded with them; (2) that science was founded on facts, and religion on something more like fancy; (3) that scientific laws, because they were quite impersonal, were irrevocable and unalterable, and left no room for the intrusion of anything spiritual. Let us consider these in turn, and ask ourselves how true they are. We shall find that they are nothing but a travesty of science as it is actually practised. This will lead us to recognize that what we conventionally call science and what we conventionally call religion have so much in common that we need fear no dichotomy of experience—when we enter our laboratory, we need not forget our religion, and when we leave it, we are not obliged to close the door on our scientific thinking. The situation is well put in some words by a distinguished German physicist: "A little science leads away from God: more science leads back to Him."

THE PRESUPPOSITIONS OF SCIENCE

The first claim about science was that it accepted no pre-suppositions and was therefore superior to a Christianity which did. This is a common belief, but wholly false. Theodor Mommsen's famous phrase, "science without presuppositions," is a hopelessly superficial description of our discipline. Let us think for a moment of some of the attitudes of mind with which any scientist comes to his search: there is honesty, and integrity, and hope; there is enthusiasm, for no one ever yet began an experiment without an element of passion; there is an identifica-tion of himself with the experiment, a partisan character about his secret hope for its conclusion which not even an adverse result can wholly extinguish; there is a humility before a created order of things which are to be received and studied; there is a singleness of mind about the search, which reveals what the scientist himself may often hesitate to confess, that he does what he does because it seems exciting and it somehow fulfils a deep part of his very being; there is co-operation with his fellows, both in the same laboratory and across the seven seas; there is patience, akin to that which kept Mme Curie at her self-imposed task of purifying two tons of pitchblende to extract the few odd milligrammes of radium; above all there is judgement —judgement as to what constitutes worthwhile research, judge-ment as to what is fit and suitable for publication. No wonder that a modern scientist—and no Christian either—has to say that "science cannot exist without judgements of value."

This is indeed true; science could not exist, and certainly is not practised, without all these qualities. They build the ethos and the tradition which every scientist must accept and to which he must conform. One could illustrate them in a thousand ways. For example, the physiologist Pavlov, in his *Bequest to Aca-demic Youth,* asks the question: "What can I wish to the youth of my country who devote themselves to science?" and he concludes his answer: . . . "Thirdly, passion. Remember that

science demands from a man all his life. If you had two lives
that would not be enough for you. Be passionate in your work
and in your searching." Or—to give a different kind of illustration—an international conference takes place; everyone has the
same right to speak; no national barriers, except the difficulties
of language, exist between the members; and, oddly enough,
when they meet together to gossip around the coffee table, they
speak much more of what they cannot do, or have failed to
achieve, than of those things in which they have been successful. What stands out most clearly, though it may never explicitly
be even mentioned, is that there really is a common search, and
it is a common search for a common truth.

If one-tenth of what I have just been saying is correct, then
science is full of presuppositions. It is true that these may be
derived from some earlier metaphysic, but science has adopted
them as its own and, like most presuppositions, their existence
is frequently not recognized even by those most affected by
them. In this case the presuppositions are such as to carry
science, properly understood, into the realm of religion. For
that common search for a common truth, that unexamined
belief that facts are correlatable (i. e. stand in relation to one
another and cohere in a scheme), that unprovable assumption
that there is an "order and constancy in Nature," without which
the patient effort of the scientist would be only so much in-
coherent babbling and his publication of it in a scientific journal
for all to read pure hypocrisy—all this is a legacy from religious
conviction. No one has put this more finely than Whitehead, in
his *Science and the Modern World:*

> I do not think, however, that I have even yet brought out the
> greatest contribution of Medievalism to the formation of the scien-
> tific movement. I mean the inexpugnable belief that every detailed
> occurrence can be correlated with its antecedents in a perfectly
> definite manner exemplifying general principles. Without this belief
> the incredible labours of scientists would be without hope. It is this
> instinctive conviction, vividly poised before the imagination, which
> is the motive power of research—that there is a secret, a secret which
> can be revealed. How has this conviction been so vividly implanted

in the European mind? When we compare this tone of thought in Europe with the attitude of other civilizations when left to themselves, there seems but one source for its origin. It must come from the medieval insistence on the rationality of God, conceived as with the personal energy of Jehovah and with the rationality of a Greek philosopher. Every detail was supervised and ordered: the search into nature could only result in the vindication of the faith in rationality.

To those who have realized the historical origins of science, the existence of these presuppositions, and their true significance, will seem the most natural thing in the world. And their reality is obvious as soon as anyone looks carefully at the practice of scientists.

All this means that the first of the three assertions about the nature of modern science—that it starts with no presuppositions—has no basis in reality. Now let us turn to the second assertion—that, unlike religion, it is founded on facts.

SCIENCE IS NOT A COLLECTION OF FACTS

There is probably a greater misunderstanding of this matter than of any other in the field of science. Facts there certainly are; for people make measurements and record their findings. But these are not science—or at any rate they are only the first stage, and have no intrinsic value until they are co-ordinated. It may be a fact that a stone which falls from the leaning tower of Pisa has taken a certain definite number of seconds to reach the ground. But this fact has significance only when it is recognized as one particular example of the universal law of gravitation. Lord Rutherford was accustomed to label the efforts of the fact-finders as "stamp collecting"—a term, however, which would be judged much too generous by any self-respecting philatelist. Science is not a collection of facts; it is what we make of the facts. Nothing could be more false than Isaac Newton at the end of his life describing himself as "picking up pebbles" on the great beach of knowledge, or than Charles Darwin writing of himself that "my mind seems to have become a kind of machine for grinding general laws out of large collections of facts." For Newton himself said that "no great discovery is ever made without a bold guess," and Darwin's magnificent contribution to science is still referred to as the *theory* of evolution—a phrase whose very wording shows that we recognize the intrusion of imagination and inspiration passing beyond the facts. Professor Beveridge at Cambridge has recently gathered together several comments on this situation which have been made by the scientists themselves. I will quote but two. First there is Huxley: "It is a popular delusion that the scientific enquirer is under an obligation not to go beyond generalization of observed facts . . . but anyone who is practically acquainted with scientific work is aware that those who refuse to go beyond the facts, rarely get as far." And then there is Pasteur: "If someone tells me that in making these conclusions I have gone beyond the facts, I reply: 'It is true that I have freely put myself among ideas which cannot be rigorously proved. That is my way of looking at things.' "

In recent years the physical sciences have underlined this necessity to leap beyond the facts in no uncertain manner; for physics is now full of atoms and electrons and protons. The nuclear physicist, who visits the Pic du Midi in the Pyrenees to expose his photographic plate to cosmic radiation, and then returns to develop it, will serve as an illustration. What he finds in his plate are a series of little tracks, sometimes nearly straight, sometimes changing their direction as if something had collided with something else. And how does he interpret all this? By saying that a π meson moves fast until it collides with some other nucleus, or spontaneously decays into a μ meson, and that perhaps other mesons play their part as well. Today there is an elaborate hierarchy of fundamental particles from which all things in nature may be said to be ultimately derived. Yet if an inquirer be so bold as to ask whether anyone has ever *really* seen a single meson, the answer has to be "No." And the same is true of electrons, and atoms, and almost all the dominant entities in modern physics. As Bertrand Russell says, physics may have begun historically with a principle of naïve realism—that things genuinely are what they seem to be—but its greatest triumphs are those associated with a leap beyond the facts. Surely no one who has seriously thought about these matters, and has recognized the outcome of these imaginative glimpses in the shape of an atomic bomb, will be tempted to assert that science rests wholly on facts. The German physicist Max Planck was not overstating the case when he said that "Science is a created work of art: for new ideas are not generated by deduction, but by a creative imagination." And Professor Dingle of London has teased us by writing that modern physics requires us to accept such a monstrous volume of unprovable improbabilities that the claims of the extreme fundamentalist seem pale by comparison. I say all this not to disparage science, for it seems to me to be plainly one aspect of God's self-revelation, and its imagery, no less than its austerity, are a living testament to the flowering of the human mind. I say it to explode the hoary myth that science rests on fact, and religion only on fancy.

THE PERSONAL ELEMENT IN SCIENCE

This leads us to the third element in the claims of scientific humanism—that scientific laws, because they are impersonal, are irrevocable and unalterable, and leave no room for the intrusion of anything spiritual. This claim is no more true than the others. In the first place, scientific laws are far from being impersonal. As we have just said, scientific laws are not *found* by men, more or less in the way that archaeologists dig up buried treasure from the past; they are *imagined* and *conceived* by men. It is only the facts, and not the laws, which are found. We need to remind ourselves that the personal element plays a large part in science—not only in deciding what things are worth studying, but, more subtly, in deciding what constitutes a "scientific proof." This last point is worth developing further, for there is a world of difference between the Q.E.D. which a mathematician correctly puts at the end of a geometrical proof, and the tentative claim of the scientist who deals, in whatever form, with nature. The mathematician starts with certain axioms, and if they are once accepted, then everything else is a drawing-out of the full implications of those axioms; and his conclusion is either right or wrong. But the scientist starts with a "hunch," which he explores. His data are always uncertain; his models, which he constructs within his mind to represent the reality behind his measurements, are necessarily either over-defined, in which case some inconsistency must inevitably appear sooner or later, or they are under-defined, in which case there remains about them an element of haziness and imprecision. And even the judgement which he brings to bear in deciding the acceptability of his conclusions has no absolute character about it. Kepler, even when saying that one reason for studying the natural world was to "discover the order and harmony impressed on it by God," was really responding to the old Greek appeal to purity of form. And his notion about the movement of the planets (that they lay on the heavenly spheres, and that the radii of these spheres were so nicely adjusted that it was possible to place the five regular solids—cube, tetrahedron, etc.—so that each solid just touched the outside of one of these spheres and itself just lay inside the next outer one) was a reflection of the thought-forms of his day. For this idea moved him to ecstasy, and "proved" to his complete satisfaction that the astronomers had done their job of observation accurately, and that, since there were only five regular solids, there could only be six heavenly spheres, and therefore only six planets. We laugh at Kepler now for this, but we should do well to remind ourselves that he was using the best scientific criteria of his time (even though, as it happened, he became the first person seriously to modify this type of approach); what he said was reckoned as scientific proof in the seventeenth century. If it looks odd to us in the twentieth century, we should remember that we may expect much of our present scientific argument to appear no less peculiar in another 250 years. It is precisely because science is not impersonal, because it lives in and is expressed by people, those whom we call scientists, that it continually grows and develops and has no finality.

The true scientist, who is aware of all this, has a humility before the incompleteness of his knowledge. It has always been so. In his *Dialogue of the Great World System,* Galileo Galilei wrote these words:

> I always accounted as extraordinarily foolish those who would make human comprehension the measure of what Nature has a power or knowledge to effect, whereas on the contrary there is not any least effect in Nature which can be fully understood by most speculative minds in the world. Their vain presumption of knowing all can take beginning solely from their never having known anything; for if one has but once experienced the perfect knowledge of one thing, and truly tasted what it is to know, he shall perceive that of infinite other conclusions he understands not so much as one.

Galileo died in 1642; but his principle still remains the same. Did not the anatomist, J. Z. Young, label his Reith Lectures of 1950 *Doubt and Certainty in Science*? And in the same year the physicist, J. R. Oppenheimer, wrote about the relation of scientific research to the liberal university as follows:

> It is a world in which inquiry is sacred, and freedom of enquiry is sacred. It is a world in which doubt is not only a permissible thing, but in which doubt is the indispensable method of aiming at truth. It is a world in which the notion of novelty, of hitherto unexpected experience, is always with us and in which it is met by open-mindedness that comes from having known, of having seen over and over again that one had a great deal to learn. . . . The nature of the discipline of science is its devotion, its dedication to finding out when you are wrong, to the detection of error.

No one who reads that quotation with an open mind can possibly fail to see how science seems to require the intrusion of things spiritual. What other significance could be given to the claim that "enquiry," and "freedom of enquiry," are "sacred"?

We must return for a moment to the assertion which was

made a little earlier, that scientific laws have a distinctly personal element in them. This will appear exceedingly odd to those who have not thought much about these things. But the biologists have recently been stressing this situation in a most interesting fashion. The true position seems to be that whereas the physicist may be tempted to assert that a true statement is one that can potentially be verified by anyone who takes the trouble to learn the necessary skill, the biologist steps in to insist that this cannot be entirely correct since no two separate observers are alike. Even the fabric of their brains differs, and, as J. Z. Young puts it: "It is not adequate to define truth as that which can be observed and verified by anyone . . . we are mistaken in this emphasis on individual observers. They are not the basic units of life. Each individual is part of a much larger system, which continues over millions of years, changing slowly by the process of evolution." So it is in this context that we must think of science; we must see it as part of the grand panorama of history, as moulding people and institutions while itself being gradually transformed, as partaking and expressing both man's spiritual character and his relationship to the material world. A scientific training which fails to do justice to this dynamic character of science and to show how it is rooted in the personal nature of science is not a sound education.

I would like to refer to an illustration of this which my father often used to recall. When he was a boy at school sixty years ago and was learning science, there were two masters whose responsibility it was to teach physics and chemistry. But they differed very radically in their approaches to their subject. "An atom," said one, "is the smallest conceivable piece of any element; it cannot be further sub-divided, as you can all see from its name, which comes from the Greek, and means 'indivisible.'" "An atom," said the other, "is the smallest piece of an element that we yet know. It has not yet been split into smaller bits." There is no doubt which of these two was the real scientist.

THE MEANING OF LAW AND MIRACLE

All this has a bearing on the nature of miracle. There can be no doubt that the existence of miracles in the New Testament is a severe stumbling-block to the science-sixth-former—and to others. We have all moved a long way from the attitude of 100 years ago when the authority and divinity of Christ were authenticated by His miracles. Many of us will feel glad that science has compelled us to take a different and more mature stand. There may be some of the miracles, particularly of healing, where we can claim to see the direction of a possible understanding in the light of modern medical knowledge. But there are plenty of others which appear to be in flat contradiction to normal scientific laws: Christ walking on the water, and the raising of Lazarus, are two examples. The Christian claim that such events as these really occurred seems to many people so contrary to the scientifically established order that it must be treated with suspicion and reserve. They are quite right in feeling like this. Miracles ought not to be admitted to the corpus of Christian belief without the most searching enquiry that can be made; to most of us, the rejection of much in the "Apocryphal Gospels" is entirely justified on this score alone. But the evidence, of a historical and psychological kind, is too strong to dismiss all miracles in this summary fashion, and we are therefore faced with the difficulty raised by science. Two lines of thought, equally honest, are open to us. On the one hand we can say, quite properly, that what we call a scientific law is really only a summary of the experience that we ourselves, and our friends, have had. There is no reason to suppose that experience must necessarily repeat itself, and in appropriate circumstances things might work out differently. In Oppenheimer's phrase, there is "the notion of novelty, of hitherto unexpected experience, always with us." For our scientific laws must not be granted a wholly objective character, and we must never fall into the error of claiming that our laws rigidly govern, or control, experiences and events. The presence of Jesus Christ in human form would surely be sufficient reason to believe that things would work out differently. And so, instead of arguing from miracles to the authority of Christ, we now argue from the authority to the miracles. But there is a second point of view that could be taken equally fairly. This is to recognize the developing character of science, the result of which is that things which appear impossible in one generation (e.g. the divisibility of the atom) become the possibilities of the next (e.g. the atomic bomb, which depends wholly upon the divisibility of the atoms of uranium or plutonium in it). Because it is the nature of science to develop, we may hope that in the course of time the events which are miraculous to us today may become not only understandable, but perhaps even reproducible, as with some of the miracles of healing. Did not our Lord say, "The things which I do, greater things shall ye do"? To take such a view is not to reduce the miracles to the status of scientific sleight of hand; it is to do justice to the penetrating awareness of our Lord, and His resulting control of Nature. It is not to reduce His stature; to many of us it is to enhance it, for it takes away the element of magic and replaces it by knowledge—and it is the knowledge of reality at the deepest possible level.

Both these points of view are scientific. Both share the characteristic properties of science—doubt mixed with certainty, and the material mixed with the spiritual.

It was necessary to say something about miracles, although it involved a break in the general argument, because they present such difficulties to the scientifically minded boy or girl. But as the reader will not have failed to notice, what we have said about them is derived entirely from our general account of science, and springs out of the critique which we have given of the claims made by contemporary scientific humanism. What we have shown so far has been (1) that science has its presuppositions, though they are often unrecognized, (2) that science is not based on facts alone, since we have no unfailing criteria for what is either a fact or an adequate proof, and (3) that scientific laws develop because there is a considerable personal element inextricably involved even in their formulation. No scientific education is acceptable which does not incorporate these three aspects.

PARALLELS OF SCIENCE AND RELIGION

But we must go further than this: for if he has got this far, the science schoolboy will want to know more about the relation between his science and his religion. In this connexion perhaps the most important thing that we can do is to point out that science, as it has been described in the last paragraph, is remarkably akin to religion. Think for a moment how close the parallel is: religion has its presuppositions, namely, that there is a God and that life's varied experiences can be made sense of only in religious terms; religion is not founded on fact alone, though it requires the historicity of the New Testament to save it from becoming sentimental and introvert; religion has its deeply personal element, since God is only apprehended by us as persons, and a satisfying religious conviction must be one whose validity, for us, lies in our own personal experience. Of course this is not all that can be said about religion, nor is it all that can be said about science. But this similarity is sufficiently impressive to suggest that these two modes of thought-and-experience are complementary to each other. We may say that they represent two ways of making sense and pattern out of our experiences, and their large common element almost forces us to recognize them as related.

We have come back to the point of view within which science grew up, where it was accepted unhesitatingly as a revelation of God; but now, thanks to the splendour of science, the revelation which it gives is infinitely more wonderful and more compelling than it could have been at the dawn of our scientific era. Science has its proper place in the whole economy of life, for it shows us God as seen and experienced from a different point of view from any other. Sir Richard Gregory, for many years the editor of the scientific journal, *Nature,* was quite right when he said: "Science is not to be regarded merely as a storehouse of facts to be used for material purposes, but as one of the great human endeavours to be ranked with art and religion as the guide and expression of man's fearless quest for truth." Science plays its part in helping us to understand our environment—to put a face on God. We ought to teach science because of this contribution that it makes. We ought to teach it in such a way that its spiritual element is not lost, in such a way that it appears as a purifying influence. For the powerful and dominant role of science today must not be divorced from the wider view. There is much to be said for the argument that when we teach science, we should stress its relation with the arts and with religion, and that when we teach the humanities, we should not leave out some account of science. It was a historian of science, George Sarton, who wrote:

It is true that most men of letters, and, I am sorry to say, not a few scientists, know science only by its material achievements, but ignore its spirit and see neither its internal beauty nor the beauty it extracts from the bosom of nature . . . a true humanist must know the life of science as he knows the life of art, and the life of religion.

It is nothing short of a tragedy that so many of our younger scientists at "Redbrick" University—though fortunately much less at "Oxbridge"—are so ignorant of the inner life and meaning of their subject that they behave as if it were the "last retreat of the philistines," and by their behaviour discourage the non-scientist from wanting to discover it. The fault almost certainly lies in the lack of any effective philosophy of scientific education in the schools.

It is this same lack of a philosophy of scientific education which has made things relatively easy for the Communist. We cannot oppose his view with any agreed view of our own; and yet his view is quite inadequate, as well as partly false. We can see this unsatisfactory character of the Communist philosophy of science, when we remember that its official description of the role of science is that provided by Engels—"the object of natural science is to control nature through understanding it." This definition fails because it completely misses out one of the chief objectives of science—what we have called the sense of revelation—and because it largely misinterprets the one objective that it does describe. For Nature is not impersonal, to be controlled; nor is it wholly materialistic, since, as we have seen, our understanding of it is in great measure the product of creative imagination. As a basis on which to build an adequate philosophy of science, or even a sufficient ethic, the Communist statement stands condemned.

A CHRISTIAN PHILOSOPHY OF SCIENCE

One of the most constructive changes that might profitably spring out of a Christian philosophy of science would be a greater emphasis on the way in which many of the most significant scientific discoveries come to be made. We have already referred to Darwin's false description of himself as a mind grinding out laws from a mass of facts. But in more positive fashion we could quote the physicist Helmholtz: "Happy ideas come unexpectedly, without effort, like an inspiration"; or the chemist Kekulé: "Let us learn to dream, gentlemen, and then we shall get the truth." All this seems to me to suggest that science is a gift, a sort of revelation which is given to that man who has prepared himself to receive it. This is important, because it underlines the claim which I made earlier, that science is one revelation of God. Few people have put this better than Sir Lawrence Bragg, Lord Rutherford's successor in the Chair of Physics at the Cavendish Laboratory in Cambridge: "When one has sought long for the clue to a secret of Nature, and is rewarded by grasping some part of the answer, it comes as a blinding flash of revelation: it comes as something new, more simple and at the same time more aesthetically satisfying than anything one could have created in one's own mind. This conviction is of something revealed, and not something imagined."

Now if science is a revelation, it is a revelation of some sort of reality beyond it, and other than it. The Christian will want to urge that this reality is nothing less than God Himself. If we once grasp the true significance of the Christian doctrine of creation—that "in the beginning God made the heaven and the earth"—then whatever we see or find in the earth must be a token of His purpose, His energy, His person. It is for this reason that science plays its part in our understanding of God, and takes its place with art and history and philosophy and even theology. There is an analogy that may be used to show this mutual relationship.[1] We can imagine a mountain, and the attempts made by various people to describe its features. Each person, to give any description at all, must stand somewhere. But from that very moment when he takes his stand, he restricts the description that he can give. The stand itself defines the terms within which his account must be given; and no one view of the mountain by itself is adequate. Yet different views will sometimes appear markedly different from each other, and some views will reveal geographical features, such as a rock or a stream, which are quite real, although they do not appear at all in someone else's view. Nevertheless, behind all the views there is one mountain, one reality which is being described, and whose character can only be fully known when each separate view has been accepted and studied. Each is necessary; none is redundant.

This is the analogy. Its meaning is that each separate discipline of study, be it art or history or science, shows us something of the reality which is God. No one view shows us everything. The fullness of the knowledge of God comes when we can place all separate revelations of Him side by side,

[1] The author has developed this in much greater detail in his Riddell Memorial Lectures, *Christianity in an Age of Science* (Oxford University Press, 1953).

recognizing their differences and rejoicing in their complementary character, by which our knowledge of God becomes three-dimensional instead of two-dimensional, as must inevitably be the case for any one view alone.

So the wheel comes full circle, and we are back again in that atmosphere in which our modern science grew. Science helps, for it is a necessary adjunct to the good life, and we may receive it as a gift of God. Our problems will not thereby all be solved, for the tensions of our day cannot so easily be relaxed, and our generation must carry the burden of the inability of our fore-fathers to deal creatively with this situation. But at least we know how to set about the integration of knowledge, and the main lines along which our thought must go. Indeed, as we go into our science, with minds prepared to receive, we shall see that the richness, the variety, the beauty, the excitement, the inventiveness and the power which it has revealed to us, become an aid to our worship, supplementing what would otherwise be incomplete. Not every scientist is supported, like Kepler, by the feeling that in discovering the ways of nature he is "thinking God's thoughts after Him"; but about those who see their work in the way in which we have been urging, at least this can be said: their work is holy, the tools and the objects that they handle in their experiments are sacramental, the material and the spiritual being most intimately interwoven. It was because he saw this so clearly, as long ago as the thirteenth century, before ever the dawn of modern science, that the last word must be with St Thomas Aquinas:

By considering what God has made, we can—first of all—catch a glimpse of the divine wisdom which has in some measure impressed a certain likeness to itself upon them. . . . In the second place, such consideration leads to an admiration of God's perfect excellence. . . . Thirdly, it inflames the human mind to love of God's goodness. For whatever goodness or perfection is to be found distributed among particular things is all united in Him who is the fount of all goodness. If therefore the goodness, beauty and charm of all things created can so gain men's affection, the very fount of goodness, God Himself, when compared with these rivulets of goodness to be seen in His separate creatures, cannot but inflame our minds and draw them wholly to Himself.

This is just as true now as it ever was. So also is the command: "Thou shalt love the Lord thy God with all thy heart, and with all thy mind, and with all thy soul, and with all thy strength." We dare not omit or diminish the second element of this quartet without grievously distorting the fullness and balance of the whole.

5

THE THREEFOLD NATURE
OF SCIENCE AND RELIGION

*Harold K. Schilling**

I. ABOUT THEOLOGY

Whenever we discuss the relations between science and religion we are sure to encounter the troublesome word *theology*. Many people react to it just as they do to the words *creed* and *revelation*. They think of it as a boring and irrelevant enterprise in verbal hair splitting, as the attempt to dogmatize in the worst possible sense and to rationalize and perpetuate fossilized ideas and prejudices. They regard the truth claims of theology as preposterous. Perhaps they have read about warfare not only between science and religion, but more specifically between science and theology,[1] and have concluded that it is theology that has caused all the troubles in this area.

* *Harold Schilling is a physicist at Pennsylvania State University, where he has been successively Chairman of the Physics Department, Dean of the Graduate School, and now University Professor. He has written extensively about methodological problems in science and religion. Like Coulson in the preceding essay, Schilling holds that the basic structure of the two fields and the attitudes they manifest are "remarkably alike." Reprinted with the permission of Charles Scribner's Sons from* Science and Religion *by Harold K. Schilling, pp. 67–87. Copyright © 1962 by Harold K. Schilling.*

[1] Andrew D. White, *A History of the Warfare of Science with Theology in Christendom*, first published in two volumes in 1895, but recently published in one by George Braziller (New York, 1955).

Now, again I plead for a different point of view. True, theology can be boring, irrelevant and intolerant. But it can also be exciting and adventurous, mightily relevant, utterly open-minded and tolerant. While at times it has split logical hairs needlessly, it has also been genuinely sensitive and creatively discriminating. Some of the greatest minds of our time are working in theology. And not a few others who are not theologians have discovered it to be a rather fascinating subject and enterprise. Moreover, its relations with science have by no means always been antagonistic.[2] As often as not theology has been an ally.

The misconceptions and prejudices to which I have referred are due to a large extent to a lack of understanding of what theology is and does, and how it is related to religion, as well as to ignorance of what the actual, rather than alleged, teachings of theology are.

Unfortunately, it is not too easy to find out what theology really is. While *in practice* theologians seem to agree rather well on what it is and what it means to theologize, when it comes to giving formal definitions and stating explicitly how it operates, they do not. The situation seems no different from science. In their talk about science scientists don't agree either. Albert Einstein is credited with having said that if one wants to know what science is one should not listen to what scientists say about it, but go and watch them at work. Apparently this can be said about theologians also. Therefore we shall proceed not by citing explicit definitions of theology, such as appear in its literature,[3] but by describing its function and its processes as an enterprise of the community of the faith.

Theology is the conceptualizing, interpreting, explaining, the-

[2] Richard S. Westfall, *Science and Religion in Seventeenth-Century England* (Yale University Press, 1958); John Dillenberger, *Protestant Thought and Natural Science* (Doubleday & Co., 1960).

[3] Roger Hazelton, *New Accents in Contemporary Theology* (Harper & Row, 1960); William A. Spurrier, *Guide to the Christian Faith* (Charles Scribner's Sons, 1952). For an excellent, annotated bibliography see Walter M. Horton, *Christian Theology: An Ecumenical Approach* (Harper & Row, 1958); Gustav Aulén, *The Faith of the Christian Church*, translation (Muhlenberg Press, 1948).

oretical part or aspect of religion.[4] It builds structures of thought or conceptual systems in response to men's desire and need for understanding and meaning. It explores the implications of revelation and faith in the realm of belief as well as that of actual life and existence. It is that activity of religion that uses formal logic and rules of evidence, and subjects creedal claims to the critical analysis of reason. It endeavors also to translate the expressive, symbolic language of faith into the discursive, precise language of the disciplines, and vice versa.

Theology is therefore important business—quite indispensable. We could not get along without it any more in religion than we could dispense with theoretical physics in physics. Its role in religion corresponds in many, though not all, respects to that of theoretical physics, which is the symbolizing, system-building part of physics.

To elucidate the role of *theory* in relation to other aspects of science and religion I should like to present a diagram—and apply it first to science.

II. SCIENCE IS THREEFOLD AND CIRCULAR

Science may be regarded as being threefold in nature and activity, as suggested by the three circles. First (circle *a*), it is *empirically descriptive,* engaging in data gathering by observation and experimentation. Second (circle *b*), it is *theoretical,* producing symbolic structures or systems for purposes of correlation of concepts, generalization, explanation and prediction. Third (circle *c*), it is *transformative,*[5] transforming man's natural and cultural environment by so-called "practical applications" of scientific laws and theories. None of these terms is completely adequate or accurate in its connotations. To give concrete meaning to them let us look at some examples.

[4] Theology is here regarded as internal, not external, to religion. This is one of the standard ways of looking at it.

[5] For this term I am indebted to my colleague Professor Paul D. Krynine, distinguished mineralogist and able philosopher of science.

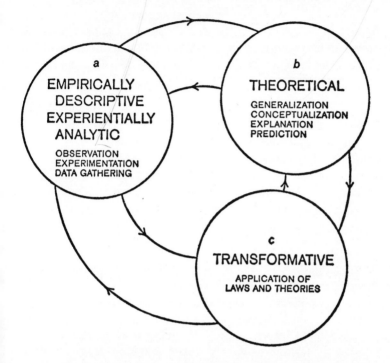

Consider the physics of gases. The part of it that provides information about the experimentally known behavior of gases is represented by circle *a*. Much of this information is formulated in the so-called gas laws, such as Boyle's Law and Charles' Law. These *laws* are expressed in mathematical equations which indicate how various measurable physical quantities are related to each other, and how they vary (change) together under different physical conditions. Thus Boyle's Law tells us approximately how the pressure of a confined gas varies with its volume, while the temperature is constant. Charles' Law shows how the volume and corresponding temperature vary while the pressure is held constant. The General Gas Law relates all three variables, i.e., the pressure, volume, and temperature, while the mass is constant. Such laws are useful in that they correlate and represent huge amounts of data. They provide information about both what has actually been observed, and what may be expected under specified conditions, i.e., for particular values of the pertinent variables.

Now physicists, like other scientists, are the kind of people who are not satisfied with having a lot of data about specific properties of gases, or even isolated laws that correlate data. What they want also is a way of correlating the laws so as to get an over-all view of the behavior of gases. Moreover, what they want especially is a mathematical structure, or theory, from which to deduce the various known gas laws and predict the existence of others not yet known. Physicists feel that when they have provided such a theoretical structure they have *explained* both the data and the laws. It is this theorizing that is represented by circle *b*.

In building such theoretical structures the physicist often proceeds by imagining, i.e., hypothesizing, a "model" which he invests with certain postulated properties. He then works out a mathematical description (system of equations) of how the imagined model works. If from this mathematical system he can deduce the laws he wants to correlate, and it meets certain other criteria of acceptability, he has a satisfactory theory.

In the case of gases, a remarkably successful theory is the so-called Kinetic Theory, which pictures a gas as consisting of a huge number of molecules that are extremely small relative to the distances between them, that are in random motion, that maintain the pressure of the gas upon the containing walls through their impact upon them. Not only does this theory "explain" the gas laws per se, but it sheds light on the laws of thermodynamics, the more general science of heat.

Circle *c* stands for the application of the empirical information about gases and the theory of gases to particular concrete situations for the purpose of controlling or transforming the physical world. There is a vast body of gas technology, which at least in its modern manifestations is to a large extent the direct consequence of this threefold activity of the physics of gases.

Another example. Chemistry is empirical and directly descriptive (circle *a*) when it propounds the laws of chemical reactions in terms of observed, measured quantities, such as weights and volumes and combining proportions, and of empirically specifiable classes or species of substances, such as elements and compounds, or gases, liquids and solids. A case in point is the so-called Law of Lavoisier, which tells us that when a chemical reaction takes place in an enclosure no weight, or mass, is lost or gained in the process. This means that in the case of a chemical decomposition the sum of the weights of the resulting components equals the weight of the sample decomposed. Thus if water is decomposed the sum of the weights of the components hydrogen and oxygen equals the weight of the water decomposed.

This is a much more meaningful and empirically useful statement than the more general one that is often called the Principle of Conservation of "Matter." This is because the term *matter* used in the latter is itself not a quantitative term, and one cannot therefore properly speak of measuring the amount of it in a container. On the other hand it is clear what it means to measure its mass or weight. Actually, like all the empirical laws of science, this Law of Lavoisier is valid only approximately, since the weights before and after a chemical reaction never do in fact add up exactly. There is always at least a small "remainder," and this may be due either to "errors" in measurement, or, say, to the presence of another, but unsuspected, component. When we take this into account we can see that in the laboratory this law, if taken precisely, functions not as a description of an aspect of nature, but as a method, an investigative tool, for the discovery of unknowns. Therefore from this point of view it could be stated more explicitly as follows: "If in the course of a change we discover a decrease in the sum of the masses of the bodies enclosed in a container, we shall say that a body having a mass of exactly the difference between the two measured masses has gone from the container in which the change took place. We shall look for this fugitive body."[6] Many a new chemical substance has been found this way. Now it is this kind of thinking that is symbolized by circle *a*.

Of course, the experimental situation with regard to chemical reactions cannot be described completely without recourse also to other laws, such as the Law of Proust, or the Law of Definite Proportions, and the Law of Dalton, or of Multiple Proportions. These are also formulated in terms of measurable quantities such as weight or mass, and of empirically identifiable chemical substances. Here we are still in circle *a*.

Now we enter circle *b*. The experimental laws of chemical re-actions—and others—are correlated and explained by the grand and remarkably successful theoretical structure called the atomic and molecular theory, which *postulates* some entities called molecules, atoms, electrons and so on and assigns to them certain properties. The growth and developments of this potent theory provide one of the most interesting and informative chapters in the history of ideas, and illustrate many features of the evolution and nature of scientific theory in general.

Chemistry is one of the sciences that illustrate most obviously the transformative activity of circle *c*. It has become not only analytical and exploratory, but truly creative. It has not only studied many substances already in existence, but has produced many new ones, such as the novel plastics, to take only one example. It has profoundly affected our mode of life and physical environment in other ways—witness its contributions in the fields of nutrition and medicine.

There was a time when science was thought to include only circles *a* and *b*, its empirical and theoretical aspects, while *c* was regarded as engineering or technology—i.e., not "really" sci-

[6] Fernand Renoirte, *Cosmology: Elements of a Critique of the Sciences and of Cosmology* (Joseph F. Wagner, Inc., 1950), p. 15. This book presents a remarkably lucid and cogent analysis of the empirical and theoretical aspects of the subject of chemical reactions.

ence at all. Today this is no longer the case. Many members of, say, the American Physical Society and American Chemical Society are engaged mainly in applying their sciences to technological problems, and yet consider themselves to be physicists or chemists, not engineers. It is becoming more and more difficult to distinguish between so-called "pure" and "applied" science.

The three components of science are, of course, inseparable and utterly interdependent. Each is meaningful only in relation to the others and to the whole. This is symbolized in the diagram by the circular arcs with arrows. Each circle is connected with each of the others by two such arcs, pointing in opposite directions to indicate action-and-reaction effects and feed-back relations. Those between circles *a* and *b* signify respectively the facts that, on the one hand, theory depends upon and comes out of observation and experimentation, and, on the other hand, observation and experimentation at their best are influenced, and often even guided, by theory. A theoretical structure endeavors to correlate and explain what one has seen. But what one sees is often affected or even determined to a considerable extent by the theoretical viewing screen through which one does the observing. Moreover, what one sets out to look for in the first place is often determined by what theory has led one to expect. We have here another case of circularity. Still another is depicted by the double connection between circle *b* and circle *c*. Theory is important in assaying the possibility of particular useful applications and indicates the direction they might well take. Conversely, theory is enlarged and enriched as one struggles with new problems in the attempt to apply it usefully. Circles *a* and *c* are similarly connected, signifying that observation and experiment often suggest or open up possibilities for useful applications without the mediation of theory; and conversely, technological needs and developments call for or suggest new areas for data gathering. The point of all this is that science is an indivisible unity. It thrives best when all three of its main components are thriving, and when there is a proper balance and interdependence among

D

them. And for present purposes it should be stressed especially that science would be inconceivable without theory.

Although in its essentials this threefold sketch depicts the nature of all the basic sciences, there are significant differences of emphasis among them. Physics and astronomy are alike in their strong emphasis upon mathematical theory—and in their quest for the grand, all-inclusive theory. But, for astronomy, circle *a* represents almost exclusively only observation and measurement, with virtually no experimentation. After all, astronomers cannot experiment with the planets or stars, i.e., intervene in their courses to manipulate them under control conditions. Nor is astronomy outstandingly transformative. Useful applications are very few indeed, and they are confined mostly to determining time and place (latitude and longitude). As we review the physical sciences, passing from physics and astronomy, through chemistry to meteorology, geology, mineralogy, and physical geography we find progressively less emphasis on precise measurements, controlled experimentation, and mathematical theory. In the biological and social sciences this trend persists and becomes even more pronounced. Moreover, the various particular science communities appear to have somewhat different viewpoints about the nature of science; that is to say, their philosophies of science are not all alike. Not only does this show up in different methodologies, but in different conceptions of basic purposes. Thus physical scientists lean more toward positivistic conceptions of theory, emphasizing their symbolic nature and predictive purpose, while the biologists seem to tend toward more realistic views about theory, regarding them as being more pictorially descriptive of nature itself.

It is therefore not too meaningful to speak of a "typical" science. They are all different in significant respects. Moreover, it is unsafe to generalize as to scientific methodology. Thus it is not true that experimentation is what characterizes all sciences. Nor do all of them think predominantly in quantitative terms.

With respect to all the sciences, however, the three circles of our diagram have this historical significance: that they represent different phases of their development. In their first stage the purely experiential, i.e., direct observation and simple data gathering, predominates. Only later do the more analytical and critical, interpretive and transformative activities put in their appearance. No doubt this is inevitable.

III. THE THREEFOLD AND CIRCULAR NATURE OF RELIGION

Turning now to religion, in many respects it also is portrayed rather well by the diagram. Certainly it too is threefold, with *a* the experiential or empirical component, *b* the theoretical or explanatory and interpretive one, and *c* the one that is transformative and pragmatic, or what is sometimes referred to as "applied religion" or "practical religion."[7] Here also we encounter the feedback interactions and circularities indicated by the dual connections between the component circles.

Theology is represented by circle *b*. It interprets and explains the faith experience of the religious community and is, therefore, largely determined by it as indicated by the arrow from *a* to *b*. On the other hand, by the concepts, doctrines and thought patterns theology develops, it profoundly affects, and partly determines, the religious life of the community (arrow from *b* to *a*). Moreover, both the life of faith and the enterprise of theology profoundly affect the transformative action of religion in the realm of ethics and morals, and in social action, while it in turn deeply affects them (opposite arrows). In a sense, then, theology (circle *b*) has a dual stance and purpose. Facing circle *a* it conceptualizes, interprets, criticizes and reacts upon the revelatory experience of the community of faith. Facing circle *c* it elaborates the implications of faith and belief for life and

---

[7] It should be noted that I am not now using some of the terms in the diagram, e.g., *experimental and data gathering*. This indicates that science and religion are not parallel in all respects relative to the diagram. There *are* significant differences.

work, and points to the responsibilities and problems of the community in the transformation of the world.

IV. EXCURSUS ON EXPERIENCE

Since all this must seem rather abstract and vague, I shall presently try to give it more concrete meaning by applying it specifically to Christianity. Before doing this, however, I must explain my usage of another troublesome word, namely *experience,* and its correlate, *religious experience.* First, I disavow completely the meaning often ascribed to "religious experience," namely, the emotional and ecstatic kind of experience often referred to as "getting religion," or "old time religion." I disavow also that usage, fashionable among certain schools of philosophers and scientists, that would restrict its meaning to only those of its aspects that are associated with physiological and instrumental perception.

What I *do* mean by it coincides more nearly with its common-sense meaning: it is what happens to people, is imposed upon them by the realities of existence. It is neither conjured up by the imagination, nor created by postulation. It is *given.* I mean what most people mean when they say: "I *experienced* the horrors of war; I did not merely read about them." "This teacher understands children through experience, not merely theoretically." "One must experience worship and prayer to be able truly to appreciate and understand their meaning and power."

My usage does not deviate far from that of contemporary empiricism, which recognizes that experience involves the whole of a man in his relation to all of his "environment." It is a broad and inclusive term. There are many kinds of experience, e. g., seeing the stars, hearing the thunder, becoming aware of the beauty of the rainbow or the beauty of holiness, falling from a ladder or falling in love, finding faith. One may experience "separation from man and God," being "born again," the revelatory disclosure of the universality of gravitation, or of the fatherhood of God. Experience includes what happens to communities as well as individuals. Moreover, experience has a variety of aspects or dimensions. Consider, for instance, how much may be implied when someone says, "Last weekend we visited Niagara Falls. It was an experience never to be forgotten." What is there about such an experience that is never to be forgotten? For many people at least this: the overwhelming impression of tremendous physical force, energy and power; the aesthetic impact of indescribable beauty and grandeur; and, for some, the sense of awe emanating from the awareness of the God (however conceived) behind it all.

So rich in content is human experience that no one discipline or intellectual endeavor is able to comprehend it in its entirety. Each one is forced to deal with it only partially, in only a restricted number of its many facets. The sciences attend to aspects of reality that can be experienced through instrumental observation and experimentation. Yet each science provides a unique kind of experience. The various arts are interested in other facets of existence, those not discernible or measurable by instruments. Again each leads to a different kind of experience. All of these are equally genuine and valid, even though they are in many respects different. *Experience* is therefore another word whose full meaning cannot be stated by intensive definition, but can be communicated only ostensively or contextually.

I disavow also the intention of assigning to experience the role attributed to it by exponents of what has been called the "religion of experience." According to this school of thought, theology is related to experience as physics is related to light and electricity. If this were true, experience itself would be the source of religion, and theology a branch of psychology or anthropology. As I see it, however, experience is the gateway to, or the transmitting mediator of, the reality experienced. The physicist experiences light and electricity. What he attempts to do is conceptualize and correlate the data of that experience in order to achieve knowledge or understanding of light and electricity. What should then be said is that experience plays the same role in religion as it does in physics. This means that theology is related to experience *as theoretical physics is related to experience*. Theological theories are to the data of the religious *experience of God and man* as physical theories are to the data of *experience of light and electricity*. From this standpoint religion, including theology, is no more a branch of psychology or anthropology than is physics, including theoretical physics.

V. CHRISTIANITY

Now let us elucidate these generalities by considering how they apply to Christianity regarded as a religion. There are those who would deny the legitimacy of this, on the ground that Christianity is not a "religion" and can, therefore, not serve as a proper example. Whether or not it should be so designated is, of course, a matter of definition, and we should not now become involved in a dispute over definitions. It seems clear that Christianity *is* a way of life, a faith, ultimate concern, *agape,* and a demand calling for commitment of all of oneself to love of God and love of neighbor. If religion is this sort of thing, Christianity is religion. It seems equally clear that Christianity *is not* a system of specified doctrine and ritualistic practice that is required of its devotees. If by "religion" is meant such a specific and specified system, then Christianity is not a religion. He whom Christians call their Lord bequeathed or enjoined no such system. What the early Christian Church carried abroad was the Gospel, news, *good news* about something that had happened— not a system of formal code.

In any case, whether Christianity should be conceived as a religion or not, let us speak of it as the way of life, faith and thought of the Christian community, in the sense that physics is the way of life, faith and thought of the physics community; and let us see whether the threefold diagram adequately symbolizes its nature at least in part.

First let us consider its experiential, empirical aspects (circle *a*). What seems to have astonished the pagan world most when it was invaded by early Christianity was not a new philosophy or novel system of ritual, but the way the early Christians loved one another, their neighbors, their enemies, and their God. And what a God! A God who loved men, who ruled by love and self-sacrifice rather than by arbitrary, monarchical and punitive power, and who was like one Jesus of Nazareth, a young Jew whom they experienced as the Christ. The lives of these peculiar, loving people were centered in and revolved around this Christ. Everything they talked about—be it nature, man or God, life or death, the past, present or the hereafter—had become and remained meaningful to them because of Him. No wonder they were nicknamed *Christ*-ians. What seemed especially odd was the fact that this Jesus was not a great celebrity. He had been known only in a very small region of the Roman empire, in Palestine. He had been in the public eye and had made his impact upon his companions and contemporaries only a very short time, not more than three or four years. After that he had been denounced and executed as a criminal. And yet these Christ-ians claimed that after His death this Jesus came back to life. Then to cap it all, they claimed that after He left them again, this time by "ascending to heaven," something tremendous happened to them that they described by saying that the Spirit of the Master, "the Holy Spirit," had descended upon them, and that thereafter this Christ had remained real to them. And finally millions of Christ-ians since then have believed all this and have testified that for them, too, Christ was—and still is—in some sense utterly alive and real.

In studying and recounting this we are operating in circle *a,* the descriptive, empirical and fact-finding part of the intellectual enterprise of the Church. To carry out this work involves various disciplines, and a variety of scholars who must be scientifically expert just as are the investigators of the history and phenomenology of the life and thought of any other community or people. Thus Old and New Testament studies require experts in the history and languages of the Near East and in textual analysis and criticism. Other disciplines involved in this empirical study of Christianity are Church history, anthropology, psychology and sociology of religion, comparative religion, comparative literature, and still others.

When Christians go forth to propagate their faith, what they are trying to do then is to share the to-them-remarkable, precious experience and way of life described in circle *a*. It is a fact of history, however, that deeply moving experience and faith always eventuate sooner or later in linguistic and theoretical expression. This is true in both science and religion. If it is an abiding, ongoing religious experience, i. e., an experience involving all of a man and touching upon his ultimate concerns, it also finds ritualistic expression. If it affects all of a man, his mind as well as his heart, inevitably it will surely be analyzed, and reasoned about. It will call forth questions and demand explanation and interpretation. It is in response to these primal demands for communication, linguistic expression, the sanctions of reason, and these urges to analyze, question and evaluate, that Christian theology (circle *b*) has come into being.

What Christian theology endeavors to *interpret* is this Christian way of life and faith, this God-man experience of the Christian community and individual. The facts or data it deals with "theoretically" are those of that experience. This basing of theology upon the body of Christian experience is indicated in the diagram by the arc-arrow from *a* to *b*. The critical function of theology, its demand that the Christian experience make sense and be under control, in short, its reaction upon experience, is indicated by the arrow from *b* to *a*.

Out of this interplay and interaction of basic experience and of critical, analytic, interpretive reflection upon it have come many conceptions of God, the world and man, that together constitute the theological doctrines of Christianity. There have been many theoretical systems, just as there have in science. Some have weathered the storms of life and others have not.

The early Christians had inherited a monotheistic conception of God from Judaism. In the light of their Christ experience this conception was immeasurably enriched. The heavenly father image took on new meaning because of the tremendously revealing Christ experience. Both His love and wrath took on new meanings, in the marvelous light of Christ's love. Sin became even more terrible in its enormity in view of the crucifixion on the one hand, and of the enriched conception of love and God on the other. The concepts of death and of the "principalities and powers of darkness in heavenly places" were transformed by the experience of the resurrection. The understanding of the nature of man and the world could never again be the same *after* the Christ experience as it had been *before*. To give all these new insights formal expression has been the task of theology.

In this connection attention is called to a series of theological treatises that exemplify with distinction the role of theology relative to the experience of the Church. It is the "Library of Constructive Theology."[8] Some of its volumes are entitled *God in Christian Thought and Experience, The Christian Experience of Forgiveness, The Christian Experience of the Holy Spirit, Redemption and Revelation, The World and God, The Christian Society, The Relevance of Christianity, Worship*. The first three of these titles in particular are directly suggestive not only of the purpose, method and spirit of the series, but of the fact that Christianity is fundamentally empirical rather than philosophical, and that a basic function of theology is to interpret the experience of faith and by reaction upon it to help shape it.

An important aspect of theology's function has been to interpret the significance of Christian insights for succeeding generations, for different cultures, and for different situations. In so doing it asks what the situation really is in a given time and culture, relative to man's relation to God and existence. It asks what it means in practice, in that situation, to love God and one's neighbor, and what action is called for, and what

[8] Edited by W. R. Matthews and Gordon Rupp, published by Nisbet & Co., Ltd., London. Most of its volumes have been reprinted many times, indicating their great significance and perennial timeliness.

duties thus devolve upon Christians in the world of affairs and in personal relations. This brings us to the relation of Christian theology to the transformative aspect of religion, symbolized by the dual connection between circles *b* and *c*. This function of theology is at least as important as the other. Here theology must analyze the ills besetting mankind, and its grave concerns and anxieties, both those that are universal and those that appear in particular situations. It must also be conscious of the great questions man asks, that reflect his ultimate concerns—for to love man significantly in the *agape* sense, one must be aware of his longings and predicaments. But more than that, theology asks which of man's questions are truly meaningful and of ultimate concern and which are not in the light of the Gospel, and what light the Gospel can shed upon the situation.

It is probably correct to say that, relative to the transformative function of religion, for a long time the primary concern of Christianity was the "salvation" of the individual "soul." Now by *salvation* I do not mean "being saved from eternal damnation and hell fire" in the once popular sense, but from the domination of sin, man's lower, egocentric self, and from the social and cosmic forces that are beyond his control and yet threaten his very existence and being. While the contemporary Church would certainly not discount the importance of personal salvation, it is preoccupied much more than formerly with the salvation of man in community and therefore with the problems of society at large. And theology has contributed in no small measure to the development of this wider point of view, and to the channeling of Christian action along appropriate lines (circle *c*).

There is probably no better exemplification of this social concern of theology than that of Reinhold Niebuhr. He has struggled mightily with the problems and terrible dilemmas facing the person who would love his fellow men in a real world. As Gordon Harland has put it, "He has sought to clarify the insights and resources of Christian faith in such a way that they may be savingly related to the structures, dynamics and decisions of large social groups. . . . His whole work serves the one concern—to relate redemptively Christian faith and social responsibility, *agape* and the struggle for social justice.[9]

Much of the work of the Church that is indicated by circle *c* might aptly be called Christian technology. Under this heading come such activities as the improvement of man's physical environment and the acquisition of the necessities of life, proper food, clothing and shelter; the conquest of disease, ignorance, superstition, slavery, and tyranny; the support of efforts toward peace and the abolishing of war; the establishment of justice and fair practices in business affairs, in labor and management relations; the improvement of race relations; the support of good government. Home and foreign missions in their various aspects come under this heading, as do many other activities. In all these fields the Church has developed experts, among both its clergy and laity, who may well be regarded as the technologists of the Church for the transformation of the world. Parenthetically it should be remarked that much of this application of the Gospel to real life needs to be effected within the Church itself. I refer to unjust social practices and other evils that are condoned or even engaged in by large sections of its membership, as well as to practices of the institutional Church itself. There is much to be done here.

It must be recognized, of course, that much of the Church's labor of love in the world is done by unsophisticated Christians with an intense love of neighbor, who are quite uninformed theologically. It might then be said that for them transformative, social action springs directly from the basic Christian faith and the sense of responsibility to God and man. This is why circle *c* is connected to both *a* and *b*. To put this into the faith language of the community, our love-action relative to our fellow men (circle *c*) is determined largely by our experience of God and man (circle *a*) and our theological beliefs about them

[9] For an able analysis of his writings, see Gordon Harland, *The Thought of Reinhold Niebuhr* (Oxford University Press, 1960), pp. vii, viii.

(circle *b*). Also, conversely, our religious experience and theological conceptions are very much affected by our actions among men.

Now a few remarks about certain approaches in theology. The need to relate the insights of the Christian faith to the ultimate questions and concerns of man is the basis for a theological method developed by Paul Tillich, which he calls the "method of correlation." "It correlates questions and answers, situation and message, human existence and divine manifestation."[10] A somewhat similar method is employed by Walter M. Horton.[11] It is built around basic perennial questions and concerns, and universal human needs, and presents answers that Christianity has to offer. Some of the problems discussed by him in this way are: the universal outreach toward some sort of deity, the universal problem of religious knowledge, the question as to whether cosmology presents a religious problem, the universal need for fellowship and inspiration, the universal need for hope, and so on. An especially valuable feature of his method is to present different theological points of view within Christianity, Roman Catholic and Protestant, conservative and liberal, and with regard to each important subject, to indicate the extent of consensus as well as disagreement among Christians.

A critical perusal of the writings of the large majority of present-day theologians will reveal them to be remarkably open-minded and far from sectarian or denominational. It should be understood more widely than it is that theology is not primarily a set, or sets, of beliefs or doctrines, but a process by which such doctrines are developed. It is no doubt true that Baptists, Lutherans, Methodists, and Presbyterians differ typically in regard to certain doctrines. There are historical reasons for this. But it makes no sense to talk of Baptist, Methodist or Episco-

[10] Paul Tillich, *Systematic Theology* (University of Chicago Press, 1953), Vol. I, p. 8.
[11] Walter M. Horton, *Christian Theology: An Ecumenical Approach* (Harper & Row, 1958).

palian theologies as such. I believe it to be true of the vast majority of theologians of today, that when they theologize they do this without conscious commitment in advance to any particular sectarian position or conclusion. My observation of theologians at work, as well as my reading in the literature of theology, has convinced me that contemporary theology does not differ significantly from science in its open-minded commitment to the free and unhampered quest for truth and insight.

VI. MORE ABOUT CIRCULARITY

Several cases of circularity have been pointed out by means of the diagram. By *circularity* of thought I mean a relationship between ideas that are so utterly interdependent that each presupposes the others and yet none is the necessary logical foundation of the others. By circularity of experience I mean a similar relationship between components of experience.

A case in point is the relationship existing in science between experiment and theory (circles *a* and *b*). Which *must* come first? Which is logically the foundation or prerequisite for the other? Should a student who is entering upon the study of a given subject, study theory first and then make experiments, or vice versa? There has been many an argument about this among scientists and they inevitably end in a stalemate. Probably there is no answer. Perhaps they are the wrong questions—like the hoary one about the chicken and the egg. The fact is that some people do—and they should—start with theory, and others with observation. This is true not only in the student laboratory, but also in the research laboratory, not only among beginners, but also among experts. There is neither logical nor psychological or pedagogical priority that must govern all cases in these matters. In the diagram this is signified by the oppositely directed arcs connecting circles *a* and *b*. Other such circularities have been pointed out.

There is circularity also with respect to the interaction of experience and thought, and therefore to the entire enterprise of science, involving all three circles. Together the latter constitute the "scientific circle." This means first, as pointed out earlier, that science is an indissoluble tri-unity, each of the three components (circles) depending on the others, and none being the logical prerequisite of the others. It means also that experientially one can enter the circle anywhere and then proceed around it in either direction—as suggested by the opposite arrows. Thus some scientists have in fact been drawn into the large circle by the fascinations of certain phenomena (circle *a*), others by an elegant theory (*b*), still others by useful technological problems (*c*). Some introductory physics courses begin with beautiful demonstrations to be observed and explained, others with an aesthetically appealing theory which suggests experiments to perform, and still others with a steam engine or a musical instrument to be taken apart and analyzed both experimentally and theoretically. Again we are confronted by evidence of the essentially non-logical and intensely human character of the scientific enterprise.

Likewise in religion. As already noted, there are the various circularities apparent within the diagram. These are illustrated by the manner in which religious experience and doctrine influence each other. But there is over-all circularity also, with complete interdependence of all three of the component circles, none being the prerequisite foundation for the others. Some people enter this "religious circle" through the gate of belief, others by experience, still others through social action. There are also, of course, other points or modes of entry. None is logically prior to the others. Once in the circle, a person may then proceed around it in either direction as his insights and experience grow.

Why belabor this matter of circularity? First, simply to portray the true nature of science and of religion, which are both much misunderstood in this regard. Second, there are methodological and philosophical implications. Some scholars would make of science—and of religion—a logical "system," depicting it not as a three-ring circle, but as a three-sectioned vertical column. At the bottom there is an allegedly impregnable a-priori, presuppositional foundation, from which confidence in the reliability and authenticity of the whole structure derives. Upon this rests logically a two-story column of the empirical and theoretical, and on top of this the pragmatic or applied. In some schemes the order of the empirical and theoretical is reversed.

As I see it, all such attempts to build systems are misguided. Neither science nor religion (or theology) can adequately be represented by them. They are not reducible or dissectible into definable entities that can be put together into philosophical or logical systems. Moreover, history seems to show convincingly that systems built upon a-priori, metaphysical foundations are built on shifting sands. Science and religion *are* non-logically circular in experience and thought, rather than logically columnar. In this respect they are remarkably similar, so much so that if we understand and appreciate the nature of the one, it will help us to understand the other. There are, of course, vast differences between them, as we have already noted. But these are not the kind that would appear in a discussion of basic structures or over-all patterns of purpose, such as our diagrams depict. Thus it is not true that the one deals with observable experience and the other does not; that one theorizes and the other does not; that one is socially applicable while the other is not. Where they differ is in the *kind* and *content* of the experiences they represent, in the kind and object of their speculations and theories, and in the kind of practical, transformative action they undertake in the world.

VII. OVERLAPPING ACTIVITIES AND IDEAS

We have emphasized that the three components of science, and religion, are not independent, but continually interact, as symbolized by curved arrows connecting the circles in the diagram. We must now recognize that in the lives of both the individual and the community these activities are usually not only interrelated and interdependent, but that they actually overlap. To depict this graphically we might in our imagination change the three-ring diagram by enlarging the circles so they overlap. This would suggest that any given investigation or development often falls in one of the areas of overlap and is rarely purely empirical, or theoretical, or even transformative. Almost always it makes contributions in more than one area.

Specialization in a science like physics or chemistry has developed to the point where many physicists and chemists regard themselves as either experimentalists or theorists. This separation has gone so far that many a theorist seems utterly at a loss when confronted with apparatus or tools; and many an experimentalist when confronted by a serious theoretical problem calls in a theorist as consultant. For this and other reasons it makes sense to think of the experimental and theoretical—as well as transformative—activies of science as significantly and identifiably different and separate, while yet realizing that they overlap, thus making it impossible to draw sharp boundary lines between them. This is not unlike the situation in religion. There too are specialists, the professional theorists (theologians) and the practitioners; though there is the same overlapping of thought and activity as in the science enterprise.

Therefore, whenever we herein use the terms *experimental, empirical* or *experiential,* and *theoretical, interpretive* or *theological,* and *technological, pragmatic* or *transformative,* it is to be understood that overlapping and fuzzy boundaries are taken for granted. If this is kept in mind we can avoid many circumlocutions and awkward qualifying phrases and sentences with respect to these terms.

6

DIFFERENCES BETWEEN SCIENTIFIC AND RELIGIOUS ASSERTIONS

*Donald D. Evans**

Two conflicting views concerning comparisons between religion and science are current today. On the one hand, both existentialist theologians and positivist critics of religion maintain that religious assertions and scientific assertions are radically *different*. On the other hand, some scientific thinkers who are keen to humanize science or to legitimize religion maintain that religion and science are essentially *similar*, and that they differ mainly in subject matter rather than in method. It seems to me that although there are a few genuine similarities between religious theory (theology) and scientific theory, there are fundamental differences between religion and science which the second view fails to acknowledge. The first view, properly qualified in

* D. D. Evans is a member of the Department of Philosophy at the University of Toronto. His book The Logic of Self-Involvement (1963) is subtitled "A Philosophical Study of Everyday Language with Special Reference to the Christian Use of Language about God as Creator." In the previously unpublished essay below, he takes issue with the kinds of similarity between science and religion which Coulson and Schilling proposed in the preceding chapters. He portrays instead a sharp contrast between the two fields. Science is logically neutral, comprehensible impersonally, and testable by observation—characteristics not present in religion, according to Evans.

response to cogent criticisms from the second, seems closer to the truth.

This paper has four parts. I shall discuss religion, then science, and then their similarities and differences. Finally, I shall summarize my conclusions.

I. RELIGIOUS FAITH AND DEPTH-EXPERIENCES

There are many varieties of religion. Some, such as classical Buddhism, are not theistic. Others, such as the modern so-called "religionless Christianity," attempt a theism without religion. The kind of religion which we shall consider is one in the Judeo-Christian tradition which equates *religious* faith with faith in *God*. Faith in God is best understood, it seems to me, by reference to "depth-experiences." This term will become clear as we look at five different kinds of depth-experience.

1. *Depth-Experiences*

a. Personal encounter. I encounter John Brown. He has an I-Thou attitude toward me, as Martin Buber would say.[1] That is, he is outgoing, open, available, and responsive. He focuses his whole self exclusively on me in my uniqueness, involving himself in my world and committing himself to me. If I respond in kind, even though less profoundly, something mysterious flashes between us, changing both of us so that we become more truly human, more real as persons. I emerge from the encounter aware of a new meaning in life, a meaning which is expressed more in a new mode of life than in any words.

This personal encounter is a depth-experience. If an agnostic

[1] My debt to Martin Buber will be evident in this section. Similarly my account of numinous experience is partly derived from Rudolph Otto, moral responsibility from John Baillie, radical despair from Paul Tillich, and indignant compassion from D. M. Mackinnon and Dietrich Bonhoeffer. In each case, however, my own account differs somewhat from theirs.

or an atheist has had a similar experience and agrees with me that it is real and important, he does not thereby agree that there is a God. He only agrees that there are mysterious depths in human relations. But he does enter a context in which I can begin to explain part of what I mean by "God." God is, in part, a hidden being whose unlimited and perfect I-Thou attitude toward me is revealed in the limited and imperfect I-Thou attitude which John Brown and others have toward me. That is, I interpret the I-Thou encounter with John Brown as a revelation of God. I look on John Brown's "presence with a meaning" as a revelation of a divine presence, an eternal meaning. I see in his I-Thou attitude toward me a revelation of God, the Eternal Thou whose I-Thou attitude toward me is complete and constant and utterly trustworthy. A believer looks on a depth-experience of personal encounter as a revelation of God and tries to live accordingly; that is, he is open to the "address" of the Eternal Thou, which comes through the words and deeds of men whom he meets in personal encounter. An agnostic or atheist interprets the depth-experience in purely human terms: "Yes, human beings are mysterious; there are depths in man which can only be known in personal encounters; but why bring in God?"

In general, depth-experiences are interpreted in one of two ways: as revelations concerning *man* or as revelations concerning both *man* and *God*. Faith involves the latter interpretation. Faith is an ongoing practical commitment to an interpretation of some depth-experiences as revelations not only of man but also of God. Sometimes a depth-experience "hits" the believer as a divine revelation, so that he is aware of no alternative interpretation at the time; but honest reflection afterwards should lead him to acknowledge the possibility of interpreting his depth-experience in purely human terms. His faith presupposes a belief that there is a hidden personal being called "God" who sometimes reveals Himself in depth-experiences. Note that his faith thus involves both commitment and belief.

Let us consider another kind of depth-experience.

b. Numinous experience. I look at a sunset or a waterfall. I have an overwhelming feeling of awe, a sense of my own littleness coupled with a joy in being so much alive and a dumfounded wonder at the mystery of beauty. Or I meet a man whom religious people call a "saint," and I have similar feelings of reverence, self-abasement, exhilaration, and bewilderment.

Such "numinous" feelings need not be interpreted in a religious way. An agnostic or atheist who is profoundly impressed by sunset or saint is not being illogical if he refrains from bringing in God. On the other hand, it is not unreasonable for a man of faith to look on the impressive features of sunset or saint as expressions of a hidden numinous being.[2] An unbeliever can understand part of what is meant by "God" in this context. God is the numinous, worshipful being who expresses Himself, reveals Himself, in such a way as to evoke numinous feelings. The man of faith interprets the depth-experience as a revelation concerning both man and God. Like many unbelievers he sometimes finds in men a mysterious depth, a capacity for awe, self-abasement, exaltation, and wonder; and in a few men he finds a mysterious impressiveness which evokes such responses in their fellows. For the man of faith, however, the depth-experience is also a revelation of God, the hidden personal being who reveals His inner nature through the numinous sunset or saint. Each element in the numinous depth-experience is correlated in meaning with an attribute of God: awe with "holiness," self-abasement with "majesty," exaltation with "spirit," and wonder with "glory." In each case the transcendence of a divine attribute is correlated with the unlimited character of the appropriate numinous response.

c. Moral responsibility. Some men have a strong sense of moral responsibility. Moral obligations come, as it were, from outside oneself, imperiously subordinating one's own inclina-

---

[2] For a detailed analysis of "impressive" and "expressive," see Donald Evans, *The Logic of Self-Involvement* (London: SCM Press, 1963), chaps. 2, 4.

tions and interests, urgently demanding acknowledgment and action.

Such moral seriousness is common to both unbelief and belief at their best. A believer differs in that he looks on his own sense of moral responsibility as a revelation of a hidden moral Sovereign who has a rightful and righteous authority over his life. He looks on the unconditional and awesome demands of the moral imperative as divine imperatives. Such faith does not equate conscience with the voice of God, for no infallibility is assumed or assured. The question, "What ought I to do?" is the same question for a believer as the question, "What does God require me to do?"—but he has no infallible method for answering his question, and his certainty and uncertainty concerning particular moral obligations may be the same as that of an unbeliever. Rather, he differs in having a sobering sense of being responsible and answerable not merely to himself or to society or to an impersonal moral law, but to a hidden personal being who is a moral Sovereign, whose wisdom is perfect, and whose demand for obedience is unqualified.

An unbeliever, however, may interpret his own moral seriousness and that of others as an indication of something profound and mysterious in human nature, without going on to interpret it as a revelation of God as well. For the believer, it reveals both man and God. Note that the morally serious unbeliever is in a position to understand part of what the believer means by "God" because they share a common sense of moral responsibility. Here again the depth-experience provides a context for meaningful language concerning God. On the other hand, to the extent to which a man lacks depth-experience he will be unable to understand such language.

We have considered three depth-experiences: personal encounter, numinous experience, moral responsibility. We now turn to a fourth.

d. Radical despair. A man is in a state of radical despair. Life seems meaningless and pointless—not only life around him, but his own life. Nevertheless he protests passionately against this meaninglessness. His despair is not a state of apathy or indifference, although he finds no basis for deciding between life and death, between right and wrong; his despair is vital and vehement; meaninglessness is for him a matter of ultimate concern.

Such radical despair is sometimes paradoxical. In such cases, the more the man protests against the meaninglessness of life, the more meaning he gives to life by his very protest. The more ultimate his concern about meaninglessness, the more meaning he gives to life by his very concern. The more vehement his rejection of this supposed meaning and that supposed meaning, the more transcendent his own sense of what a meaningful existence would be. The more profound and vital his anxiety in the face of meaninglessness, the more profound and vital his own courage in facing this anxiety.

Radical despair, like other depth-experiences, is open to alternative interpretations. The man of faith interprets his own concern for meaning as a revelation of a being who is the source of meaning in life. He interprets his own existential courage as a revelation of a being who is its source, and his own passionate yearning for an ultimate as itself a revelation of the ultimate. The man of faith believes that Pascal was right when he put those famous words into the mouth of God: "You would not be seeking me unless you had already found me." The unbeliever, however, interprets his radical despair in terms of man alone. His concern for meaning, his existential courage, and his passionate yearning for an ultimate may reveal mysterious depths in human personality. But the unbeliever does not share the believer's conviction that there is also a revelation of God, that both God and man are active in the depth-experience.

   e. Indignant compassion. Some believers and unbelievers have this in common: they identify themselves compassionately with other human beings in their suffering, sharing in it, but also grieving and rebelling against it. Like Dostoievsky's atheist Ivan Karamazov, or Camus' atheist Dr. Rieux, their compassion is compounded with a sense of outrage and revulsion that nature and men should inflict mental and physical torture on human beings. Karamazov and Rieux focus their revolt on the alleged God who made a world in which children can be torn to pieces by hunting dogs as a sport, or in which children writhe helplessly in the pains of the plague.

This atheistic protest is, for some believers, supreme blasphemy; but for other believers it is an admirable attitude which can be a profound revelation of God. For example, D. M. Mackinnon of Cambridge says, "The man who revolts, determined somehow to affirm in this most desperate situation that God did not so make the world, is met by the mystery of God's own revolt against the world He made."[3] On such a view, a man interprets his own indignant compassion as a revelation of the infinite indignant compassion of a hidden personal being, as well as an indication of mysterious depths in human nature. For the unbeliever, however, it is only the latter.

Belief in a God of indignant compassion involves a belief in a God who suffers, God as depicted by Bonhoeffer when he wrote "Christians stand by God in his hour of grieving." Bonhoeffer's image is vivid and daring. In a Nazi prison, he interprets his own grieving for humanity as a participation in God's grieving. It is as if he were standing by a friend who grieves over the sufferings of the friend's child. His own grieving is as nothing compared to his friend's. His own compassion for the child is a sharing in his friend's compassion. Similarly a man's finite concern for others is a way of sharing in the infinite divine concern.

We have considered five kinds of depth-experience. There are others which might have been included, but I shall not discuss them in this paper. Let us now examine depth-experiences more closely in relation to religious faith.

2. *Religious Faith*

Religious faith is a practical commitment to an interpretation of depth-experiences as divine revelations. Such faith presup-

---

[3] D. M. Mackinnon, *Christian Faith and Communist Faith* (London: Macmillan & Co., 1953), pp. 247–48.

poses a belief that there exists a hidden personal being who reveals himself in these ways. This being, who has the proper name "God," reveals Himself as the Eternal Thou, the awesome numinous, the moral Sovereign, the source of meaning, and the grieving friend. The believer holds that in each case the depth-experience has limitations and imperfections, but that the God who is thereby revealed does not. For example, the I-Thou attitude of the Eternal Thou is *perfect* in its constancy and openness. Although I am far from being clear as to what I mean when I describe God in these ways, and although I assume that any attempted description will be inadequate, and although the meaning of the descriptions cannot be understood in abstraction from elusive and mysterious depth-experiences, my faith does involve a *"belief-that."* I stress this, because I want to make clear my disagreement with those religious philosophers who rightly stress the element of commitment in faith, but who wrongly deny that the commitment presupposes a *belief-that*.

I also wish to distinguish my account of religious faith from some which resemble it in taking a depth-experience seriously and in finding common ground between believers and some unbelievers, but which differ in *equating* a depth-experience with faith or with God. Paul Tillich, for example, says that faith *is* the state of being ultimately concerned.[4] He also says, in a passage made famous by being quoted in *Honest to God,* "If you know that God means depth, you know much about him. . . . You can not think or say: Life has no depth! Life is shallow. Being itself is surface only. If you could say this in complete seriousness, you would be an atheist; but otherwise you are not. He who knows about depth knows about God."[5] Elsewhere Tillich seems to equate faith (his "absolute faith") with the radical despair which protests against meaninglessness.[6] I reject

---

[4] Paul Tillich, *Dynamics of Faith* (New York: Harper & Row, 1958), p. 1.

[5] J. A. T. Robinson, *Honest to God* (London: SCM Press, 1963), p. 22.

[6] Paul Tillich, *The Courage to Be* (London: Nisbet & Co., 1952), esp. p. 167.

Tillich's equation.[7] God is not the same as the depths in man, and faith is not the same as an experience of these depths. If Tillich wants to use the words "God" and "faith" in a peculiar way which abolishes any radical distinction between belief and unbelief he is free to do so, but both believers and unbelievers have a right to protest, indeed to protest with Tillichian passion! Similarly it is a mistake to equate faith with numinous experience or personal encounter or moral responsibility or indignant compassion. Faith involves an interpretation of a depth-experience as a revelation of God.

The various descriptions of God are indirect. God is a being such that various unlimited depth-experiences are appropriate responses to Him. This does not mean that God *is* a depth-experience. Such an account would be an unwarranted reductionism, similar to a reduction of material objects to sense-data or a reduction of other minds to observable public behavior. The meaning of a statement is linked with its method of verification, but the two need not be equivalent. Nor is an indirect description of God a matter of *acting-as-if*. Religious faith is not an *acting-as-if* there were a God to whom various responses would be appropriate if He really did exist. No, there really does exist such a God, though what is meant by talk about Him cannot understood in abstraction from human depth-experiences.

3. Christian Faith

Thus far in this paper I have talked about a religious faith which is not specifically Christian. A Christian faith differs in that depth-experiences are interpreted in relation to Jesus, the man of Nazareth whom Christians believe to be now alive and present in the depth-experience. For example, in the case of personal encounters, the Christian looks on another man's "presence with a meaning" as a revelation of Jesus Christ. In the words of Hopkins:

[7] Sometimes Tillich does not equate God with a depth-experience or a depth in man; God is the "ground" or even the "source" of these. This strand in Tillich's thought is not in conflict with my approach.

[The just man]
Acts in God's eye what in God's eye he is—
Christ—for Christ plays in ten thousand places,
Lovely in limbs, and lovely in eyes not his
To the Father through the features of men's faces.[8]

Also, the Cross of Christ transforms our ordinary notions of what is supremely *numinous*. A Christian looks on the Cross as the normative expression of divine glory: transcendence revealed in humility, majesty revealed in sacrifice, life and spirit revealed in death, mystery revealed in agony. Others, both believers and unbelievers, may look on the Cross as the unfortunate death of a good man; but the Christian looks on the Cross in such a way that, more than sunsets and saints, it arouses his awe, his self-abasement, his exultation, and his wonder. In other words, the Christian worships Christ crucified.

The Christian also interprets his moral experience in relation to Jesus Christ. His sense of moral responsibility to the divine sovereign is modified in various ways because of this. For example, in so far as a man is a Christian, he looks on his status before God as something which he cannot earn, something which he receives as a gift from God through Christ. He is justified by grace, and so his moral seriousness has an underlying joy and an absence of anxious strain.

I shall not try to indicate the specifically Christian interpretation of radical despair and indignant compassion. Perhaps I have said enough to show that the Christian reinterpretation of a depth-experience may involve a more or less radical revision of a man's religious interpretation. We should also note two additional points. On the one hand, my conviction concerning Jesus of Nazareth may reinforce an original decision of faith. Indeed, some elements in a step from agnosticism to faith may seem implausible unless the Christian claims for Jesus are true; for example, the interpretation of one's own grieving as a revelation of God's grieving may seem implausible unless one

[8] *Poems of Gerard Manley Hopkins,* ed. W. H. Gardner (New York: Oxford University Press, 1948), p. 95. Reprinted by permission.

believes that Jesus was divine, so that the Cross reveals God's grieving. On the other hand, my conviction concerning Jesus is in some respects not a basis for faith but rather something which itself requires a basis. It is only rational to interpret depth-experiences today in terms of Jesus if there is an adequate basis for believing two things about him: that as an historical figure he was a normative medium for God's self-revelation, and that he conquered death in such a way as to become a living presence in the depth-experiences of multitudes of men. These beliefs concerning the character and the resurrection of Jesus depend, in turn, partly on historical evidence. But this cannot be explored further here.

II. SCIENTIFIC LANGUAGE AND OBJECTIVITY

Some writers have claimed not only that some science is nonobjective but that objectivity is not even a tenable ideal for science. Such a claim may contain many valid objections against popular notions of scientific objectivity, but it is far too extreme. There are three important ways in which scientists actively, and often successfully, seek for objectivity. In each of these ways, as we shall see, science differs radically from religion. A scientific assertion should be *logically neutral, comprehensible impersonally,* and *testable by observations.* The first requirement has to do with the logic of scientific assertions, the second with conditions for understanding them, and the third with their method of verification.

Before we consider each requirement in turn, I should indicate how I am using two terms: "assertion" and "objective." "Assertion" will be used in a very loose and general way so that it covers scientific observation-reports, laws, hypotheses, or theories; the differences between these will be noted only when necessary. An "objective" assertion is one whose truth or falsity can in principle be established on the basis of maximal intersubjective agreement.

1. Scientific Assertions Are Logically Neutral

The term "neutral" can mean a great many different things. The meaning which I shall select and refine is one which makes "neutral" the opposite of *"self-involving."* A self-involving assertion is one which commits the person who asserts it or accepts it to further action, or which implies that he has an attitude for or against whatever the assertion is about, or which expresses such an attitude. For example, in saying "I promise to return this book tomorrow," I commit myself, logically, to a specific future action. In saying, "I commend Jones for his restraint," I imply that I approve of Jones' restraint. In saying, "I look on you as a father," I express an attitude toward you. In each case I *cannot* deny the self-involvement. I cannot deny that "I promise . . ." commits me, or that "I command . . ." implies a favorable attitude, or that "I look on you as a father" expresses an attitude. The "cannot" is a *logical* one. It is based on part of the *meaning* of the utterance, namely its performative force: what one is doing in saying such-and-such.[9] This meaning or force depends on public linguistic and institutional conventions, though it sometimes also depends on special contexts of meaning or on the special intentions of the speaker (what *he* means in saying such-and-such).

Of course a man may be deceitful when he promises or commends or expresses an attitude. Although he implies that he intends to return the book or that he has a favorable attitude toward Jones, he may have no such intention or attitude. Similarly an utterance which expresses an attitude may be quite insincere. But deceit or insincerity does not affect the meaning of the utterance. Although the speaker does not "mean what he says," what he says *has* a meaning; his deceit or insincerity depends on this linguistic fact. As I propose to use the terms

[9] See *The Logic of Self-Involvement*, pp. 27–46, which depends on J. L. Austin's account of "illocutionary force" in *How To Do Things with Words* (Oxford: Clarendon Press, 1962).

"self-involvement" and its opposite "neutrality," they have to do with matters of logic and meaning rather than introspective psychology.

Let us now consider scientific assertions. It is a requirement of science that scientific language should be *neutral*. In asserting or accepting a scientific theory, law, or observation-report, I give assent to it without committing myself to future conduct (other than verbal consistency), and without implying or expressing any personal attitude for or against what is asserted. If the scientific assertion were not neutral, agreement between scientists would depend partly on each one's personal commitments and attitudes, especially his moral commitments and attitudes. For example, if the Kinsey report says, "Such-and-such sexual behavior is normal," and the word "normal" here does not mean "average" or "usual" but "normative," a scientist's assent to the assertion would depend partly on whether or not he approves of the behavior. Scientists rightly seek a language which is as neutral as possible in order to minimize any dependence on such considerations. The objectivity which can be achieved through intersubjective testing in science depends partly on the logical neutrality of scientific assertions. Science can discover what *is* the case, what *is* being done, only if scientists do not have to agree concerning what *ought* to be the case, what *ought* to be done.

Logical neutrality must not be confused with *psychological neutrality*. A particular scientist may be a bitter opponent or an enthusiastic practitioner of the sexual conduct which he is reporting; or he may be very detached and disinterested. In each case, however, his report can and ought to be logically neutral if it is to be a scientific report. Which attitude tends to promote scientific progress, scientific "detachment" or scientific "passion"? Whatever the answer to this question (my own answer is "both, but in different ways and different contexts"), the issue has nothing to do with the requirement that scientific language be neutral in its public meaning. Nor does the logical neutrality of scientific language mean that science is doomed to be existentially trivial. A scientific report (for example, the results of a test for cancer) may be both logically neutral and profoundly important.

Logical neutrality must also not be confused with *absence of belief*. In making a scientific assertion, a speaker usually implies that he believes it. The strength of the belief implied varies according to the type of assertion. Where a scientific hypothesis is presented, no belief need be implied at all. But where a belief is implied, this belief is not itself an attitude for or against something, nor is it a commitment to a future pattern of conduct. The belief may provide a basis for such an attitude or commitment, but it is not itself an attitude or commitment. Furthermore, whether or not a speaker actually *has* the belief which he implies is an empirical or psychological matter. He may be sweating with conviction or inwardly sneering with scepticism, but the kind of belief which he *implies* depends on conventions of language concerning the meaning (performative force) of what he says. If a scientist is testing a new hypothesis, will his work be better if he passionately believes in it or if he cautiously entertains it as a mere possibility? Whatever the answer to this question—and there are conflicting answers given—the issue has nothing to do with the requirement that scientific language be logically neutral.

One final clarification concerning logical neutrality. Critics of objectivity-claims for science often point out that all investigations involve a *selection* of subject matter and that these involve implicit *judgments concerning importance*. This seems to me to be a legitimate point. No investigation, whether scientific or nonscientific, deals with everything or with every aspect of an event, and what is included is presumably regarded as being more important for the investigation than what is omitted. But this point does not show that logical neutrality is impossible. When I say, "The litmus paper has turned red," my assertion may involve some implicit judgments concerning the importance of such color changes, but I do not imply that I have a pro-attitude or a con-attitude. The term "implicit" may mislead us here, for I do not *imply* a judgment (or attitude) concerning importance in the way that I *imply* a pro-attitude when I say, "I commend you for your restraint." The so-called "implicit judgment" is one which a speaker might make in giving a *reason* for having selected changes in *color* rather than, say, changes in *shape*. Furthermore, any implicit judgment concerning importance—assuming there are such judgments—could itself be logically neutral. In saying, "X is important" I imply no pro-attitude or con-attitude toward X. We should also notice that the scientific importance of X lies in its relation to other matters in science. X may *also* be of profound personal relevance to the investigator, but this is not necessary.

2. *Scientific Assertions Are Comprehensible Impersonally*

Obviously *all* comprehension or understanding, including scientific understanding, is "personal" rather than "impersonal" in the sense that it is *persons* who understand. But we also say, "He's an unusual person, he deals with every problem so impersonally." In a somewhat similar way we can say, "Scientific assertions are understood by persons, but they are understood impersonally." That is, if a man has sufficient intelligence and scientific training, he should be able to understand a particular scientific assertion regardless of his personal attitudes concerning what the assertion is about, and regardless of his moral, aesthetic, or spiritual appreciation of what the assertion is about. The conditions for understanding are scientific, not intimately personal. For example, let us suppose that John Brown does not understand what is meant by "Light travels in straight lines." If he has enough brain power and if he studies enough physics he should be able to understand the assertion. This understanding should be possible whether or not light is something that matters tremendously to him, whether or not he is a self-centered or an altruistic person, whether or not he has ever contemplated a beam of light with the eye of an artist. The conditions for understanding a particular scientific assertion are independent of these variable personal factors. It is a matter of intelligence and scientific training.

Scientific training, however, involves a good deal of *attitudinal* training, especially for people who have not grown up in a scientific culture. There are various scientific virtues to be inculcated if a student is to become a scientist: industry, patience, curiosity, open-mindedness, detachment, self-discipline, rigorous and orderly thinking, scrupulous honesty in reporting results, etc. These virtues are conditions for understanding science. If too many are lacking, a student will not make any progress in understanding. Thus he may fail to understand "Light travels in straight lines," not because of his attitudes toward light or his failure to appreciate light aesthetically, but because he is lazy—or more generally, because he has not been sufficiently interested in science to continue his studies. When I say that scientific assertions are "comprehensible impersonally" I am not denying that the understanding of a particular scientific assertion depends *indirectly* on the fulfillment of prior personal conditions.

Science does differ from many other disciplines in that its indirect dependence on personal conditions is, on the whole, less; and the conditions themselves are less profoundly and intimately personal than those in some other disciplines; obviously they differ from basic conditions in aesthetics, morality, or religion. But the main point is that the understanding of a particular scientific assertion does not depend *directly* on personal conditions. There is no direct relation between the meaning of a particular scientific term and a particular scientific virtue or attitude. The meaning of "electron" is not correlated with an attitude of detachment, or with any other attitude. The meaning of "holy," however, *is* correlated with an attitude of reverence; that is, "X is holy" means (in part) "X is such that an attitude of reverence is an appropriate response." More generally, the meaning of "God" is correlated with various attitudinal depth-experiences.

The requirement of impersonal comprehensibility (like that of logical neutrality) is rightly designed to minimize the relevance of personal factors in science. It is an attempt at maximal mutual understanding in spite of the profound and numerous personal differences which exist among men, especially differences in aesthetic, moral, and spiritual attitudes. There are limits, of course, not only because of variations in degree of intelligence and kind of scientific training, but also because of variations in *kind* of intelligence. Also, the more theoretical and frontier-exploratory the nature of the scientific work, the fewer the scientists who can, at the time, understand one another fully.

We should also notice that there are a great many different levels of understanding; a man only gradually gets to "know his way around" in a field, grasping more and more of the significance of various terms or theories. Nor is all scientific language easily intelligible because precisely defined; the fertility of some theoretical concepts depends partly on their open texture. In short, the requirement that scientific assertions be comprehensible impersonally does not mean that all science should be like a ten-year-old's scientific textbook! It does nevertheless mean three things. First, the indirect dependence on personal conditions is less than in many other disciplines. Second, these conditions are less profoundly personal than those in many other disciplines. Third (most important), the comprehensibility of a particular scientific assertion is not directly dependent on profoundly personal conditions.

We have considered two requirements of scientific assertions, each of which in a different way is designed to promote the objectivity of science: logical neutrality and impersonal comprehensibility. The first is a matter of logic, and can be stated with precision. The second is a matter of conditions for understanding, and is much less clearly statable. The third requirement, which also is designed to promote objectivity, has to do with methodology; it is fairly clear, but complex.

E

3. Scientific Assertions Are Testable by Observations

A scientific assertion should be, in principle, testable by observations. That is, a scientist should be able to specify the observable states of affairs which would verify his assertion—or at least help to support it. And he should also be able to specify the observable states of affairs which would falsify his assertion—or at least help to undermine it. He may not be able to test his assertion at the moment; he may have to wait until further evidence comes in, or until technicians build an apparatus. But he must be able to say what observable states of affairs *would* verify or support his assertion, and what *would* falsify or undermine his assertion; his assertion must be testable in principle. It must not be compatible with any and every possible state of affairs.

In the early days of positivism, the requirement that scientific assertions be testable by observations was mistakenly regarded as the key to the whole of science. Today, however, philosophers of science set forth many qualifications and objections concerning it, so much so that there is considerable danger of its being ignored in comparisons between science and religion. Let us consider some of the qualifications and objections which have been propounded, looking successively at four different kinds of scientific assertion: observation-reports, theories, paradigms, and presuppositions.

a. Observation-reports. The claim that scientific assertions are testable by observations needs to be qualified, since all observation involves interpretation. There are no "pure" observations, "given" perceptions, or "raw" experiences. Human minds impose various conceptual frameworks on all observations, perceptions, or experiences. What we "observe" depends on the conceptual framework which we bring to the observations; we can never disentangle observations completely from interpretations so as to "test" interpretations by reference to "pure" observations. Scientific observations, moreover, involve a special kind of interpretation. They are "theory-laden"; that is, what one observes as a scientist is already interpreted in terms of concepts drawn from scientific theory. Where common sense observes a swinging stick, the scientist observes a pendulum. Where common sense observes a flash, the scientist observes an electrical discharge.

Does this mean that scientific assertions are not testable by observations? Surely not. It means that there are differing levels of interpretation of experience, and that "higher" levels cannot be reduced to lower ones. That is, if we consider a common-sense observation-report ("The stick is swinging") this involves terms such as "stick" which are not reducible to lower-level talk about sense–impressions. Above the common-sense level, a scientific observation-report ("The pendulum is swinging") involves terms such as "pendulum" which are not reducible to lower-level common-sense talk about sticks. At a still higher level, a scientific theory will use terms like "gravity," which are not reducible to terms used in scientific observations.

At each level, including the "bottom" level of sense-impression reports, there is an element of interpretation. Yet the different levels are linked. Although a higher-level assertion is not reducible to a lower-level one since it is *not equivalent in meaning,* the *truth* of the higher-level one depends partly on the *truth* of the lower-level one. This hierarchical picture of language is an oversimplification; however, it does seem to me to provide a way to avoid a possible misunderstanding of the testability requirement. The requirement need involve neither reductionism nor a belief in an uninterpreted basis for all knowledge. It does not depend on a crudely empiricist epistemology.

More important, the testability requirement is part of scientific practice as this is described even by such antipositivists as Harold Schilling.[10] There is an accumulation of established scientific knowledge which has been tested by observation and

[10] Harold Schilling, *Science and Religion* (New York: Charles Scribner's Sons, 1962), esp. chaps. 5–8.

which is permanent (or virtually so) *because* of this testing. Such knowledge includes experimental (that is, observational) laws which are not undermined by changes in scientific theory.[11] It is true that the laws may be reinterpreted by being explained in relation to new theories, so that the newly interpreted law is not equivalent in meaning to the old one; nevertheless the law also has a relatively uninterpreted meaning, and its truth in this form has been established by reference to observations. Probably the observations would not have been made were it not for the existence of a scientific theory, but this does not show that the testability requirement is unnecessary. It is also true that the observations are usually reported in a language which includes scientific terms that are relatively theoretical or interpretive as compared with the everyday language of common sense. But the scientific terms are linked to common-sense terms, though they are not reducible to common-sense terms. If a nonscientist in the laboratory sees no spark or feels no tingling pain on touching a wire, the scientist's report concerning an electrical discharge may be undermined or even falsified.

b. Theories. Someone might concede that perhaps experimental laws are testable by observations, but insist that theories are not. It is clear that the evaluation of a theory involves various criteria which are not observational.[12] There are *formal* criteria: internal consistency, coherent conceptual relations, and simplicity or relative independence from *ad hoc* assumptions. There is an *aesthetic* criterion of "elegance"; although minimized by some scientists, it is stressed by others. Then there is the *explanatory power* of the theory in displaying a pattern in many previously unrelated states of affairs. Some would stress the role of scientific models in this respect. Then there is the *"fertility"* of the theory in stimulating the invention or discovery

[11] Cf. Schilling, *op. cit.,* and Ernest Nagel, *The Structure of Science* (New York: Harcourt, Brace & Co., 1961), chap. 5.

[12] Most of these are outlined in Ian Barbour, *Issues in Science and Religion* (Englewood Cliffs, N.J.: Prentice-Hall, 1966), pp. 144–50. I am greatly indebted to Dr. Barbour for his balanced and lucid discussions of various issues throughout his book.

of new theories, concepts, and experimental laws, and its consistency and coherence with other highly rated theories. Since there are many different criteria, there is no such thing as a "knockdown" falsification or a "conclusive" verification of a theory by reference to observations.

This objection is extremely important in destroying crude positivist conceptions of scientific "verification." But with reference to the testability requirement, all it shows is that the requirement is only one among many. A theory may pass observational tests as well as its rival does, and yet be rejected because it is inferior when appraised by reference to its fertility, say, or its internal coherence. If, as some experts claim, it is true that *no* theory ever fits *all* the relevant observations, then obviously the testability requirement is not as strict as one might imagine. Also, if it is true that no theory is ever "falsified" by observations, this is an important point in understanding the requirement properly. But none of this shows that no theory is ever *undermined* by observations. A theory is not compatible with any and every conceivable state of affairs that might be observed. Finally, however much philosophers of science may insist that scientific theories are not evaluated *solely* in terms of whether or not they enable scientists to make precise and specific *predictions* of observable states of affairs, or to *produce* these at will, surely these features of science are important; and surely they mark important differences between scientific theories and theories in metaphysics or in theistic religion.

A different, but related, objection to the testability requirement is that scientific theories are not representations of the real world at all, but are merely useful fictions or regulative maxims. A theory can be neither true nor false, it is said, so it can be neither verified nor falsified; indeed, observations can neither support nor undermine the alleged truth of a theory, for a theory cannot be "true." This objection is relevant only if we accept a nonrealist view of scientific theories. Yet even if we do, we need not reject the testability requirement. Rather, we understand the "test" of a theory to be a test of usefulness rather than of truth.

c. Paradigms. The term "paradigm," as used by Thomas Kuhn,[13] refers to a type of scientific theory which has a special role in science. The paradigm theory, together with certain laws which it explains and perhaps an exemplary application and instrumentation, dominates a whole area of scientific investigation. It not only provides solutions to scientific problems; it largely determines what *counts* as a scientific problem and what *counts* as a scientific solution. It provides a framework of presumptions within which detailed scientific investigation can flourish. When a paradigm is replaced by another paradigm, this is no minor change; it is a scientific revolution. An established paradigm is scarcely affected at all by some of the observations which do not fit in with it. In the overthrow of a paradigm, nonobservational criteria play a major role, and these criteria themselves may be modified or reinterpreted.

It is clear that in the paradigm we find science in a form most remote from observational testing, from "knockdown" falsification or "conclusive" verification by means of specific observations. Paradigms are very different from restricted generalizations such as "All the boys in this room right now have blue eyes." Nevertheless, even Kuhn says that "observation and experience can and must drastically restrict the range of admissible scientific belief, else there would be no science."[14] More specifically, in his account of the "anomalies" which force scientific revolutions he notes that a paradigm makes possible a precision of observational expectations which renders it specially sensitive to possible undermining by anomalous observational findings.[15] Without the paradigm, one would not notice that such-and-such an observed state of affairs is anomalous, yet the paradigm is put in question by this observed state of

13 Thomas Kuhn, *The Structure of Scientific Revolutions* (Chicago: University of Chicago Press, 1962).
14 Thomas Kuhn, *op. cit.*, p. 4.
15 *Ibid.*, p. 65.

affairs. When Kuhn says that paradigms "provide all phenomena except anomalies with a theory-determined place in the scientist's field of vision,"[16] he is indicating both a way in which paradigms are relatively *immune* from being undermined by observations and a way in which they are peculiarly *sensitive* to such undermining. Indeed, his account of paradigm sensitivity helps to explain a fact noted by Nagel:

Prescientific beliefs are frequently incapable of being put to definite experiential tests, simply because those beliefs may be vaguely compatible with an indeterminate class of unanalyzed facts. Scientific statements, because they are required to be in agreement with more closely specified materials of observation, face greater risks of being refuted by such data.[17]

d. Presuppositions. Antipositivist writings on science, especially those which stress alleged similarities between science and religion, often maintain that science involves unfalsifiable presuppositions which constitute the "faith" of a scientist. The argument goes as follows: a scientist believes that the world has an order, that it has regularity, that it is dependable. No observable state of affairs could falsify this claim. His faith is not testable by observations. So if a religious faith is not testable by observations, this is not a feature of religion which distinguishes it from science.

Later I shall indicate the one strength and the many weaknesses of this argument. Here I shall distinguish between two different kinds of scientific presupposition. First, there is the paradigm, which we have already considered. A paradigm involves belief in a specific kind of order, regularity, and dependability within a specific area to be investigated by a subcommunity of scientists. Investigations which are carried out within the framework of a paradigm involve a great many implicit or explicit presuppositions. We have seen that paradigms are remote from "knockdown" falsifiability by observations, but nevertheless have not only a resistance but also a

16 *Ibid.,* p. 96.
17 Ernest Nagel, *op. cit.,* p. 9.

sensitivity to possible undermining by observations. It would be misleading to say that paradigms are in principle unfalsifiable, for old paradigms *are* replaced by new ones, and this happens partly because of anomalous observations.

Although I suspect that most of what practicing scientists might mean by "scientific faith" arises from paradigms, there is a second type of presupposition which also has a role to play. It has the general form, *"Every* X *has a* Y," where it is possible to verify "This *X* has a *Y*," but not to falsify it. Consider, for example, *"Every event has a sufficient condition."* Whenever scientists discover an experimental law and apply it to a particular event which is covered by the law, the proposition "This event has a sufficient condition" is verified. But what if scientists cannot find a sufficient condition for an event, for example, the particular movement of a particular electron? They may go on looking, but they may abandon the search. The proposition "Every event has a sufficient condition" is not falsifiable, yet it may be so undermined by failure to verify that it is abandoned—at least in a specific area of science. In so far as scientists believe in a world "order" or a "regularity," where these terms have a definite sense, the belief is not immune from being undermined by observations, though observations alone do not suffice to overthrow it.

In this section we have examined the requirement that scientific assertions be testable by observations, and we have noted various ways in which it needs to be qualified. Observation involves interpretation. Theories are not tested solely by reference to observations. Paradigms and presuppositions are not falsifiable by observations. In previous sections we considered two other requirements of scientific assertions: logical neutrality and impersonal comprehensibility. Before we move on to see whether religious assertions fulfill any of the three requirements, I should note one important omission in my account: I have not considered the requirements in relation to *social* science. My own view is that special difficulties arise only in relation to the second requirement. Some assertions in social studies, though logically neutral and testable by observation, are not comprehensible impersonally. In that respect, they are not "scientific," though they are nevertheless respectable and important. I am referring to assertions concerning how an agent views his situation, where the agent's view may be very difficult for an investigator to understand unless there is some affinity or rapport between the two men. But I cannot discuss this matter further here.

III. RELIGIOUS LANGUAGE AND OBJECTIVITY

1. *Religious Assertions Are Not Logically Neutral*

Religious faith, as it was described in Part I, is expressed in such assertions as the following:

"I look on this man's I-Thou attitude toward me as a revelation of a hidden being whose I-Thou attitude is complete and constant."

"I look on the impressive beauty of this sunset as an artistic expression of a hidden numinous being."

"I look on this unconditional moral demand as a command from a hidden being who has rightful authority over my life."

"I look on my concern for meaning in life as a revelation of a being who is the source of the concern and of ultimate meaning."

"I look on my indignant compassion as a revelation of a hidden being whose compassion is infinite."

These assertions are not neutral, but *self-involving*. Each is an expression of attitude, a commitment to interpret a depth-experience as a revelation. In religious assertions where the word "God" occurs, the meaning of the word "God" is roughly "the hidden being who is such that various attitudinal depth-experiences are appropriate responses." God is the hidden being who is worthy of worship. In using the word "God," a member of a religious community is using self-involving language. He may, of course, be insincere. He may be, as a matter of fact, psychologically neutral. But his language is not logically neutral. It is a requirement of the religious community that his language be self-involving in its meaning.

There are two important exceptions to this. First, many *theological* assertions are second-order statements *about* religious assertions, and are not themselves self-involving. Talk about self-involving assertions need not itself be self-involving. In saying, "I promise . . . ," I do promise; my utterance is self-involving. But in saying, "I promised . . . ," or "He is promising . . . ," or "Promises are self-involving," I do not promise; nor are my utterances in any other way self-involving. Similarly if a theologian says "What Christians mean by 'God' is 'the being worthy of worship,' " the assertion is not self-involving. And even when he says "God is the being worthy of worship," although his assertion is not *explicitly* a second-order statement about religious assertions, it may be second-order implicitly, especially if the context is descriptive.

This leads us to the second exception. The context in which self-involving language is used may be artificially made a "descriptive" one. That is, there may be an implicit agreement among speakers or writers that self-involving elements are to be set aside. A man can use the word "God" to mean, say, "the [alleged] being whom [some] people believe to be worthy of worship," without implying or expressing any religious attitudes himself. In this way it is possible for unbelievers or wavering members of the religious community (or theologians!) to talk about God without insincerity.[18]

Neither of these exceptions detracts from the self-involving character of primary religious assertions. The secondary theological or descriptive uses of religious language are parasitic on the primary use; that is, they depend on the primary use for their meaning. Similarly second-order talk about promises depends on the existence of first-order promise-making, and descriptive uses of the word "good" depend on self-involving uses of the word "good."

[18] For a further discussion of "descriptive" contexts see *The Logic of Self-Involvement*, pp. 50–51, 160–62, 183–85.

2. Religious Assertions Are Not Comprehensible Impersonally

The main point can be dealt with briefly. The account of religious faith in Part I and of this requirement in Part II have already indicated my conclusion. Religious assertions require special personal conditions for understanding. Each depth-experience is an elusive and mysterious experience which a man will not have had unless he has fulfilled various personal conditions. In order to understand what an I-Thou attitude is, one must be responsive to it in others, and this depends on one's own basic life-experience and attitudes to people. Similar conditions apply in the case of other depth-experiences. There are intelligent men, well-trained men, for whom some or all of the descriptions of depth-experiences have little meaning. Yet one can understand the meaning of talk about "God" only to the extent that one understands talk about the depth-experiences. Religious language is directly correlated to depth-experiences in its meaning. So religious assertions are not comprehensible impersonally.

This conclusion, however, needs some clarification and qualification. What constitutes an "understanding" of an assertion? A man may be able to use the words of the assertion without making any gross mistakes concerning its relations with other words. A psychopath, for example, might pick up much of what Wittgenstein calls the "logical grammar" of the word "conscience" by listening to other people talk. Yet in terms of his own experiences he does not understand what a conscience is. Similarly a deprived but intelligent child might learn how to use the word "love," without having had any deep experience of what it is to love and to be loved. Similarly a man of no depth-experiences might learn how to use religious language, for example, that "God" is connected with "worship"; he need not have had a personal experience of worship in order to do this. We seem to need a distinction between *"verbal"* and *"experiential"* understanding or comprehension of language. I cannot explore this further here, but some such distinction is required if the comprehensible-impersonally requirement is to be properly clarified. A man needs depth-experiences for *experiential* understanding of religious language.

3. *Religious Assertions Are Not Testable by Observations*

In Part II we saw that scientific assertions should be testable by observations. We also noted that science has a presupposition, "Every event has a sufficient condition," which is unfalsifiable. Are religious assertions testable by observations? Are there any unfalsifiable religious presuppositions of the form "Every X has a Y"?

My answer to the second question is, "Maybe." Some believers do hold, for example, that every event has a divine purpose. But religious faith is fundamentally a conviction that *some* depth-experiences are divine revelations. The word "faith" is appropriate for two different reasons. First, "This depth-experience is a revelation" is *unfalsifiable,* like "This event has a sufficient condition." Second, "This depth-experience is a revelation" is *"verified"* only by presupposing the existence of God. The second reason is what distinguishes religious faith from so-called scientific faith.

Do religious assertions resemble scientific assertions in being testable by observations? In four important ways they do not. We shall consider these ways in turn, considering scientific assertions first in each case.

First, although scientific presuppositions, paradigms, and theories are evaluated in terms of various nonobservational criteria, they are also open to support or undermining by *observational tests*. And although scientific observation-reports are not reducible to common-sense observation-reports, they can be supported or undermined by common-sense observation-reports, which thus provide a base on which the whole hierarchical superstructure of science is built. The superstructure of religious and theological assertions, however, is based on reports of elusive and mysterious depth-experiences rather than on common-sense observations. Although talk about God is not reducible to talk about depth-experiences, the former cannot be understood in abstraction from the latter; and if there had never been any depth-experiences, there would be no empirical basis for religion.

Second, scientific observation-reports are in principle open to *intersubjective testing* by anyone with the requisite intelligence and scientific training. If I think I observe an electrical discharge, but no other scientist does, my observation-report is radically undermined. The intersubjective element in religion, however, is very different. Suppose that other people report fewer depth-experiences or very different ones, or that other people stop having depth-experiences which seem to them to be divine revelations. As a believer I am committed to go on believing in spite of this. I may, as a matter of fact, falter, especially if my own spiritual life has gone dry. But I ought not to falter, for this runs contrary to my religious commitment. Depth-experiences depend on elusive personal conditions, and those which are divine revelations also depend on the free action of God. Men ought not to try to test God; it is God who "tests" men by sometimes withdrawing His presence. There is, to be sure, an intersubjective element in religious faith. The believer holds that God has revealed Himself to other members of the religious community in the *past*. Moreover, the believer's convictions concerning what counts as revelation are derived mainly from the religious community. Faith is a trust in God which is based partly on a trust in intersubjective testimony. But it is not a matter of intersubjective testing or experimenting similar to that in science, for there are two open "variables" in the venture of faith: God and human sin. If God seems to be absent (or dead!) this is either because He has chosen to withhold His presence or because men are not responsive to it.

Third, the interpretive move from common-sense descriptions of events to scientific descriptions is so designed as to enable men to make *precise predictions of observables*. Covering laws are discovered: whenever conditions *C1* to *C5* hold, an event of type *T1* occurs. And if men can produce conditions *C1 to C5,* they can thereby produce events of type *T1*. (They can explode an H-bomb.) Scientific theories work not only in that they make the world more intelligible, but also in that they make possible such prediction and control. In religion, however, the interpretive move from depth-experiences to divine revelations does not enable men to make predictions on the basis of covering laws, and still less to produce divine revelations at will.

Fourth, the move from common sense to scientific observation-reports begins with an ontological assumption that there is a real external world which we can observe. A *realist* view of scientific theories may involve some further ontological conviction concerning the nature of the world. No further ontology, however, is entailed. In religion a further ontology *is* entailed. The move from reports of depth-experiences to religious assertions involves an assumption that there exists a hidden divine being, distinct from the world but revealing Himself through the world, a being such that various human attitudes are appropriate responses. This assumption differs even from the scientific realist's assumption concerning the world, a world such that various scientific theories "work." Religious theory, for those who make the crucial assumption that God exists, works in two ways. On the one hand it meets *intellectual needs* by making more intelligible the various depth-experiences-interpreted-as-divine-revelations; for example, it might link the numinous aspect of God with the moral aspect. On the other hand, it meets *spiritual needs* by helping to promote those depth-experiences and interpretations which are believed to bring men into right relation with God; that is, it promotes faith.

In four important ways the testable-by-observations requirement in science thus differentiates science from religion. We should note, however, that religious theory (theology) *may* resemble scientific theory in so far as various nonobservational criteria are used to evaluate it. I say may, because theologians disagree moderately concerning the extent to which theology should be appraised in terms of consistency, internal coherence, and simplicity, and they disagree greatly concerning the attempt to fit theology into a consistent and coherent relation with other disciplines. Even more generally, the spiritual-need emphasis in theology may become more and more dominant in contrast with an intellectual interest in producing a system. The more this happens, the more remote becomes the analogy between theology and scientific theory.

Before I close this section of the paper, I should expose a major weakness. I have failed to grapple with one way in which religious faith *is* in principle testable by observations.[19] Since revelation is a divine *action,* it should make a difference to what happens. A depth-experience must be partially *caused* by God if it is to be a *revelation* of God. Of course some convictions concerning God might be true even though God did not produce them. A critic of religion is committing the "genetic fallacy" if he attacks the truth of some religious convictions by exposing their nondivine causal origin. It is possible that a Freudian explanation of my belief that God is like a father could be correct, yet my belief might nevertheless be true, by a happy coincidence. Or perhaps it is not a coincidence; perhaps God the Creator made the world in such a way that natural causation would lead to my having this true religious belief. But if my religious conviction is that *God sometimes actively reveals Himself* in depth-experiences, this specific conviction involves a causal claim concerning God. If *all* religious convictions of this specific kind could be accounted for by reference to nondivine sufficient conditions, then faith in an actively self-revealing God would be falsified. Such falsification is not possible in practice, only in principle. But a substantial and rightful undermining of religious faith is a possibility. If this were not so, the religious believer would not be making any claim concerning a God who *acts* in the world. Nothing ventured, nothing claimed.

---

[19] *Christian* faith, as we saw at the end of Part I, is also testable by observation (i.e., historical investigation) in so far as it depends on beliefs concerning the man Jesus.

What kind of *causal claim* is involved? The nearest analogy, I think, is something like "Without your encouragement, John, I could not have done it" (or "would not have done it" or "would not have felt it"). Such a claim can be undermined by behavioral evidence, yet the basis for the claim is not simply a Humean constant conjunction. The recipient of the action is in a privileged position to back his claim by referring to his own private experience. Yet his claim may become untenable in the face of overwhelming contrary evidence. Similar issues arise when a man claims that God actively revealed Himself in a depth-experience, so that a human action or a human feeling was partially caused by God. The recipient of the divine action is in a privileged position to back his claim, yet it may become untenable in the face of overwhelming contrary evidence.

For some philosophers no problems arise concerning the need to test claims concerning divine action by reference to observations. These men hold that there are two complementary and nonconflicting ways to talk about some events: as the action of a personal agent (human or divine) and as an effect of a set of nonpersonal sufficient conditions. I do not think that this account will stand up to scrutiny. I do not think that we can have our cake of agent causality if we eat it up with a determinism of natural causality. Perhaps I am mistaken concerning this, but if I am not, then my faith in a God who sometimes acts by revealing Himself in depth-experiences is a faith which is open to undermining by reference to observations.

IV. CONCLUSIONS

Three conclusions can be drawn concerning differences between religious and scientific assertions. *First,* religious assertions are self-involving, though second-order theological assertions may be logically neutral, and there may be special descriptive contexts in which self-involving elements are set aside. Scientific assertions are logically neutral. *Second,* religious assertions are understood experientially only to the extent that men have had various depth-experiences. Scientific assertions are not directly or indirectly dependent on such conditions for their comprehensibility, and they are indirectly dependent on different and less personal conditions. *Third,* religious assertions are not testable by observations, except where they involve causal claims concerning divine actions (or where they depend on historical claims concerning the man Jesus). Scientific assertions are testable by observations, although many are evaluated by reference to nonobservational criteria as well, and many are not falsifiable solely by observations.

7

SCIENCE AND THE
DEATH OF "GOD"

Frederick Ferré *

> The empiricist in us finds the heart of the difficulty not in
> what is said about God, but in the very talking about God at
> all. We do not know "what" God is, and we cannot understand
> how the word "God" is being used. . . . The problem of the
> Gospel in a secular age is a problem of the logic of its appar-
> ently meaningless language, and linguistic analysts will give us
> help in clarifying it.
>
> —From Paul M. van Buren,
> *The Secular Meaning of the Gospel*

In the midst of a lot of loose talk about the "death of God" it
helps to restate the issues, as van Buren does, linguistically. It is
the intelligibility of the *word* "God" that seems to have expired
for a great many people. And without the capacity to make
sense any longer of the word it becomes impossible and irrele-

* *Frederick Ferré is Chairman of the Department of Philosophy at
Dickinson College. He has written extensively concerning linguistic
analysis and religion, including* Language, Logic and God *(1961),* (*with
Kent Bendall*) Exploring the Logic of Faith *(1962), and* Basic Modern
Philosophy of Religion *(1967). In this unpublished essay he examines the
influence of scientific empiricism in both science and religion, and discusses the problem of "verification" in religion.*

vant either to affirm or to deny the "death" (or continued "life") of—you know Whom.

Why has this fate overtaken theological language? It is, as van Buren says, because most of us have become thoroughly secular in our general outlook, and especially in our basic assumptions about how any meaningful assertions of fact ought to be established or refuted. We assume, that is, that for every factual proposition advanced there ought to be some evidence that can be pointed to; and we take the expression "pointed to" seriously. *Evidence,* to be evidence, should be public and visible (the root of the word, after all, is *video*). We are, in a word, *empiricists;* and in so far as "God" is an incorrigibly nonempirical word we find it puzzling or—more likely—just uninteresting.

Over the years I have gathered a good deal of statistical data to confirm this diagnosis of the theological situation. I have made it a practice to assign a paper, due in the first week of class, to beginning students in philosophy of religion. The topic has been "The Primary Obstacle to Religious Belief," and I have kept score of the frequency of different types of answer. By far the commonest "obstacle" has been the absence of empirical verification for religious claims, particularly claims about God. My students repeatedly ask a question that goes to the heart of things: "Why, just because the area of belief happens to be religious, ought we to abandon the critical concern for solid evidence that we have been taught as a basic obligation of responsible thinking in other areas, especially (but not exclusively) the sciences?"

This appeal to scientific attitudes as providing the model of good thinking is very pervasive, and with reason. Just as scientific achievements have transformed the world we live in, so scientific methods of thinking have fundamentally influenced the ways we think—or acknowledge that we ought to think. The appeal to scientific method as the paradigm of responsible thinking is not only pervasive, therefore; it is also highly persuasive. It would be absurd to ignore man's most obviously successful instrument for understanding and controlling reality. The mind of the world—the secular mind—is rightly impressed with the critical rigor of empirical science. If this makes for difficulties in continuing to use language about "God," then so be it.

I think we should be very clear, however, about the precise nature of these difficulties. They have in recent years been much too crudely stated, and as a result the available options have been obscured. If there has been logical crudeness in philosophy of religion, however, it is largely due to a parallel situation in philosophy of science. We had better take our start there.

SCIENCE AND THE VERIFICATION PRINCIPLE

Given the empiricist "common sense" of our modern world, it goes almost without saying that all the assertions of the sciences require an empirical footing, somehow or other, in the givenness of human experience. But when we get beyond such a platitude and attempt to define precisely the relationship between scientific language and actual or possible sense experience, we encounter conflicting schools of thought. Must everything that a scientist says be *reducible* to statements about sense experience? A major philosophic tradition—I shall call it *verificational analysis*—has answered this question affirmatively. Every scientific assertion, this tradition holds, is an empirical hypothesis, and empirical hypotheses are reducible to actual or possible experiences. Thus even categorical statements, such as the assertion: "Sharks' skeletons are made of cartilage rather than bone," should be understood as a covert hypothesis: e.g., "If you examine a shark skeleton you will have sense experiences of a specifiably different sort from the experiences you would have in examining a man or a whale." And what is *meant* by "cartilage" is finally exhausted by a list of the kinds of experience (seeing a translucent substance, feeling its flexibility, etc.) that would confirm such a hypothesis. Once replaced with such a list, nothing factual is left for the expression to mean. Thus, from this understanding of the language of science it is plausible to move to the generalized conclusion, commonly called the verification principle of meaning, that the whole factual meaning of any proposition is equivalent to the method of its (sensory) verification. The apparent capacity of the verification principle to illuminate the language of the sciences, coupled with what we have acknowledged to be the very reasonable acceptance of scientific thinking as paradigmatic for all good thinking, worked strongly in its favor.

Problems, however, immediately arise for verificational analysis as a philosophy of science. One obvious problem is in understanding *universal law* statements, if the whole factual meaning of any proposition is taken to be equivalent to the method of verifying it. It is one thing to say, "All sharks are cartilaginous," and mean only that experience (so far) of shark skeletons has been such-and-such; but it would seem to be quite another thing to use "all" and *intend* to refer to much more than "some" sense experiences. The problem is compounded when scientific assertions go beyond the level of empirical generalization (as illustrated in our shark example) to the level of universal-law statements. How is the logic of *scientific law* to be translated, without residue, into statements with sense experience as the sole referent? Is there not a lot more meant by a law than could ever be expressed in what *has* been or *might* be experienced? Does a law not have the force of stating, somehow, what *must* occur under given circumstances? And how, in principle, can that extra force, that additional modality, be reduced entirely to statements about perception, since one can never *perceive* the difference between a "had to be" and a "happened to be"?

A related problem arises in attempting to interpret the meaning of statements referring to the *non*occurrence of events covered by known laws. What, in terms of the verification principle, can be meant by *"counterfactual conditionals"* assuring us that if such-and-such *had* happened, so-and-so *would have* resulted? There is no way, in principle, to confirm in experience a nonevent. Must all "would have" expressions be abandoned as having no factual content? This seems strange, since one of the prime functions of law statements would appear to be to license assertions of the type: "I know (as a matter of fact) that if I had dropped the weights, they both would have fallen at the same rate of acceleration." It may even be argued that the sciences are much more interested in knowledge that can be stated in this form than in mere reports of particular happenings, however clearly verifiable; and if so, then a theory of scientific meaning which rules out this sort of statement from the class of factually meaningful expressions would be worse than strange: it would be inadequate to interpret scientific thinking.

Other problems, as well, follow from a verificational analysis of scientific discourse. One of these has to do with the built-in limitations of the practical process of "verifying" or "falsifying" various types of scientific assertion, and the other has to do with the logical status of theories and their associated "theoretical entities."

First, it is generally conceded that no hypothesis, however simple, is ever *verified* or *falsified* in total isolation from other beliefs, assumptions, methodological presumptions, and the like. If the hypothesis in question is a relatively "low-level" one—on which very little else in the science depends—a negative result from an experiment designed to test it will lead very quickly to its abandonment. But the sciences rightly refuse to count every assertion as equally vulnerable to abandonment. If a student in Physics 101 measures the gravitational constant at double what has hitherto been printed in textbooks as its value, his teachers are not likely to rush out to announce his finding to the world. And even the most carefully run experiments by respected professionals are suspect if they purport to falsify well-established laws. Other beliefs will be abandoned, if necessary, much sooner. And the basic principles of a science *will not be verifiable or falsifiable at all,* in any straightforward sense, within the science itself. The vindication of a science's basic principles will be in the success of the science as a whole. Therefore if the meaning of scientific assertions is held, with verificational analysis, to be equivalent to the specific sense experiences that would tend to verify them, it becomes quite unclear what some of the most important assertions of the various sciences can mean. Reduction to sense experiences alone will not do; and the more important the assertion, the less readily interpretable in these terms it would appear to be.

The very notion of the *"importance"* of a scientific proposition, relative to other propositions, requires one to look beyond the verificational analysis of meaning. "Importance" is not gauged simply in terms of the weight of sense experience that may be piled up behind a given law (though very widespread public confirmation is certainly one measure of importance); rather, the strategic location of a law or concept within the complex web of thought that constitutes any science is the more significant index of its importance. If many strands of what is often called the "nomological net" run to or through or from it, if it serves to tie together otherwise loose elements, then it is rightly valued as highly important for the part it plays in scientific theory—no matter how indirect or problematic its verification or falsification in public sense experience.

Second, this mention of the theoretical role of science brings us to one last problem that confronts a verificational analysis of scientific meaning and method. Within the language of the *theories* of the sciences there often appear terms which seemingly refer to things that are *not directly observable*. "Atoms," "electrons," "alpha particles," "pi mesons," "genes," and the like, and logically derivative expressions referring to things that can be directly observed, like "particle track," "gene mutation," "absorption line," and so on, crowd the discourse of scientists. If the whole factual meaning of any proposition consists in a class of statements referring to actual or possible verifying sense experiences, then all statements purporting to make assertions about "atoms," which are not directly observable, are either about something else or are factually empty of content. On the basis of the verification principle of meaning, indeed, some philosophers of science have attempted to do away with the persistent view of scientists that their theoretical terms refer to unobservable entities of some kind; they have attempted to translate theoretical language into an "observational language" without loss of content; they have experimented with "phenomenalistic" reductions, "sense-data" reductions, and "physicalistic" reductions. But despite the ingenuity of these attempts, they have failed to be convincing either to most working scientists, who remain stubbornly wedded to the view that what they mean by such a term as "alpha particle" is more than a convenient summmary of a large collection of pointer readings and counter clicks; or to other philosophers who (especially in recent years) have looked with less reverence on the verification principle itself.

I have discussed the problems facing the verificational analysis of science because this position has until recently represented a kind of orthodoxy in the philosophic representation of our modern paradigm of good thinking. The philosophic representation and the scientific reality, however, need to be kept distinct. The respect that the successes of firsthand scientific thinking have rightly earned while shaping the modern critical consciousness does not necessarily need to be transferred to the comparatively much cruder secondhand accounts of these successes given by philosophers. Nor is it fair to attribute the problems implicit in the second-order accounts to the primary scientific enterprise itself. Instead we should work at providing better accounts.

THE FUNCTIONS OF SCIENTIFIC LANGUAGE

This attempt is exactly the task that a number of philosophers, many of them refugees from the dwindling ranks of verificational analysis, have recently been setting themselves. Instead of starting with a homogeneous view of the various statements of science, resulting in the glorification of the empirical generalization or the low-level empirical hypothesis as the single paradigm of scientific discourse, a more pluralistic approach is now being tried. "What is the actual role of this expression?" becomes the first question, not "What sense experiences would tend to verify or falsify it?" Thus this philosophical approach, which I will call *functional analysis,* asks first for the *use* of an expression rather than for its "meaning" in any a priori or doctrinaire sense of that highly ambiguous word. Precisely in finding its use—most broadly understood not only in terms of linguistic customs but also in terms of human purposes and "forms of life," as Ludwig Wittgenstein put it— we shall be discovering its meaning in the fullest, most important sense.

What are the uses, then, of scientific discourse? What are the primary human purposes behind the forms of language and conception that have fashioned the normative mentality of the contemporary world? No doubt there are a great many answers to these questions, but for simplicity I shall propose two primary *functions of scientific thought and speech:* they are, first, the determining of our expectations for experience and, second, the satisfying of our demand for understanding. Now add a third function which is no more (but no less) than the blending of the first two: expectation is to be set in the context of intelligibility, and understanding is to be disciplined by future experience.

Many of the problems we noted for a verificational analysis of science turn out to be based on an important half-truth concerning the purposes and functions of science. The earlier approach tended to ignore the role of scientific conceptions in satisfying our demand for *understanding;* the whole of scientific meaning (and thence all factual meaning) was equated with the genuine, but not exhaustive, scientific interest in *predicting* specific types of experience. The verification principle works— and sometimes clarifies very helpfully—when applied to statements which are *meant* to function to determine our empirical expectations. Successes in this area of scientific purpose (for example, eliminating as empirically meaningless such words as "phlogiston" or "aether" from the scientist's lexicon) were taken as justification for excluding other purposes, however, with the serious results we have observed. Above all the role of *theories* and *models,* which function mainly for the provision of understanding, were distorted by being pressed exclusively into the service of the interest in predicting or summarizing specific sense experiences. The distortion was possible because the scientific quest for intelligibility is never released from its responsibility, at some point, to empirical consequences; but that this was a distortion remains clear to all who are familiar with the labyrinthine indirectness of the passageways between theoretical schemes and the world of gross perception, or with the massive indifference of working scientists to the absence of perceptual interpretations for their crucial theoretical terms, or with the actual types of consideration that tend to support or undermine the acceptance of theories.

What are these considerations? A detailed functional analysis of the modes of understanding which theories interpreted by their models are expected to satisfy is beyond the scope of this chapter; but perhaps I may be allowed, for the purposes of this book, to define *understanding* most generally as *the provision of a conceptual form* with certain ideal characteristics as follows:

First, the form should hang together, it should *make a pattern,* it should be *integral.* Contradiction or disconnection is a defect in a conceptual scheme if its function is to aid understanding. No doubt some disconnection will be found, in real life, even in the best of our scientific patterns; but this fact simply reminds us that I am describing an ideal by which theories are and should be judged.

Second, the theoretical pattern should *extend widely* or at least *be exemplified repeatedly* in various contexts. This is the sense in which it is legitimate to look for "familiarity" in explanatory schemes. We must not insist that our best intelligibility-bearing conceptual structures will be modeled only after aspects of ordinary experience or exclusively after objects found within the narrow boundaries of human perceptual capacities. What is "familiar" in this sense is contingent on too many logically irrelevant factors. But formal familiarity is a major element in the quest for theoretical satisfaction.

Third, the conceptual candidate for such a theory must *cover the given data;* it must *be adequate to the evidence.* If it fails to include in its pattern, no matter how integral or how pervasive, the raw stuff which initially demands intelligible explanation, then it is to this extent a failure. Granted, this too is an ideal that is immensely hard to realize in practice. Every theory has its limitations of scope and its empirical "margin of error"; most theories must further suffer the existence of "anomalies" or, at the very least, statistical deviations from the data most naturally patterned by it. Just how wide the deviations, how many the anomalies, how gross the margin of error—these are questions to be decided in the context of actual inquiry, in the light of the theoretical alternatives, the purposes and needs at hand, and what is loosely called "the state of the science."

In a similar way judgments are made about other desirable characteristics a good theory should possess, such as simplicity. Some degree of *simplicity,* some *limitation on sheer complexity,* is an indispensable requirement of any conceptual form that is to be useful to human minds, which can comprehend only so much complexity. But how much is too much? This cannot be answered in the abstract; there are no quantified measures of simplicity, nor are there mechanical solutions to the question whether to prefer a theory with pervasive patterning but some internal disconnection or a theory with tight internal coherence but a rather *ad hoc* form. Extremes are easy to decide; but the real issues arise where equally competent and thoughtful men differ.

For this reason the considerations that support or threaten *the acceptance of theories and models* do not lend themselves to the crisp, clear-cut decision techniques that for long have been supposed to be the hallmark of scientific thought. There *are* considerations for the reasonable assessment of theories; that much is quite clear to those who observe the practice of the scientist with the unprejudiced eye that befits a philosophic analysis. But it is also clear that the logical character of these considerations makes it highly dubious that we should stretch the terminology of "verification" to this type of enterprise at all. Hypotheses are subjected to procedures of verification. Theories are weighed.

Unfortunately, this rather basic logical distinction—obvious when the different functions of the various conceptual strands composing the fabric of scientific thought are given due attention—has been largely obscured in the popular image of science, particularly as that image has been filtered through verificational analysis. In consequence many persons—including many of high intelligence and high motives—have been misled in their assumptions of what constitutes responsible thinking. Their paradigm purports to be science but in fact is a cartoon of science, not wholly wrong but crude. They suppose that secular morality in thinking requires them to adopt *"seeing is believing"* as their universal motto, and to conclude that anything "unseeable" eliminates the logical possibility of belief or disbelief. And so, sometimes reluctantly, they feel obliged to put aside as "noncognitive"—and therefore not in the least amenable to reasonable assessment—their utterances about values or about *ex hypothesi* nonobservational terms like "souls" or, finally, "God."

"GOD" AND VERIFICATION

The philosophic problem about "God," therefore, has tended to be couched in unsophisticated verificationist terms. What specific sense experiences, theists have been asked, are logically crucial for the expression "God loves little children"? We can specify what expectations are promised by the empirical hypothesis that "Mr. Brown loves little children": e.g., he will attempt to prevent children from serious injury, etc.; and if we should have the ill-fortune to observe Mr. Brown standing calmly doing nothing to save an innocent child from some disaster, we should count the statement of alleged "love" either false or so horribly redefined and qualified as to have lost its meaning. But it seems that theists consider their utterances about "God's love" to be compatible with an indefinitely extensive list of specifiable observations, including the sufferings (surely preventable by omnipotence) of innocent children. Therefore such utterances do not function to predict specific observations, since an expression compatible with *every possible* evidence is logically unable to determine *any specific* evidence. But if seeing is believing, then there is nothing specifically conveyed by theological language that can possibly be believed. Talk about God, therefore, is factually empty (so this argument concludes) and must be treated as *noncognitive*—as the expression of an emotional attitude or commitment to a way of life, or the like—rather than as the assertion of anything that might be open to rational argument.

This argument is by now a modern classic. It has in one form or another set the primary problems in philosophy of religion for nearly a generation and it has more recently presented the main starting point and challenge for theologians who, like Paul van Buren, insist on adopting the requirements of responsible secular thinking for any modern restatement of the meaning of the Christian gospel. Van Buren maintains that the empirical elusiveness of "God"-talk forces Christians to look for nonfactual interpretations of what their language actually means. The verification principle has undermined any factual significance for sentences containing "God" or synonymous terms; therefore the Christian theologian must rebuild on "basic attitudes," "fundamental perspectives" (for which R. M. Hare invents the term *bliks*—and, van Buren adds, "there is no arguing about 'bliks' ").

The problem with this argument, of course, is that it involves a bald *nonsequitur*. To be sure, we should grant that modern analysis has clearly shown that sentences containing "God" do not normally (among educated modern theists) function as low-level empirical generalizations nor as empirical hypotheses. But this premise does *not* by itself entail the conclusion that such sentences cannot function in *any* factual or cognitive way. To pass validly to such a conclusion requires a further assumed premise: viz., that the *only* factually cognitive function for language is the conveying of implicit observational data. And this assumption we have seen already to be false, even with respect to the language and thought of the sciences.

Our alternative, after our earlier discussion of scientific logic, ought to be obvious. "God" language does not need to be put aside as noncognitive, logically unbelievable, and radically unarguable, if it can be shown *capable of performing a theoretical function* within the theological enterprise. Uncovering such a function, of course, would be very far from suggesting that this is the *only* function of "God" and related terms; functional analysis of meaning has taught us that language can perform many, many roles—even quite different ones at the same time. One need not reject van Buren's descriptions of the profound attitudinal functions performed by theological discourse, therefore, in order to affirm additional theoretical possibilities for belief and argument. We can accept what he affirms but still insist on more.

There is indeed, an interesting parallelism between the verificational analysis of science, which we have already set aside as too partial and crude, and the verificational analysis of theology. Both are reductionist positions. Both begin from an a priori assumption as to the one kind of factual meaning there can be. Both discard what their simplistic categories cannot readily handle. And both interpret the purposes of the enterprises they analyze in a one-eyed way. The *verification analysis of science,* we recall, tended to ignore the side of science interested in satisfying our human quest for understanding. It put its emphasis exclusively on scientific interest in reliably determining human expectations for experience. And in so doing it inevitably distorted its treatment of those types of scientific language, theories, and models which are not primarily used for the predictive so much as for the interpretative side of science. In a strikingly similar manner *the verificational analysis of theology* tends to emphasize, again, only one side of religious concern: the attitudinal, the ethical, the emotive. The theoretical side of theology, like the theoretical side of science, tends on this philosophical account to be an embarrassment. But neither theological nor scientific interests are purely "practical"; both are human enterprises involving the unquenchable human thirst for *intelligibility*. It is, indeed, this thirst, this desire for understanding, that represents the main area of overlap between science and religion—the overlap that has made possible all those unfortunate battles between them. The battles may be unfortunate, I should add, but the overlap is not; it is what also makes possible our hope for an eventual unification of the human consciousness.

Both science and religion can be represented with initial plausibility by verificational analysis, I believe, because the features that verificationists point out are in fact present in the subjects concerned. Science *is* profoundly interested in predictions; religion *is* a deeply attitudinal phenomenon. Scientific language is full of empirical hypotheses; theological speech does function to affirm basic commitments to whole ways of life. But in addition to giving descriptions of empirical regularities, the scientist attempts to provide some conceptual means of *understanding* why the regularities in our experience are as they are. Here he employs terms that are not merely predictive of more experiences; they are interpretative of experiences already known or expected. And, similarly, the theologian is apt to be interested in more than the evocation and expression of attitudes; he wants (at least sometimes) some conceptual means for making intelligible the totality of the nature of things at least well enough to be able to show why the attitudes he nourishes are fitting. Again, the terms employed will not be expected to predict specific observations so much as to put all experience into a pattern that is *whole,* that is *pervasive,* and that is *adequate*.

One of the functions of some types of Christian "God" language, I believe, is to attempt to provide this kind of *patterning for the whole of things*. The vivid *imagery* of Scripture and tradition, first, provides the model for what would otherwise remain—without some such model—imaginatively indefinite. It is a model which, like all religious organizing images, specifically indicates the place of mankind within the pattern, and the kinds of attitudes and policies of life that are appropriate if "the whole of things" is given conceptual definiteness in this way. But, second, there is another type of discourse including "God" that functions in a more systematic way to achieve *propositional* integrity, to work out the many contexts of exemplification of the familiar patterns, and to relate the whole structure of beliefs to the pervasive and unavoidable given data of human experience. This more systematic discourse is the relatively more abstract conceptual scheme which the imagery of the theistic model interprets concretely. "God," as both the focus of supremely intensive valuational attitudes and the key concept in the theoretical structures of Christianity, is far removed by the internal logic of theological thinking from any simple or direct process of verification or falsification. But schemes of thought including this term may still function *cognitively* to refer. And in this role they are functioning factually though not empirically. Language involving "God" is not appropriately liable to be verified or falsified; instead, it should be weighed.

Here, then, is where I locate the real problem of "God" in our time. It is not, as cruder analyses have indicated, in the absence of some cognitive import for theological language; it is in the more subtle—and perhaps even more dangerous—issues that arise in *the weighing of the whole theoretical scheme* of theistic religion. We are now at last in a position, I think, to appreciate what options are left.

THE CRITICAL EVALUATION OF THEISM

The first option is one that I consider closed; but because of its apparent attractiveness to so many religious devotees today, despite much brave talk of the "world come of age," it must not be passed over in silence. This option would be *to refuse to accept the obligations of responsible thinking* according to the best standards available to our age. Here I urge all Christians to side unequivocally with the secular world. The canon of critical responsibility is no "respecter of persons"—or of privileged positions. Theologians like Paul van Buren, therefore, are wholly right in their basic intention. We are and must be "worldly" in our methods of thinking. Anything less than the best that the world can provide is a dereliction in our duty, and we know it. Christianity is not worth saving if it depends upon a ghetto mentality; nothing that violates our basic integrity—or even tempts us to do so—can qualify as "good news." And for exactly this reason my students, in raising the challenge against "religious fudging" that I mentioned at the start, were and are completely right. The only possible reply to them is: "Of *course* there can be no question of abandoning the basic obligations for responsible thinking we have learned as perhaps the most precious part of our modern heritage. *Critical concern for evidence* can be no less in approaching religion than in any other important area of life."

But in answering this way, and in siding squarely with van Buren's intention, it is crucial that we not slip carelessly into popular half-truths in defining the requirements of the secular standards we endorse. The critical method of contemporary consciousness at its best demands that our beliefs be based on adequate grounds and weighed according to the assessment of appropriate considerations. But while good thinking of any sort demands this basic rule of evidence, the gist of our discussion has shown that there are *various kinds of thinking* even within single fields of inquiry, and in consequence there are a variety of types of grounds that may be adequate and many sorts of consideration that may be assessed for different orders of beliefs. The mistake of some well-meaning theological secularizers is to be railroaded, through a commendable desire to be faithful to the best of secular thought, into philosophic stances that turn out, ironically, to be far from the best: inflexible,

F

incomplete, and already largely outworn. Critical responsibility, *sí!* Verificationism, *no!*

The second option assumes *the critical necessity of verificationism,* and so is closed to any who have been convinced by my argument to the contrary. But critical responsibility requires me to admit that I, too, may be wrong! And since there seems to be a good deal of life left in the verification principle, it would be foolish to ignore this option, which involves the motto that "there is no arguing about 'bliks.' " Ultimate commitments, being *noncognitive* on this view, simply "grasp" one; and modification of basic perspectives is always a matter of *"conversion."* This position, however, even apart from my attempt to show that verificational analysis is not critically compelling, strikes me as untenable. It is *unnecessary,* since attitudes and acts are just as subject to *intelligent assessment* as are beliefs. It is possible to give an analysis of an unreasonable attitude no less than of an unreasonable theory. Even if theological discourse is noncognitive in every respect, it still does not follow that "there is no arguing about 'bliks.' " We may not use the vocabulary of factual assessment, but a vocabulary of assessment there still remains. Even those who say that "there is no arguing about 'bliks' " admit that some bliks can be termed "right or wrong" or even "insane."

Moreover, it would be radically *irresponsible* to exempt religious commitments, even if found to be noncognitive, from careful examination. *Commitments have consequences,* and basic commitments have the most far-reaching consequences of all. To throw critical reflection to the winds in just the most important aspects of life would be the ultimate example of penny-wisdom and pound-foolishness. It would be the conscious acceptance of radical heedlessness at the motivational springs of one's life. I cannot conceive a more perfect definition of the unexamined life. Finally, since attitudes and policies of life have consequences not only for one's self but also for others, the option we are now considering is *dangerous.* If religious positions shape basic policies of action and attitudes of the profoundest sort, and if concerning them "there is no arguing" by rational means of adjudication and weighing, then incompatible commitments have no recourse but to the methods of mental or physical coercion. When the practical implications of nonarguable positions conflict, the consequence becomes the moral equivalent of a state of warfare. There is no logical difference, once reasoning has been put aside, between intense propaganda, brainwashing, and bayonets: they all function to persuade.

The social dangers and moral shortcomings of a position are not to be confused with its logical inadequacies, of course. Those inadequacies I have attempted to present in the main body of my argument. But I believe it is incumbent on us not to overlook the immense *practical consequences* of the issues we are examining. We sometimes fail to appreciate the barbaric terrors implicit in the abandonment of hope for the application of reasonable standards to basic issues of life. Thus the second option, though starting from the putative acceptance of critical method, shares with the first option a common practical readiness to exclude critical intelligence from matters of religious concern. As usual, anarchism and dogmatism go hand in hand. Let us hope, for civilization's sake, that neither option wins the present crucial struggle for this generation's mind.

The third option, one that I consider open to those who insist on *thinking both comprehensively and critically* with the best tools of our age, involves some radical theological reforms. Assessing the cognitive strength of "God"-talk will, if my analysis is correct, involve the careful weighing of the theoretical merits and weaknesses of theistic imagery and the various abstract propositional formulations which articulate it. "Weighing," we recall, is to theories as "verification" is to empirical hypotheses. Both involve *norms of inquiry* relative to the subject matter and to the conceptual functions under consideration; but both do involve identifiable norms of inquiry such as I have attempted to spell out in the foregoing. Given this understanding of the logical situation, I see three major areas of theological reform: all potentially painful and perhaps simply hopeless. What are they?

THE REFORM OF THEOLOGICAL LANGUAGE

First, without attempting to go into any of the specifics involved, there will be the need to make whatever *alterations in doctrine* prove necessary for increased theoretical strength. If theological theory contains identifiable contradiction or incoherence, the theologian who is determined to think with the full resources of secular responsibility must have the courage to abjure "fudging" appeals to paradox and mystery, as though they were somehow cognitive virtues in disguise. He must work, with all the skill and dedication of the scientist, to overcome such defects in the *integrity* of his conceptual scheme. Granted, the whole scheme is not to be condemned out of hand because of unsolved problems (this would be imposing a standard far more rigorous than is ever applied even to the theories of physics); but they must be recognized as the defects that they are, to be retained only because of specifiable overwhelming requirements of the given human data, to which the scheme must somehow remain adequate as best it can. Likewise, theological schemes must be open to revision by the demand of *adequacy*—even at some cost of the systematic requirement, if necessary. A theological theory is not simply or directly "falsifiable" by specific sense impressions, as we have seen; but it must not be insulated from the ground of basic, long-term human intuitions of life. To lose touch with this ground in experience would be to abandon its primary function and, sooner or later, its own vitality. This first general reform, then, calls for the recognition of the *radical revisability* of theological structure. And if this should entail the vulnerability of cherished dogmas—the Trinity, the natures of Christ, the impassibility of God, etc.—then let the chips fall where they may. But since doctrine fulfills other functions than the theoretical, it may be that this kind of reform will prove too painful to be carried through. If so, Christian thought is not worthy of modern secular belief.

The second general area of theological reform would be found in the need for believers to take a *radically different attitude toward their beliefs*. Belief, we remember, is to be proportioned to the strength of the considerations supporting such belief. There are "strong" belief-claims and "weak" ones. A man is in violation of critical propriety if he adopts "strong" cognitive attitudes toward matters that are very weakly warranted. But theological theory is at best supported only by the most delicate and cognitively uncoercive considerations. In weighing a scientific theory, as we have seen, there are all sorts of intangibles with regard to "enough" simplicity, "satisfactory" pervasiveness of pattern, "acceptable" balance between internal coherence and adequacy of coverage, and the like. Even more clearly, then, when it comes to weighing theories that are as all-encompassing and as dependent upon primal and inchoate intuitions as are theological ones, there is no present prospect of any of the candidates sweeping the board clean by obvious theoretical superiority to all other concepts for representing the whole of things. Believers in God, therefore, will have to learn to hold their concepts with *a new tentativeness* appropriate to the extreme uncertainty of the considerations relevant to the warranting of their beliefs. But since certainty of mind as well as commitment in act is one of the greatly valued elements in traditional theistic faiths, it may again prove that the needed reform is out of reach. If so, then the best thinkers of the modern world, who know the dangers of unwarranted cognitive closure, will rightly hold aloof from this form of dogmatism.

The third reform I envision will be *the acceptance of genuine pluralism*. A reformable and tentatively held theory does not exclude other theories of the same subject matter. A multiplicity of theories, in fact, that weigh approximately equally in the balance may be very welcome. By virtue of their number we are freed from slavery to any one of them and can in this way retain our hold on the distinction between our representations and the realities represented. And by taking care to hold onto this distinction we shall be more likely to be spurred into efforts at continually improving our conceptions. Unanimity is the surest lure to complacency, and complacency puts a stop to growth. Believers who choose to follow this option will need to set aside all pretensions to sole possession of truth and welcome, instead, all other critically held rival theories of ultimate reality. But, of course, the satisfactions of exclusivism have sunk so deep into the fabric of actual theistic traditions that it is perhaps mere dreaming to speak of this reform. Still, it is required if "God" is to be kept in contemporary currency. If the reforms entailed by the option of thinking responsibly while remaining a theist are indeed impossible, then "God" had better be dispensed with by lovers of truth.

A NONTHEISTIC POSSIBILITY

This last, pluralistic reform within Christian thinking, if taken as seriously as I intend to urge it, must (to remain authentic) make room for a reverent and open nontheistic religious position. All our conceptual schemes and value-organizing imagery are, after all, human instruments which quickly become idols if maintained with unconditional loyalty.

For some contemporary people, as we all know, "God" imagery and its associated theory blocks the sense of intellectual and valuational integrity that is a prime objective of mature and responsible religion. For these persons the centrality of anthropomorphic imagery even in reformed theistic belief is less an asset for supporting central human values and providing a familiar structure for understanding the universe than a liability compounded of offensive human vanity and outmoded conceptual parochialism. For these persons, again, present-day theological theories attempting to interpret how three-story imagery and mythical accounts of nature and supernature can square with the best of current knowledge are more ingenious than convincing; these persons weigh theistic theories, that is, and find them wanting in the balance.

It is not in the least surprising that differences in judgment in the weighing of theological theory should appear among men of equal virtue and equivalent competence. As we saw earlier, such differences are common, even in the sciences, whenever real issues and live inquiries are at stake. What is perhaps unusual is my contention that this is a natural and perfectly acceptable situation when it comes to disagreements over theistic versus nontheistic interpretations of the ultimate nature of things.

I hope I will not be misunderstood. I am not abandoning my long-held view that reformed theistic religion may be a responsible option for those who, despite its dim prospects for widespread popularity, are themselves able to adopt it. Much of my effort here has been spent precisely in battling the bad reasons sometimes given for ruling this out. Theism remains a responsible possibility.

But the logic of the situation, as I have found it, does not turn this possibility into a coercive requirement for all men of good will and good brains. There may well be good reasons, as well as bad ones, for resisting theistic language. And Christians, I believe, should be among the first to have the grace to say so. The main positive reason for withholding assent from theistic theories and images is, I believe, the obligation to remain sensitive to evidence, to openness, and to the possibility of theories and models of even greater adequacy and integrity than present theistic religion can offer.

This recognition may have the important value of freeing us from the threat of premature cognitive closure that familiar patterns (especially cherished patterns) may foist unconsciously upon our minds. Ours is a revolutionary and transitional age in which we need above all to be open to the intuitions, the data, the glimpses of the real and the ideal, that constitute the evidential-experiential pole of human thinking. Ours is an age, I believe, when we are above all obliged to remain alert to the prospect—or, at least, the hope—of more adequate patterns by which to represent ourselves and the total environment in which we think and act, and by which to provide both wholeness (integrity) and fullness (adequacy) to our basic thoughts and values. The constant, often unwitting, temptation of Christians whose minds have been nurtured in the expectation of a warmly familiar, all-encompassing picture of reality is to discount the importance of the posture of watchful waiting, of reverent openness to the data of life, of ambiguity-tolerance before the new, the disturbing, the unclassified, the potentially richer and fuller. There is nothing, I am convinced, in the best of the central Christian tradition to prevent a contemporary Christian from adopting such a stance; too often the therapeutic agnosticism implicit in the positions of many giants of creative Christian thinking is overlooked.

This secular age, shaped (for better, I think, not for worse) by the scientific spirit of critical responsibility, is in large part no longer satisfied to go for theoretical and valuational nourishment to images and theories inherited from ancient cultures and fitted for alien world-views. It may be that a return to theistic imagery and theories—refreshed and reshaped—will eventually turn out to be the long-term hope of human integrity before what might still prove the ultimately most satisfying truth open to men. But it may equally well be that, whatever our future, "God" (traditionally pictured and traditionally defined) will have to die for us today, for the sake of a rebirth of more effective, contemporary ultimate images that can bring new dimensions of understanding and satisfaction to postmodern life.

PART THREE: EVOLUTION
AND CREATION

8

EVOLUTION AND THE
DOCTRINE OF CREATION

Langdon Gilkey[*]

During the past year the intellectual world of the West has been celebrating the centenary of the publication of Charles Darwin's *Origin of Species* and seeking once again to estimate its significance for our cultural life. It is appropriate that the church attempt to make an evaluation of her own in relation to Darwin's influence. The church must continually re-think her relation to culture, of which relation the impact of Darwinism remains a potent symbol.

[*] *Langdon Gilkey is Professor of Systematic Theology at the Divinity School of the University of Chicago, and has published many articles and books in the field of theology. The selections below reflect the neo-orthodox position which until recently has been dominant in Protestant thought. The first portion of the chapter appeared as an article entitled "Darwin and Christian Thought," copyright © 1960 by the Christian Century Foundation and reprinted by permission from the January 6, 1960 issue of* The Christian Century. *The second portion is taken from Chapter 2, "What the Idea of Creation Is About," of his book,* Maker of Heaven and Earth, *which is the most extensive recent treatment of the doctrine of creation by a Protestant theologian. Copyright © 1959 by Langdon Gilkey; reprinted by permission of Doubleday & Company, Inc.*

I

The relations between Christian faith and the Darwinian theory of evolution have been complex. The simple picture, dear to the secular mind, of a head-on clash between prejudiced religionists and open-minded scientists is about as inaccurate historically as is the fundamentalist's view of the clash as one more joust between God and Satan. Actually, the Christian religion in significant ways prepared the ground for the theory of evolution.

The Christian concept of creation provided one of the necessary foundations for the development of Western empirical science, of which Darwinism is certainly an important result. The biblical view that time is both linear and irreversible, and therefore capable of cumulative development, is perhaps the most crucial of all the distant progenitors of the concept of evolution. It is no accident that evolutionary theories of origins appeared within a culture saturated with biblical concepts of creation and of Providence.

It is true however that three notions, derived from and supported by biblical ideas, had to be dislodged if evolution was to be intelligible to Western minds. First, the limited time-span of the biblical view needed extension if natural scientists were to think of a gradual development of the forms of life. Largely on biblical grounds, most intelligent men before the end of the eighteenth century assumed that the world was only about 6,000 years old; Thomas Browne, for example, asserted in 1635, "Time we may comprehend; 'tis but five days elder than ourselves." Clearly, if there had been so little time since the beginning, no slow development of the forms of life by gradual changes was possible or even conceivable.

The second biblical notion in conflict with evolutionary concepts was that the present forms of life had come into being all at once at the beginning through a single act of divine creation. Western thought had always assumed that whatever we see around us had been put there once and for all by God. Thus John Ray was in 1695 able to affirm that the "universal opinion of divines and philosophers" is "that since ye first Creation there have been no species of animals or vegetables lost, no new ones produced."

Closely associated with this notion of a single initial creation was the concept of fixed, unchanging species or forms of life. The assumption that there are certain immutable "kinds of things" is as old as Greek philosophy, but for Western minds it received its most fundamental sanction from the biblical account of creation. At his initial act of creation God, in the biblical view, made all the present species of plants and animals, and since then they have not substantially changed. Each species represents an essential and eternal structure in the nature of things, purposed from the beginning, and while there may be variety here and there in details these essential natures remain immutable. This general concept of certain fixed forms of life, certified by revelation and confirmed by early biological studies, was the common assumption of most scientists, philosophers and theologians until the latter part of the eighteenth century.

II

In estimating our attitude to Darwin it is important to recall that the orthodox religious and scientific picture of the origins of species had undergone steady attack from the newer sciences of geology and historical biology long before Darwin appeared. The development of geological inquiry and speculation at the turn of the nineteenth century had generally established the immense age of the earth—an intellectual change almost as significant as the advent of Darwinism. Instead of the traditional estimate of a 6,000-year span, scientists now offered the awesome picture of time stretching backward almost to infinity: "We find no vestige of a beginning," said James Hutton in 1795. By the 1820's the simple, homely biblical time-span had been rigorously challenged; the Flood was consequently removed as a significant event in geological history. Scientists, intellectuals and clerics alike accepted the new "unbiblical" age of the earth. As Lyell, the real founder of geology, showed in the 1830's, the earth was given its present form neither by recent divine acts of creation nor by the simple miraculous cataclysm of the Flood, but rather by the gradual working of natural forces controlled by immutable laws over ages of time. With the rise of the science of geology, the biblical view of creation suffered its first real defeat, for now for the first time the endless world of uniform natural law really impressed itself on the Western mind—a fact to be remembered by fundamentalists who castigate Darwin and yet hire geologists to find oil, coal or water.

The concept of the fixity of species, moreover, was shaken if not yet dislodged by the new understanding of fossilized bones which, when reconstructed, revealed species long since extinct. Geological discovery had shown that even the firm earth was subject to change; now, with horrendous skeletons of long-vanished reptiles rising in every museum, men became aware that the forms of life also could change, realizing that behind our brief age there lay mysterious reaches of time in which species had appeared and then died, to be replaced by other species which eventually would also disappear. And cats, dogs and cows and all the Ark's medley of animals were nowhere to be found in the distant past; their day was yet to come.

Thus by 1850 the "biblical" account of creation, and with it the three concepts we have noted, was already radically questioned in countless Christian minds. A new view of nature and of her early processes had been in slow formation in the early nineteenth century, a view which contradicted at almost every point the concrete picture of origins in Genesis. The result was that long before 1859 there was widespread doubt about the inerrant validity of Scripture, accompanied by an anxious search for some new basis of faith. Before 1850 such literary figures as Alfred Tennyson, Thomas Arnold and George Eliot both reflected the doubt and carried on the search, and the great theologian Schleiermacher formulated a new interpretation of religion to resolve the problem. Thus the *Origin of Species* does not represent an initial or isolated challenge to the biblical view of origins, and no disproving of Darwin's theory of evolution could lead to re-establishment of the biblical world view as literally infallible. In order to re-establish that early view of the world, one would have to reject almost every major scientific hypothesis on which our present culture has been nourished.

III

If the literal biblical history had already been widely questioned by 1859, why was it that Darwin's theory raised such a storm among scientists, philosophers and churchmen? The answer lies not so much in the particular scientific theories of Darwin, although they were certainly unacceptable to the older patterns of thought, as in the deeper philosophical and religious assumptions that the new understanding of origins seemed to imply. First, Darwin's theory completed, confirmed and radically symbolized the new scientific world view. As astonomy and physics had explained the origins of the solar system by uniform and mechanical law, and as geology had explained the formation of mountains and valleys by a similar set of uniform laws, so Darwin explained the one seemingly unexplainable mystery, the origins of living species, by the same sort of uniformity of mechanical law. Men can with some aplomb regard stars and rocks as merely "caused," as products of purposeless change. But Darwin's explanation not only completed the system of natural explanation, it brought man's own existence under such laws of change. And the inclusion of man was a step having not merely quantitative but qualitative significance; now even man had become engulfed within the blind flux. With the inclusion of himself in the reign of endless and purposeless law, man found himself a citizen of an entirely new and alien world.

Darwinism implied that just as rocks, mountains and even stars are caught in endless change, so is life itself; species come and go, dinosaurs rise and fall—and so does man. In a world of endless change, man's existence itself suddenly became but a moment within that change. Also, in Darwin's theory man is regarded as the temporary product not of the providential activity of God but of random factors and causal sequences in the shifting realm of nature. According to Darwin the sources of man's life are twofold: chance variations within the passage of countless generations and selection of the most favorable of these variations by the requirements of survival within the universal struggle for existence. Random variations plus natural selection of the fittest mold the fluid forms of life into types more and more adaptable to their environment.

Man, then, was seen as arising not from the purposive providence of God but out of the conflux of the random novelty of variation and the ineluctable law of survival—strictly and solely the child of chance and determinism. The dinosaurs rose and passed away for no reason at all except the whim of chance and the laws of survival; so it will be with the whole human enterprise, which has arisen and will disappear at the dictation of the same two blind goddesses.

Unlimited change and unqualified purposelessness were thus the twin philosophical implications of Darwinism that sent shudders through the nineteenth-century soul. These philosophical concepts had been equally implicit in every scientific advance since Galileo, but Darwin brought them into the open when he applied them to the hitherto sacrosanct topic of the origin and destiny of man. With Darwin's book the meaningless sea of endless, mindless nature seemed to close forever over man's existence. Philosophical naturalists often say that the nineteenth century was not immediately attracted to Darwin's thought because he "made man an animal" and thus compromised man's presumptuous sense of superiority. This is to miss the real issue: it was because Darwinism seemed to make man a child of blind Fate, rather than of God, that it became the center of heated if short-lived controversy.

IV

What rescued the nineteenth century from the despair implicit in Darwinism? It was the fact that quite quickly in scientific and philosophical minds blind Fate was transformed into a benevolent cosmic Progress. The new secular religion of progressive evolutionism made it possible for Victorian culture, both religious and irreligious, to absorb evolution with truly astounding serenity and speed; believing firmly in inevitable Progress they were able to forget the deeper implications of Darwinism. In our own day, when the faith in inevitable progress has almost completely disappeared, those implications have finally come home to roost. It is our age, not the nineteenth century, which has had aching acquaintance with the void of meaninglessness.

From the foregoing we can see that in the Darwinian controversy, ideas clashed on two levels: the level of specific scientific theories about origins and the level of fundamental philosophical comprehension of the ultimate character of existence. On the first level such ideas as the limited age of the world, the fixity of species, and specific divine acts of creation confronted the Darwinian view of an unlimited past in which random variations and natural selection transformed the mutable forms of life into their present species. On the second level philosophical and theological ideas affirming that existence is created and guided by the divine Providence clashed with an implicit philosophical affirmation that only chance and determinism rule in the universe as a whole. It was the conjunction of the scientific with the philosophical-religious level that made the controversy so significant. The difficulty was that to both sides of the argument controversy over the first level really involved at each point controversy on the second level, and leading scientists as well as bishops took issue with the Darwinian theory both because of its particular scientific hypotheses and its philosophical implications.

V

In seeking to understand the controversy it is necessary to remember that Darwin's theory actually contains two closely associated but distinct elements. The first element is the hypothesis that evolution has in fact happened, that species have developed by evolving from other, now extinct, forms of life. An affirmation of evolution in this general sense clearly contradicts the earlier biblical and scientific concepts of an original divine creation of species each of which is independent of other species and fixed in its nature. The second element in Darwin's theory is the hypothesis that the process of evolution is to be explained by random variations and natural selection. In Darwin's own work these two elements are so intertwined as to be almost inseparable—for good historical reasons. Many theories of evolution had appeared in the 100 years before 1859, but Darwin's was the first which purported to give a natural and scientific cause for evolution. It was the theory of the cause of evolution that made the theory as a whole scientific, hence Darwin kept the two elements together in the closest possible relation. But in the development of the theory since Darwin's time a tacit separation has taken place; while the fact of evolution has been generally accepted and is the foundation for all present sciences of life from biology to medicine to agronomy, the understanding of its causes has been continuously subject to scientific debate, criticism and transformation.

The distinction between the fact of evolutionary development and the understanding of its causes is important for the relation of the theory to religion. The fact of evolution certainly challenged certain views defended by orthodoxy: the short time-span of the earth, the once-for-all creation of species and the fixity of species. But as most theologians now agree, these views are "religious" only in the limited sense that they are the theories of the origins of species implied in Genesis. This aspect of Darwin's theory is a challenge to Christian faith only if one insists on the verbal infallibility of Scripture and the literal truth of all of its statements, "scientific" and historical as well as religious. As we have shown, such a view of religious truth had been under scientific attack well before Darwin. Anyone who uses the science of geology to find oil or coal has already implicitly abandoned the literalist view of Scripture. In any case it is not at all certain that belief in God as the Creator and Providential Ruler of all of life necessarily involves a belief that the world is only 6,000 years old and that all present species were named by Adam in the first days.

The issue of the causes of evolution, however, is more complex. Here the two levels of the controversy—the level of particular scientific hypotheses and the level of philosophical implications—meet in the most subtle manner. On the one hand science can deal only with what have generally been called "secondary causes": explanations of phenomena and events in terms of other finite causes interpreted according to the known relations of natural experience. Scientific inquiry can investigate only the interrelations between finite events. Divine power cannot be brought into the laboratory to be tested; by definition the "causes" of a miracle are beyond human investigation. Science as a mode of inquiry is not equipped to understand an event in theological or religious terms as the work of God; it must understand an event as the work of finite and hence nondivine causes. This is just what Darwin sought to do; by explaining the evolution of species solely in terms of natural, finite causes, his theory is a prime example of scientific method.

VI

If scientific understanding is thus incurably *un*theological, is it then also *anti*theological? This question raises the most fundamental issue in the controversy over Darwinism. To many moderns a scientific explanation does preclude the activity, the "causality" of God. To them an adequate explanation of the origins of life in terms of secondary causation seems to make both irrelevant and unintelligible an additional "higher" explanation. If all the causes of a thing have been assembled, there can be no other causes. For example, if the science of meteorology can specify in scientific terms all the relevant causes of a thunderstorm, does this not preclude the simple biblical causality which holds that God willed and brought forth the storm? Similarly is not the assertion that random variations (or mutations, as geneticists now call them) plus natural selection "caused" the rise of man another way of saying that God did not create man? Especially does this implication appear valid when the two types of causality seem to be directly opposed. Darwin's essential emphasis on *random* variations denies effective purpose in the variations and the natural selection that mold life. The essence of God's activity is, of course, its purposive character. Thus the explanation in terms of secondary causes seems not only to make unnecessary and irrelevant further theological understanding, but actively to exclude it as contradictory to science.

The implication that secondary causality excludes the primary causality of God is at the center of the position known as philosophical naturalism; the real debate raised by Darwin revolves about this philosophy, Two things should be noted about this implication of Darwinism. First, both the naturalistic opponents of religion and the religious opponents of evolution should recognize that to rule out God's activity because it cannot become a part of a scientific explanation of events is to draw a philosophical conclusion which is not itself a part of the scientific hypothesis. The naturalistic world view is an extension of scientific understanding beyond the range of science. It is an extension into metaphysics, into a general description of the ultimate nature of the universe. Though naturalistic philosophy has been a clear implication of Darwin's theory to many of his followers, it is not part of this theory as that theory appears in the field of biological science—which can no more establish the absence of God from the universe than it can certify his presence in the biology laboratory.

Religious antievolutionists, furthermore, should note that the scientific method itself—and thus every particular hypothesis—*if* expanded into a philosophical viewpoint, carries the same threat as does Darwin. If scientific explanation excludes divine activity—and this seems to be the terror which Darwinism held for those Christians who feared it—then no hypothesis of physics, chemistry, geology or meteorology is acceptable to Christian minds, and no faithful Christian can plan his morrow on the basis of a scientific weather forecast. Again we see that Darwin is not alone in supplying problems for religious thought. His theory is merely the most powerful and poignant symbol of the challenge which all of modern science raises for Christian faith when scientific understanding is made into an all-embracing world view. It is not the specific theory of evolution, any more than any other specific theory, which challenges the truth of faith; what is at issue is the philosophical conclusion which contends that scientific hypotheses provide an all-sufficient understanding that excludes Providence.

VII

What then does the Christian say about Darwinian thought? He will neither reject it nor give it unqualified endorsement. The theory of evolution can in itself be accepted by any Christian willing to question the verbal infallibility of Scripture and the specific theories of time and of species contained in it. In fact on these terms it is possible for evolution and Christian thought to cohere with surprising and even dangerous ease. Liberal theology effected such an amalgamation, interpreting the theological concepts of revelation, creation and redemption in accordance with the fundamental idea of the evolutionary development of the cosmos, of life, of culture and of religion. In the late nineteenth century, far from being antithetical to all religion, evolution became the bulwark of liberal religious thought. As Lyman Abbott said: "The history of the world, whether it be the history of creation, or providence, or of redemption, whether the history of redemption in the race or of redemption in the individual soul, is the history of a growth in accordance with the great law interpreted and uttered in that one word evolution."

Contemporary theology has had a more ambiguous relation than did liberalism to scientific and philosophical notions such as evolution. Unlike liberalism it has carefully tried to construct its theological concepts on the basis of revelation rather than on that of either science or philosophy; it does not use the concept of evolution as a means of interpreting the religious ideas of creation, providence or revelation. On the other hand, unlike the older orthodoxy it has sought to interpret the realities of Christian faith without denying any specific theories of the various sciences. Most contemporary theologians accept the theory of evolution as a probably accurate biological description of the way in which life has developed, just as they accept the hypotheses of physics, chemistry or geology. But they maintain that this biological understanding of man, while providing illumination of man as "creature," does not produce a total understanding of man in all the dimensions of his existence. Thus modern theology affirms that man is not only a creature evolved from nature but also a child of God made in his image and destined through faith for eternal life with him. Evolution is accepted as a scientific concept, but like all such it is regarded as neither in conflict with nor determinative of theological concepts.

If Christian thought accepts evolution as the most probable description of the natural origins of man's life, how are Christians then to understand the causes of evolution? Specifically, how are we to think about God's creation of man in God's image if we also recognize the biologist's explanation of human origins in terms of random mutations and natural selection? What is the relation of God's primary causality to the secondary causality of natural and historical life? Modern theology by and large has side-stepped this difficult question, partly out of concern for the issues of revelation and redemption and partly out of fear of domination by science and philosophy. But it cannot be permanently avoided, for on a sound answer depends the intelligibility of the central Christian affirmation that God is the Lord of nature and the Sovereign of history.

If Christians are to accept the modern world of scientific inquiry and technology, they must learn to think of God's providence as working through and within the finite relations of things to one another and not, so to speak, alongside of and separate from those relations. Divine causality, whether it concern the movements of natural forces in climate and weather or of historical forces in the doings of men, does not push aside the activity of finite agents—as if God would cause a storm without the contributing meteorological factors or bring about an historical event without the action of men or effect our salvation without the activity of our wills. Rather, divine causality works through the finite; in regard to origins, God works through all the secondary causes that have played their part in the development of life on earth. Science studies by its empirical methods these finite causes—in the case of evolution, genetic mutations and natural selection—in the workings of which religious faith discerns, however dimly, the mysterious activity of God's providence. And just as the events of history or of an individual's life seem from the outside to be "random," yet in them the eye of faith can discover the workings of God, so the processes of natural development seem to the inquiries of science to be entirely random, yet to the mind of faith they manifest the mystery of God's creative and providential will.

For the Christian, then, the inquiries of science—and with them the theory of evolution—do not conflict with his faith. The scientist is studying the finite causes through which God's providence is acting on the world; Christians should not be surprised when the scientist, who by his method can find only those finite causes, does not discover God's activity therein. But the Christian does not concur with his inquiring friend if he abandons his scientific role and extrapolates from the explanations of scientific inquiry the philosophical doctrine which maintains that only finite causes are at work, that nature is self-sufficient and provides the sole source and environment of man. The naturalism that denies the category of the divine is, however, not a part of science, but a philosophical extension of it. Let us recall that such a naturalistic view of reality, far from being a new product of modern science, is as old as philosophy itself and that the controversy of religious faith with this ancient view is as old as human culture.

In summation evolution as a scientific hypothesis presents no new or fundamental challenge to Christian faith. In its biological aspect it illuminates extensively the creatureliness which is a God-given aspect of our being. And in its deeper implications the theory of evolution embodies for us a reminder of two of the perennial tasks of the church: the task of rethinking our faith in God and his works in the light of all we know and the task of carrying on in as intelligible terms as we can the continual debate with a cultural wisdom that knows nothing of God.

.   .   .   .

WHAT THE IDEA OF CREATION IS ABOUT

The best way to understand what is the subject matter of the doctrine of creation is to distinguish between certain basic kinds of questions that men ask. People ask many kinds of questions about the origin of things, and these are often radically different from each other in meaning and intention. Consequently the answers to these questions can be in quite distinct realms of discourse. It is, therefore, in terms of the differences in kinds of questions men ask that we can most easily see the distinction between scientific, philosophical, and theological answers, and can most easily apprehend the different kinds and levels of truth that each one seeks.

First of all there is the scientific question about origins. Here we are inquiring about "causes" or developments preceding a "state of affairs" in nature that we may now know something about. We are pushing our inquiry further back in time by asking about the factors which brought about the state where our last inquiry left us. Thus we can in scientific knowledge move back beyond the formation of the seas and the mountains to the cooling of the earth, back from there to the whirling gases which formed the earth, and back beyond there to the nebular hypothesis, and so on. The question of origins here asks merely about the character of the preceding "state of affairs," about the circumstances among finite things that brought about our present situation, about the unknown finite "causes" that produced the known effects. Scientific hypotheses and statements are thus by definition *about* relations between finite things in space and time. They assume that the process of events in space and time is already going on, and they ask about their character and the laws of their interrelationships. They cannot and do not wish to ask questions about the origins of the whole system of finite things. Therefore, while science may be able to push its inquiry back *toward* an "ultimate origin of things," if there be one, clearly it can never find or even inquire about such an ultimate origin. For the question of an *ultimate* origin asks, if it asks anything at all, about the cause of every finite state of affairs, including each preceding one. It is the question of the origin of the whole system of finite relations, and thus can never be found by an inquiry that restricts itself to the relations within that system. In science there is nothing that corresponds to or can conceivably conflict with either a metaphysical understanding of origins or with the theological doctrine of creation.

Another kind of question people ask about "origins" is more strictly philosophical or metaphysical in character. It goes something like this: "In or behind the changing things that make up existence as we find it (trees, rocks, stars, people, ideas, sensations, etc.) is there any sort of thing (or substance or principle) which is always there, which always has been there, and so from which all these things can be said (by analogy) 'to come'? Is there any basic, fundamental, permanent substance, being, or set of principles which underlies them and so which gives them all the reality they possess? Is there a Really Real at the origin of things, and if so what is it?"[1]

This is the question that tantalized the early Greek and Indian philosophers and so incited the great tradition of speculative philosophy. It is the question of what it means for anything "to be," of what must be there if something is to exist at all, and so the question of that upon which changing existences ultimately depend—it is the "ontological" question of "being" or "existence." And the answers have been fascinatingly various in the history of thought: there are the water, air, and fire principles of the earliest Greek thinkers; there are the Boundless, the Unmoving Being, and the atoms of more sophisticated thinkers; the Ideas of Plato, the One of Plotinus, the transcendent, unnamable Brahman of Hinduism—and so on to the *Natura Naturans* of Spinoza, the Monads of Leibnitz, the elaborate categorial factors of Whitehead, and the "Nature" of contemporary naturalistic philosophy. In each case, in order to find the "origin" or foundation of experienced existence, the mind asks about an underlying level of reality beyond and yet within sensible experience. This is the metaphysical question of origins.

Now as one can easily see, this is a very different sort of question from the scientific question we noted above. Here we are not asking about the finite "causes" out of which a given state of affairs arose. And the reason is that the metaphysical question would apply with equal cogency to that preceding set of circumstances. In fact, as philosophy quickly realized, our question is not really concerned with what happened "beforehand" at all. Rather we are asking: "Assuming *all* the various

[1] An attempt has been made to phrase these basic "metaphysical" questions without prejudice for any particular kind of systematic answer. Although the phrasing may seem to imply a transcendent monism as the "Really Real," nevertheless, in theory these questions are such that they could be the starting point for an immanent, naturalistic pluralism such as has been formulated by Whitehead.

'states of affairs' that have characterized the universe of finite things, on what fundamental structure of relationships or substance or being do they all depend for their existence and reality? What is the source and 'origin' of their total being?" Thus even substantial changes in the answers to scientific questions about origins need not have a fundamental effect on metaphysical viewpoints. A man can remain a positivist, a naturalist, an idealist, a pluralist, or monist, whatever the present status of the nebular hypothesis or the idea of evolution.

Finally there is another kind of question that involves the issue of "origins." This is a much more burning, personal sort of question than the scientific or metaphysical ones, which are rightly motivated by a serene curiosity about the universe we live in. Here we ask an ultimate question with a distinctly personal reference. We are raising the question of "origins" because we are asking about the ultimate security, the meaning and the destiny of our own existence. It is the metaphysical question of being in an "existential" form, a question about the ultimate origins of our *own* being, and so a question in which we ourselves are deeply involved. For when we ask about the security and meaning of our own life, we are not asking about something else (a nebula, or even a first substance) outside of us; our question is about ourselves as we are caught within the mighty forces that impinge on us, determine our life, and mete out to us our fate. Consequently, we can never back off from these issues and gaze at them objectively. Rather they come to us in the midst of our involvement within them. Thus we experience them not as spectators but as participants—and so the problems of security, meaning, and destiny, partly engulfing us, become something we can never completely conquer and reduce to intelligible size. They are, as Marcel points out, "mysteries" and not "problems"[2]—something we must think about, but not something we can control, dissect, measure, test, or even contemplate objectively and define clearly. They elude our easy intellectual grasp because they grasp us.

[2] Gabriel Marcel, *The Ontological Mystery*.

This kind of question comes to us all at certain times. We are aware of them especially when our security has been somehow rudely shaken, as in a sudden brush with death on the highway, and we realize the arbitrary and precarious hold each of us has on existence and life. We suddenly sense our own creaturely dependence on things and events beyond our control, or we feel with a shudder our own life span slipping away from us—and, wondering how long we will be here, we ask if there is anything that is truly dependable and secure, not to be removed by anything, upon which our own existence depends. Or this kind of question can come when we can find no apparent purpose or meaning making coherent our existence amidst the baffling events of life, and we wonder why we are here. Then we ask (with Pascal) "Who has put me here?" What is the meaning behind my own being at this concrete moment and place? Have I merely been hurled into existence at random by blind forces of parentage and environment as the planets were hurled off into space by the whirling sun? Is there no Creator who has placed me here and given my concrete life a purpose, a destiny, and a ground for hope? Or again, we may ask: "What ultimately determines my life—who or what is in charge here? I see my life determined by powerful, often meaningless, and surely blind forces: outside of me there are floods, wars, conquests, and economic cycles; within me are hereditary weaknesses, neuroses, fatal flaws, and the corrosion of the years. Are these, then, the Lords of my existence? Am I dependent solely on them, and on my own strength to defeat or control them, in order to find a purpose and direction in all I do? Am I merely a cork tossed about on mighty waves, since so clearly I am not able to be captain of my own destiny? Is there no sovereign Lord of all, who is Creator and Ruler over all these powers that rule over me?"

Such questions about the ground of our contingent being, about a transcendent purpose for our short life, and about the Lords of our destiny, are a part of the life of us all. Here we ask why *we* exist, and on what power that existence depends. This is not a speculative question for us, but a deeply personal question about the meaning and security of *our* existence. Such questions, therefore, do not spring from intellectual curiosity so much as they come from anxiety about the mystery of the existence in which our whole being is involved. And they must be answered somehow, if any human being is to live free of insecurity and frustration. Sometimes they are answered superficially in terms of immediate securities and small "meanings"— such as a new car, a paid-up mortgage and an insurance policy. But when these little supports are shaken by some shattering natural, psychological, or historical event, the ultimate questions of the origin, the meaning and destiny of life itself, rush powerfully to the fore and seem to blot out all our other questions. We live in such a time today.

Two things should be said further about questions of this sort. First of all, they are peculiarly "religious" in character. That is, they ask about the ultimate ground and meaning of our existence, they search for a faithful and healing answer to our deepest problems, and they are answered in terms of affirmation and trust, rather than in terms of proof and demonstration. Let us look at this last point for a moment; we shall return to it often again. As we have pointed out, these questions represent "mysteries" and not "problems." What brings these questions on us pell-mell is not usually an intellectual problem which arouses our curiosity and calls for an intellectual solution.[3] Rather they rush up within us because we find ourselves in some personal crisis that has created inner anxiety and a sense of utter lostness. It is our anxiety, our frustration, our futility, our guilt—not our curiosity—that must be assuaged and satisfied. In such a situation an intellectual solution, or even demonstration, may be quite irrelevant. An academic proof of God's

[3] "The question 'Why should anything exist at all?'. . . does not present itself to us as a conceptual question: our motives for trying to answer it are not those of logical tidiness." A. Flew and A. Macintyre, eds., *New Essays in Philosophical Theology* (New York: The Macmillan Co., 1955), p. 19.

existence will not help a man who is overcome with futility or guilt. His problem is not ignorance or unclarity of mind, so much as it is turbulence and anxiety of spirit. What he needs, therefore, is not a demonstrated concept of deity in his mind, so much as an experienced encounter with Almighty God. For only in such an encounter, and the living relation that flows from it, can a man find the courage and conviction, the purpose and inner strength to accept and to conquer the "mysteries" of existence. Certainly our answers to these questions must satisfy the mind with regard to validity. But because they stem from transforming experiences that are deeper than proof and demonstration, real answers to existential questions primarily tend to promote confidence and serenity in facing life, rather than intellectual satisfaction at resolving a "curiosity" problem. When, therefore, an answer to these questions is received, we speak more meaningfully of faith and trust than we do of knowledge or complete understanding;[4] and so we call these "religious" questions and answers.

Secondly, although these religious questions are centered upon immediate problems of meaning in our contemporary personal or group life, nevertheless inevitably they too imply the question of ultimate origins. The question of the meaning and destiny of our present life can only be answered if we can have confidence in the fundamental goodness of life as promising fulfillment; and such confidence in the promise of life is possible only if we have some basis for trust in the source of all being. The religious question of the meaning of our being drives us to the religious question of the origin of all being in God. To the anxious question: Why are we, and on what do we ultimately depend? the Christian faith gives the answer: We are creatures of God dependent utterly upon His sovereign power and love. Thus in asking the religious question "Who created the world?" men are not so curious about how or when the universe came to

___

[4] "Whence we conclude, that the knowledge of faith consists more in certainty than in comprehension." J. Calvin, *Institutes of the Christian Religion,* Book III, Chapter 2, Section XIV (Allen's translation).

be as they are deeply concerned about the goodness and meaning of their life, and so about the character of the ultimate source and ruler of their life. The religious affirmation that God created the world is, therefore, fundamentally concerned to give a positive answer to the baffling mystery of the meaning of our life here and now as finite, transient creatures. For it asserts above all that our present existence is in the hands of the One Almighty Lord whom we know as love. The theological idea of creation is first of all an answer to the religious question of the meaning and destiny of man's historical life.[5]

Now if there is anything upon which contemporary theology agrees, it is that the biblical belief in creation derives from an answer to this "religious" question, rather than from an answer

---

[5] This connection between the "existential" question, "Who rules our destiny?" and the religious doctrine of creation is clearly brought out in the three following quotations:

"The doctrine of creation is not a speculative cosmogony, but a confession of faith, of faith in God as Lord. The world belongs to Him, and He upholds it by His power. He sustains human life, and man owes Him obedience." Quoted from R. Bultmann, *Primitive Christianity* (New York: Meridian Books, 1956), p. 15.

"In the last analysis, the Old Testament doctrine of creation expresses a sense of the present situation of man. He is hedged in by the incomprehensible power of Almighty God. The real purpose of the creation story is to indicate what God is doing all the time." *Ibid.*, p. 18.

"God rules. He exercises control in every part of this visible universe, and particularly in the affairs of men. If this is true, how does it come about? What is that relationship between God and the world, between the spiritual and the material, which makes such control possible? The Hebrew answer is simplicity itself. God can rule the world because He made it. 'The sea is His and He made it, and His hands prepared the dry land.' 'By the word of the Lord were the heavens made, and all the host of them by the breath of His mouth.' God is not dependent on the world; the world is wholly dependent upon Him." S. C. Neill, *Christian Faith Today* (Penguin Books, Inc., 1955), pp. 72–73.

By associating these ideas or doctrines with human religious questions, we do not mean at all to imply that "religious truth" is merely a matter of human questions and human answers. Religious truth is first and foremost a matter of divine revelation. Our point is that revelation is always received and understood as the answer to the specifically religious, and not the scientific or even the philosophical, questions a man asks about his life.

either to a scientific or a metaphysical question. The Israelites, who expressed this doctrine in psalms, history, and prophecy, were not prompted by a scientific curiosity about the exact series of events, or the set of relations and circumstances which accompanied the origin of the world. Nor were they concerned with the speculative question of an underlying substance which would explain the world of changing things. They were overwhelmingly interested in the mystery of the purpose and meaning of their history as a people, and so with the nature of the Ruler of all history. Correspondingly, they sought, in calling God "Creator," to affirm the total sovereignty and the almighty power of the God who had revealed Himself as the author of Israel's destiny and the executor of Israel's fulfillment. They, and the Christians who followed them, confessed God to be the Creator and Ruler of all things, because each had received a vivid answer to fundamental religious questions: Who has put us here; who has fashioned us and for what purpose; who is the ultimate power over our existence; and who claims us as the Lord and Ruler of our life and destiny?

Their doctrine of creation, then, is an affirmation of faith that despite the mystery and anxiety of their creaturely dependence and temporality, they, as biblical people, have found God revealed to them as the Almighty Power who created them and all that seemed to threaten them, and created them for such a purpose that they might through Him have confidence and trust in life and in its meaning.

The Christian doctrine of creation, therefore, expresses in theoretical language those positive religious affirmations which biblical faith in God makes in response to the mystery of the meaning and destiny of our creaturely finitude. These affirmations are: (1) That the world has come to be from the transcendent holiness and power of God, who because He is the ultimate origin is the ultimate Ruler of all created things. (2) That because of God's creative and ruling power our finite life and the events in which we live have, despite their bewildering mystery and their frequently tragic character, a meaning, a purpose, and a destiny beyond any immediate and apparent futility. (3) That man's life, and therefore *my* life, is not my own to "do with" merely as I please, but is claimed for—because it is upheld and guided by—a power and a will beyond my will. This is what the Christian means when he says, "I believe in God the Father Almighty, Maker of heaven and earth." This is what the idea of *creatio ex nihilo* is essentially "about."

G

9

CREATION AND THE
ORIGIN OF LIFE

*William J. Schmitt, S.J.**

The possibility of life arising from nonlife is once again the subject of much discussion. Universities noted for their scientific accomplishments are sponsoring symposia; scientists of outstanding reputation are undertaking serious research programs dealing with Spontaneous Generation. Unfortunately, a great deal of the literature on this subject, especially in book form, is unscholarly sensationalism. There are some also who, exhuming a long-dead line of argumentation, claim that Spontaneous Generation does away with any need for "the hypothesis of God."

.   .   .   .   .   .

The first step in the construction of the hypothesis of Spontaneous Generation of life on this planet is to consider the

* W. J. Schmitt is a chemist who has written for a number of research journals. He was formerly on the faculty at Fordham University and is now Chairman of the Chemistry Department at the Ateneo de Manila, Philippines. In this selection he discusses the origin of life and indicates reasons for believing that there was no "gap" between the nonliving and the living. On the theological side, he defends the neo-Thomist conviction that God's "primary causality" operated not by intervention but by establishing a system of natural causes which produced life. Reprinted by permission from Thought, Vol. 37 (1962), pp. 269, 275–77, 281–87; sections dealing with the earlier history of the problem are omitted.

conditions under which life could have arisen. Paradoxical as it might seem, the absence of life is one of these conditions. The very statement of the question supposes this but, in addition, we find it a necessary condition for any Spontaneous Generation. Considering the fate of complex organic molecules in the world today, which is to be rapidly broken down by bacteria and other living organisms, we know that only in the absence of life could the postulated evolution of molecules take place, for only on an earth still sterile would they be safe from the devouring hordes of organisms.[1]

As regards temperature, moisture, pressure and illumination, it is accepted by many that the conditions on the primitive earth were much what they are today. The atmosphere, however, was made up primarily of methane, ammonia, water vapor and hydrogen. Another difference was in the solar radiation. It was probably richer in high-energy ultraviolet radiation, at present screened out by layers of ozone in the upper atmosphere. Other sources of energy would be electrical discharge and radioactive decay.

THE EVOLUTION OF ORGANIC MOLECULES

The first step in the proposed evolution of life must be the formation of simple organic molecules. Without these life as we know it is impossible and inconceivable.

The simplest organic compounds, the hydrocarbons, are readily formed by the action of minerals called carbides on water, which minerals could easily have arisen from the action of carbon on metals. The initially formed hydrocarbons could evolve into more complex ones under the influence of ultraviolet energy or electrical storms. Oxygen-containing compounds would also form, the oxygen coming from the dissociation of water.[2] The reactions involved here are simple and well known. They are not mere speculation. Thus we can be sure that, in the

[1] A. I. Oparin, *The Origin of Life on the Earth,* translated by Ann Synge (New York: Academic Press, 3rd ed., 1957), pp. 78–79.
[2] *Ibid.,* p. 182.

conditions described, the primitive earth would have a supply of alcohols, aldehydes, acids, amines and other simple organic substances.

Let us consider, as an illustration, the manner in which the amino acids, the building blocks of proteins, might have been formed under the primeval conditions. Various approaches have been suggested, the most striking that of Stanley Miller. He exposed a mixture of ammonia, methane, hydrogen and water vapor (the primitive atmosphere) to a spark discharge for several days. At the end of this time he found a number of amino acids, as well as other organic compounds.[3] From analogous experiments, it can be shown that even the more complex substances such as sugars and polyenes could have arisen naturally under the conditions of the primitive earth.

The problem of explaining the primordial generation of proteins presents more difficulty, though not insurmountable. We have seen that the amino acid building blocks could easily have existed on the primitive earth, but the vastly more complex proteins are another matter. Various mechanisms of protein synthesis have been suggested, but much more important for our consideration is the very statement of the problem. On this point there is a marked difference of opinion between Oparin and most other writers.

The proponents of what may be termed the "lucky protein" theory give most of their attention to the problem of protein synthesis. Admitting the very serious nature of the obstacles to spontaneous protein synthesis, they solve this difficulty by an appeal to time. Calvin points out that the period of chemical evolution probably occurred between 2.5 and 1 billion years ago. In this "great deal of time . . . many improbable events can occur. . . . This, of course, is one of the saving graces of the problem."[4] The argument is based on the fact that a statistically improbable event (the spontaneous synthesis of a

[3] Stanley L. Miller, *Science 117*, 528 (1953); *Journal of the American Chemical Society 77*, 2351 (1955).
[4] M. Calvin, *American Scientist 44*, 248 (1956).

protein), given a sufficient number of tries, can become statistically very probable. It is argued that the billions of years available for chemical evolution permitted many attempts and thus enabled a statistically improbable event to take place.[5]

The proponents of the "lucky protein" hypothesis feel that, having explained the origin of one protein molecule, they have explained the origin of life. They argue that once such a complex material as a protein, even one molecule of it, was formed, it would guide and direct the synthesis of like molecules. This reproduction would be the first manifestation of life.

.   .   .   .

The present hypothesis of Spontaneous Generation postulates the evolution of elements and simple organic compounds to the highly obscure point where the nonliving becomes living. This study is a legitimate pursuit of scientists since they use their particular tools and can reach conclusions in their own field. Some remarkable experimental results have already been obtained. It would be false, however, to say that the road is clear, that it is only a matter of performing certain experiments. Most scientists working on this problem admit to a hope that their efforts will be successful, but there is no certainty; and this is generally admitted. This much, perhaps, can be said: if life did arise spontaneously on the earth, the feat can probably be duplicated in the laboratory.

THEOLOGY AND THE ORIGIN OF LIFE

Any explanation of the origin of life on earth is also of theological interest since it would have a relation to the teaching of the Church on creation and conservation. Even in Origen's time, the concept of Spontaneous Generation had been used by atheists. We are not surprised, therefore, to find modern authors

[5] George Wald, *Scientific American 191,* No. 2 (1954), pp. 45–53.

who preface their writings on this subject with a sly reference to the "myth of creation."[6]

As will be shown, the Church has taken no official stand on the hypothesis of Spontaneous Generation. Individual theologians, of course, have discussed the question and should continue to do so. In such discussions, it would seem proper to avoid any hasty or overstrong reaction of either joyful acceptance or horrified rejection. Both extremes can do a disservice to theology.

Yet both extremes have existed. Because certain atheists and agnostics have used Spontaneous Generation as an argument in their favor, we have not lacked those who completely reject this hypothesis as incompatible with Catholic teaching.[7] On the other hand, one theologian has gone so far as to "prove" from Holy Scripture and from the writings of the Fathers of the Church that Evolution and Spontaneous Generation are part of Catholic doctrine.[8] Such wholehearted endorsement of a scientific theory which later may be discarded is, to say the least, imprudent, and it has rightfully brought severe criticism.[9]

Nowhere does the Church officially discuss the hypothesis of Spontaneous Generation, but we can get some idea of the mind of the Church by considering her teaching on the doctrine of creation.

The whole Christian attitude toward the world is that it resulted from the activity of God. In the early ages of the Church this was affirmed against the errors of Gnostic and Manichean dualism, which attributed the material world to the evil principle. The dogma of creation was considered so impor-

---

[6] *Ibid.*

[7] Felix Ruschkamp, "The Origin of Life," in *God, Man and the Universe,* ed. by Jacques De Bivort De La Saudée (New York: P. J. Kenedy and Sons, 1953).

[8] E. C. Messenger, *Evolution and Theology* (London: Burns, Oates & Washbourne, 1931).

[9] E. C. Messenger, Editor, *Theology and Evolution* (London: Sands and Co., 1949).

tant that it was incorporated into most creeds.[10] It has been discussed and defined in various ecumenical councils.[11] In our own time this dogma is opposed to materialism in its many forms, all of which deny the existence of a transcendent God · Who is distinct from the world and Creator of the world. Catholic dogma teaches that the material universe is completely dependent on God, that all things were created either mediately or immediately by Him, the true and only efficient cause of the universe taken as a whole.

Nowhere in these sources do we find either a condemnation or an approbation of Spontaneous Generation.

The only time an official pronouncement touches our question, it does so indirectly. This we find in the encyclical *Humani Generis* where direct reference is made to the theory of evolution. The Church very wisely points out that, since we are dealing with theory rather than fact, and since the evolutionary concept can be so misemployed as to lead to serious philosophical and theological errors, prudence is required when dealing with the subject. We are further cautioned not to express as facts conclusions which go beyond the evidence. This, however, is merely one of the principles of the scientific method and is recognized, at least in principle, by all scientists.

But, after giving voice to these words of caution, the stand of the Church remains clear: "Thus, the teaching of the Church leaves the doctrine of evolution an open question. . . . In the present state of scientific and theological opinion this question may be legitimately canvassed by research, and by discussions between experts on both sides."[12]

Certainly, therefore, the theologian should be careful not to espouse too heartily a mere hypothesis. Nor should he forget

[10] Henricus Denzinger *et al.,* (ed.), *Enchiridion Symbolorum* (ed. 29; Freiburg: Herder, 1953), No. 6; *ibid.,* No. 86.

[11] *Ibid.,* No. 428; *ibid.,* No. 706; *ibid.,* No. 1805.

[12] *Humani Generis,* translation appearing in *The Church Teaches,* prepared by St. Mary's College (St. Louis: Herder Book Co., 1960), p. 154.

that often the doctrine of the Church is merely a negative norm. The fact that the Church does not teach Spontaneous Generation does not make it untrue. Furthermore, where a scientific hypothesis leads men into error it is necessary to examine whether the hypothesis does this *per se* or only because of improper application of the hypothesis.

Turning to the Holy Scriptures, we again find the absence of any statement which can be understood as either approving or condemning Spontaneous Generation. Today we realize more clearly than ever before that the message of Genesis is spiritual and theological; the Bible is not trying to teach science. Furthermore, science can neither affirm nor deny the answer to the religious questions contained in the Bible. Therefore, no matter how far back science can push its investigations of the origin of life, it will never reach the level of the message of Genesis.[13]

With regard to the testimony of the Fathers of the Church, certain distinctions must be made. The Fathers, like the authors of the various books of the Bible, were not attempting to teach science. At best they accepted the teaching of the philosophers (scientists) of their day to illustrate theological doctrine. Therefore, along with their contemporaries they did accept Spontaneous Generation, not the chemical theory of today but the crude biological theory that was held in some form until the work of Pasteur. But it is not proper to cite them except to show that the general concept of Spontaneous Generation is not inimical to Catholic teaching.

In all the official sources of Catholic doctrine, therefore, we find neither condemnation nor approval of Spontaneous Generation. On the other hand, the Church recognizes the validity of scientific theories which attempt to give a more proximate explanation of facts concerning which theology gives us more fundamental information. Only those hypotheses which *per se* oppose revealed truth must be rejected.

[13] John L. McKenzie, S.J., *The Two-Edged Sword* (Milwaukee, Wis.: Bruce, 1956), pp. 73–75.

A THEOLOGICAL SPECULATION

Revelation is complete, but our understanding of it is ever growing. Scientific facts and hypotheses have assisted this understanding in the past and they can do so now. In particular, the theory of Spontaneous Generation can illumine and broaden our understanding of the creative activity of God.

God's purpose in creating the world is to manifest and communicate His perfections.[14] Or, to look at it from the viewpoint of the created world, the whole purpose of the world, its *rationale,* is to show forth the perfections of God.[15] It would seem reasonable to conjecture that the perfections of God are manifested more splendidly and to a greater extent by the spontaneous origin of life than by a mechanism which requires a special intervention of God.

In our human lives we are quite familiar with the concept of "making." When someone makes something, we attribute the object to the maker. The more elaborate, useful, beautiful and pleasing the object, the more we admire the one who made it. In general, the more perfect the object, the more it manifests the skill and perfection of its maker. Thus we admire Michelangelo for his magnificent "Moses." We also admire the skill of the glassblower who turns out a crystal goblet. These products certainly manifest the perfections of the one who made them. But for Michelangelo to have invented a machine that would have done the entire sculpturing for him would certainly have been a greater feat and would have manifested more perfection in the artist. For the same reason, Michael Owens, the inventor of the first automatic bottle-blowing machine[16] might be thought worthy of greater tribute than the glassblower who turns out individual bottles which vary in uniformity.

[14] Denzinger, *op. cit.,* No. 1783.
[15] *Ibid.,* No. 1805.
[16] Freda Diamond, *The Story of Glass* (New York: Harcourt, Brace & Co., 1953), p. 85.

The more God has given to creatures the power of causality, the more they can reveal the dignity and power of His creative act. When we contemplate the world God has made, we see a magnificent spectacle. This magnificence is enhanced when we consider that God does not "make" in the same way that man does. Among other things, it is not sufficient that God once and for all creates the world and then leaves it alone. Since He is the cause not only of the essence of things, but of their very existence, His creative activity must endure in a positive manner. Without this conservation the world would simply cease to exist. Hence we say that God continually creates the world. His activity never ceases and the products of this creative activity continually manifest the divine perfections.

Since God is the cause of the creatures' existence and perfections, He is also the cause of all created activity. Therefore, whenever a creature "makes" something, it is manifesting, in a limited way, God's creative activity. The creature-action is an image of the Creator-action. When molecules react according to the design and plan of God, they also manifest the perfections of God. The more perfect their activity, the more perfectly they manifest the divine activity.

Since molecular evolution that would result in a living organism is more perfect than the common molecular activity, such a process would more perfectly manifest the divine perfection. Indeed, it would manifest not only the creative activity of God, but also His very life. Vegetable life is an admittedly weak image of the perfectly immanent activity of God, but it is an image and hence cries out the perfections of the Living God.

All of this is said, not to prove the existence of Spontaneous Generation from theology, but to show that it is more compatible with Christian theology than its opposite postulate. Spontaneous Generation manifests more perfectly the divine perfections of creative activity and life than does the postulate that God had to intervene in a special way to bring life on the earth.

In our daily life we become quite used to the process whereby a living organism takes nonliving matter and transforms it into its living self by the process of anabolism. Theologians do not postulate a special intervention of God in this wonderful process. Under the ordinary conservative power of God, Who keeps in existence both the food and the living being's active nature, the nonliving becomes living. It would seem that only our imagination[17] is in the way when we accept the fact that life from nonlife is possible under the directive influence of a living being, yet refuse to accept the same possibility under the directive influence of normal material activity which operates under God's provident care.

Spontaneous Generation in this context can never substitute for creation, since the entire course of it is within the created sphere. But it can enhance creation and make clearer God's perfections. Charles Darwin, it seems, had the vision of this, for he concludes his great work as follows:

It is interesting to contemplate a tangled bank, clothed with many plants of many kinds, with birds singing on the bushes, with various insects flitting about, and with worms crawling through the damp earth, and to reflect that these elaborately constructed forms, so different from each other, and dependent upon each other in so complex a manner, have all been produced by laws acting around us. . . . There is grandeur in this view of life with its several powers, having been originally breathed by the Creator into a few forms or into one; and that, whilst this planet has gone cycling on according to the fixed law of gravity, from so simple a beginning endless forms most beautiful and most wonderful have been, and are being evolved.[18]

Such a concept of God's activity can bring us very close to the Creator. In the climax of his spiritual teaching, St. Ignatius

---

[17] It has often been objected that Spontaneous Generation goes contrary to the principle that the effect cannot exceed its cause. Since the philosophy of Spontaneous Generation will be published elsewhere, it will suffice for now to point out that the principle quoted applies only the field of *efficient* causality and presupposes that you are dealing with the *adequate* efficient cause. It can be shown that Spontaneous Generation does not conflict with this principle.

[18] Charles Darwin, *The Origin of Species.*

presents his "Contemplation to Obtain the Love of God." After pointing out that love ought to manifest itself in deeds rather than in words, and that love consists in a mutual sharing, he turns to consider the blessings of creation and redemption. He reflects how God dwells in creatures, giving them existence and sometimes life, and how He works in creatures.[19] The contemplation of these truths can help prepare a man to make an act of love of God. The more wonderful God's ways, the more His perfections are manifest to us, the easier is that love. We do not know whether God is the author of life by a special act of His Almighty power or by the intrinsically more perfect way of His ordinary creative causality; but the latter seems more in keeping with His dignity and providence: "By his providence God watches over and governs all the things that he made, reaching from end to end with might and disposing all things with gentleness."[20]

[19] Ignatius of Loyola, *The Spiritual Exercises,* Fourth Week.
[20] Denzinger, *op. cit.,* No. 1783.

IO

CREATION AND THE CREATOR

L. Charles Birch*

The doctrine of evolution is now almost universally accepted by biologists as a description of the process of creation of the variety of plants and animals which now inhabit, or in some past ages have inhabited, this earth. Christianity also has a doctrine of creation, and, at least in enlightened theological circles, this doctrine is not regarded as incompatible with the biological doctrine of evolution. This being the case, the biologist may justifiably ask at what point in his understanding of evolution of life does the theological doctrine become relevant. And he may wonder whether the theologian has anything to learn about creation from the biological doctrine of evolution. Are we dealing

* L. C. Birch is Head of the School of Biological Sciences at the University of Sydney, Australia, and is a noted evolutionary ecologist. In addition to many scientific articles and books, he has written Nature and God (1965), in which he maintains that creation was not an event in the past but a continuing process still in progress. In the following essay he criticizes the neo-orthodox viewpoint of Emil Brunner, which is not unlike that of Langdon Gilkey in Chapter 8 above. Birch defends the process philosophy of Alfred North Whitehead and Charles Hartshorne, in which he finds a coherent metaphysics that allows for chance, order, and creativity in nature as well as human freedom and divine initiative. The essay first appeared in the Journal of Religion, Vol. 37, No. 2 (April, 1957), pp. 85–98, and is reprinted by permission of the University of Chicago Press.

with two fields which meet without overlap, or is the description of the history of creation rather one field in which biologist and theologian overlap without necessarily coinciding? The first view is strenuously argued by Brunner in his *The Christian Doctrine of Creation and Redemption*.[1] It is not unrepresentative of the viewpoint of many theologians. The second view seems to find stronger support among scientists who are Christians and among philosophers of religion, for example, Hocking, Hartshorne, and Tillich.

TWO CONCEPTS OF GOD'S CREATIVITY

This division of opinion hinges on the concept of God's creative activity, of his relation to his creation. In the one, God stands in relation to the world as a carpenter to a table which he has made. The Creator and the creation are two distinct entities. God is conceived as a being alongside the world, spectator of the world he has made. In the other view there is no such sharp distinction between the act of creation and the created object. The object of creation in some way incorporates the ever present creativity of God, without becoming identified with it. This view avoids the error of pantheism but yet is not dualistic. If God's activity were withdrawn, the object of his creation would no longer exist. The carpenter may presumably leave his table without imperiling its existence, but not so the God who participates in the life and being of his creatures. He is never merely the spectator of the world.

The first view claims that what the scientist finds out about the nature of creation has nothing to do with what the Christian knows about God's creativity through revelation, or at least it adds nothing to what he already knows; the clash between scientist and theologian in the past has been due simply to a failure to recognize which field belongs to the scientist and which to the theologian. Because it is dualistic, it denies the

[1] Emil Brunner, *The Christian Doctrine of Creation and Redemption* (New York: Westminster Press, 1952).

possibility—nay, even the desirability—of a synthesis. The second view, by contrast, seeks to open ways of conversation between theologian and scientist in the belief that the sacred and the secular, the natural and the divine, are not uniquely separate divisions of reality, desirable though it may be at times to separate them for didactic or analytical purposes. By contrast, too, it is a view which labors in the hope of attaining some sort of synthesis of religion and the rest of culture, while preserving the most precious insights of both. This paper is written in the particular conviction that theology has everything to gain and nothing to lose by appropriating the insights of the modern theory of evolution.

Some of us who are scientists and Christians have, rightly or wrongly, an earnest desire to bring the learning of our specific discipline into the light of Christian convictions and vice versa. We are unable to believe that the one part of our lives has nothing to do with the other. These lines are being written while that concern is uppermost in the minds of some of us who are at present studying the processes of evolution in tropical forests of South America. Our concern does not mean that we believe there is a "Christian biology" or a "Christian physics" as opposed to secular biology or secular physics. But it is possible for me to say as a Christian that the discovery of the processes of creation and the personal experience of redemption are mutually illuminating experiences. They seem to be two lights which come to one focus. In some way we may catch a glimpse of the same God active in the natural world as we experience more vividly in our human lives.

That the two kinds of experience are not identical must be granted. God as Redeemer is an existential experience for me. It is I who experience forgiveness and grace. It is I who in some way participate in the life of God. Through a divine encounter I discover God, and that is personal. Such knowledge is vivid and demanding. But I have no such direct access to God the Creator in the non-human world. There I am observer rather than participant. The non-human world is external to me. I can only know it from the outside except in so far as it is possible for me to project myself imaginatively within. But does this mean that the non-human part of the world leaves us without a witness? Alternatively, is it possible that we can catch a glimpse of the same God there whom we experience so vividly as Redeemer? If such glimpses are possible, then they are probably of the nature of imaginative flights, the result of intuitive insight. But this is not to say that they are mere fancy. They are built on the substantial foundation of experimental science. Perhaps the most rigorous and all-embracing synthesis ever attempted is the philosophical system which stems from Whitehead. For some of us it is the one which makes more sense than others. It presupposes that every entity, from electron to man, has its own private "feelings" or experiences of God. This presupposition helps us to see the relation between our existential experience of God and the world's experience of God. We cannot claim to have the world's experience of God. On the contrary, that is denied us. We do not have the experiences of the electron or even of an individual muscle or bone cell in our bodies. We can only infer that they may exist. Such knowledge is speculative and stands or falls by the validity of the system of which it is a part. It stands in contrast to the sort of knowledge that we can have through the impact of God in our own lives. We could only know the God of the electron or the cell in the same way if we were indeed an electron or a single cell. Yet the glimpse we catch is enough to excite wonder and awe and to provoke the most searching questions of the world we investigate.

The revelation of God in human experience leads to a thirst to discover the same God active in the rest of creation. We admit as Christians that our view of life and the universe is partial and colored as a result of our experience of God. It cannot be otherwise. How can we fail to be conditioned by the most vivid experience of our lives? The Christian is no longer objective in the sense of being detached from the object of his interest, namely, God. But he is objective in the sense of including the object. We would claim that it is not possible to have any substantial knowledge of God in human life or in the non-human part of the world without some experience of him whom we seek to know. It is then less appropriate to seek God by starting with the electron or the amoeba and then working up to man or the saint than it is to reverse the process. But it is a restricted adventure which starts with man, only to end there.

It is my own conviction that the evolutionary hypothesis naturally leads to this point of view, which the tradition of Whitehead has elaborated. But it would be to give quite a false impression if the reader of these lines were to suppose that this view is general among biologists. On the contrary, it is almost certainly a minority opinion. The facts of evolution are certainly not dependent upon any philosophical system; but I would be false to my convictions were I not to indicate that system which to me makes most sense of these facts.

METAPHYSICS AS THE MEETING GROUND OF THEOLOGY AND SCIENCE

It is not the purpose of this paper to develop in speculative thought details of how God may be active in the natural order. That is the task of Christian metaphysics. Those of us who believe that there is such a task to be done are not prepared to accept the premise or conclusion of some scientists and theologians that the world is a mechanism in its entirety or that the creative process is to be understood entirely in mechanical terms or that the mechanical processes are irrelevant to an understanding of creation. As biologists, we discover some of the mechanisms of evolution, such as mutation and the principle of natural selection. That is our special task as scientists in the laboratory or in the field.

The mechanical pictures which the physicist and biologist build are only schematic representations or pictures of reality. Some have called them "models." The scientific investigator tries to construct as accurate and as complete a picture as he can. With the advance of science, these pictures become more complete and closer to an adequate representation of the reality they purport to describe. Some scientists work in the faith of eventually obtaining a perfect picture of the reality they are dealing with. And some of our scientific pictures are probably valid representations of a part of reality. Other scientists are less willing to concede that science can ever get beyond the model. There will always be a gap between the model and the reality. Physicists and biologists seem to differ in this respect. Physicists seem prepared to grant that their concept of the electron is only a model—at best, a mathematical model. The model is not the electron. The real nature of the electron goes deeper than that. Biologists seem less willing to consider their pictures of the cell or the nervous system, for example, as models. Sometimes these larger objects are more tangible, and the pictures we build of them are perhaps more real. But we should not be too confident that this is really so. The biological concept of the cell or the nervous system may be incomplete on two grounds. There is the admitted fact that we just do not yet know all about the physics and chemistry and biochemistry of these entities. But in addition to this inadequacy of our knowledge there may be something in the nature of these entities which escapes analysis in the laboratory. And cells and nervous systems consist of electrons and other "particles" which the physicist assures us can be decribed only in highly abstract models. In his McNair Lectures the mathematician Coulson has given an admirable analysis of this aspect of modern science. He maintains that this is an aspect that science has in common with religious thought:

It is becoming clear that, whether in science or history or religious experience, facts are never known fully and can never be completely correlated. As a result our models—in science, the atoms, the genes, the complexes and repressions of the mind: in religion, the nature of God and His mode of working in the world—can never be wholly satisfactory. For at least they must suffer from one or two complaints. Either they are over-defined, leading to internal inconsistency and contradiction; or they are undefined, leading to "fuzziness" and imprecision. This is true both in science and in religion.[2]

To mistake the model for reality is to be guilty of what Whitehead called the "fallacy of misplaced concreteness." It is the besetting sin of scientists. Perhaps the greatest failure in our teaching of modern science is the extent to which our students get caught in this trap. They become dogmatic in their belief in the model as reality itself. The trouble is that in our laboratories the model is our working hypothesis. It is a handy way of describing what we are doing. But we believe more about these models than is warranted. This mistake should never have been made; for the history of science is a history of how one model after another has been revised or modified or replaced. Newton's model is succeeded by Einstein's, and so on. Each step in the history of science sees an attempt to find a yet more adequate model of what we think to be reality. But even the best models (and these are in physics) still seem to leave a gap between our knowledge and reality.

Some scientists who have thought deeply on these things (for example, Sewall Wright[3] in biology and Max Planck in physics) believe that the inner nature of reality, as distinct from the model, escapes the scientific investigator and that it is not his task to penetrate beyond the visible. Max Planck granted to metaphysics the task of discovering more about this inner nature. If this is not a wrong point of view, then metaphysics is the ground on which scientist and theologian can meet. There is a task for metaphysics which should be the active concern of theologian and scientist and philosopher. Indeed, it has been the active concern of some metaphysicians, including Whitehead, Hocking, and Hartshorne in the United States.

The knowledge so reached is surely different from that which is strictly analytical. Brunner says that it is possible to know

---

[2] C. A. Coulson, *Science and Christian Belief* (Oxford: Oxford University Press, 1955).
[3] Sewall Wright, "Gene and Organism," *American Naturalist,* LXXXVII (1953), 5–18.

one part of the world (the scientific part) without knowing the Creator and that in the sphere of natural science it makes practically no difference whether a scholar is a Christian or not. In so far as science deals exclusively with technical details or the "external aspects" of reality, Brunner is doubtless correct. But this aspect of our knowledge is an abstraction. It is knowledge with fuzzy edges, leading off in many directions from the clearly visible to the invisible. Perhaps it is the task of the scientist to penetrate only as far as this indefinite boundary. But the scientist who is also a Christian often feels unwilling to leave his knowledge there. He craves for meaning which reaches beyond the visible to the invisible, and sometimes he ventures there alone or, better still, in company with the philosopher. When he returns to the everyday tasks of his laboratory, the technical details take on a new hue. They are no longer "mere" technicalities. What were ashes are now invested with life and meaning which go beyond that which he knew before. If what he now possesses is a more complete picture of reality, then I cannot see how the scientist who is a Christian can be content with less than this. To be sure, he will know, and should let his students know, just what he finds in the laboratory and what is to be explored with less tangible tools than balances and microscopes.

The position I have attempted to outline has been clearly stated in other terms by Hartshorne[4] when he speaks of two ways of describing reality—the "mind way" and the "matter way":

Mind and matter are not two ultimately different sorts of entity but, rather, two ways of describing a reality that has many levels of organization. The "mind" way I take to be more final and inclusive, so that my position is the opposite of materialism. However, I recognize that the material mode of description is that part of the complete mode which is capable of scientific precision and that, accordingly, materialism, or the restriction of attention to this mode, is a natural bias among scientists. Much depends on seeing that what I have

4 Charles Hartshorne, "Mind, Matter, and Freedom," *Scientific Monthly*, LXXVIII (1954), 314–20.

called the complete mode—that is, an ultimate idealism or psychical-ism—does not exclude any scientific procedure, but merely opens our eyes to the beyond that tends to escape any save a vague, intuitive apprehension. No exact analysis or observation in physical or spatio-temporal terms is forbidden, but rather we are enabled consciously to experience the world *both* with all possible accuracy *and* with the dim background (which, consciously or not, is always there anyway) of invincibly indefinite feelings for the "life of things" (Wordsworth). In the end, this may actually increase the extent of our accurate knowledge, and it is sure to increase our enjoyment of the world, peace of mind, and understanding of ourselves.[5]

If our Christian convictions lead us to reject materialism, then it is incumbent upon us to seek to penetrate beyond the veil to a more inclusive conception of reality, to what Hartshorne calls a more "complete mode" of description than materialism alone can give. Then, to be a Christian with all our minds, as well as with all our hearts, is to see reality, even the reality of evolutionary creation, in a clearer light. It does then make a difference whether a scholar is a Christian or not.

CRITIQUE OF BRUNNER'S CONCEPTION OF CREATION

Before proceeding to categorize more systematically some of the possible points of meeting which concern both biologist and theologian in their understanding of the natural creation, let us first examine more closely the thoroughly different point of view elaborated by Brunner in his *The Christian Doctrine of Creation and Redemption*. He draws the contrast in describing God as one who stands "before and above" the world, a view which he says is "in direct opposition to the view of Greek philosophy and its later exponents, namely that there is a correlation between God and the world, just as there is between left and right, i. e., that the one cannot be conceived apart from the other." According to Brunner, we must drop this idea altogether, and try to draw out the full meaning of the opposite

5 *Ibid.*

conception. We are to think of God as the God who is "there, apart from the world, who indeed Himself posits the world, to whom the world is not His *alter ego:* and when we think of the world we must think of it as something which does not naturally, essentially, and eternally, belong to God, but as something which only exists because it has been created by God. If it were otherwise, God would not be the *Lord* of the world at all, but, so to speak, its double."[6] And later he writes: "The fact that God 'called the world into existence'—this expression is genuinely and exclusively of Biblical origin—means that He has created something other than Himself, 'over against' Himself."[7] Having affirmed a rigid dichotomy between the Creator and the Creation, Brunner proceeds to state that of ourselves we do not know that God is Creator but that, like every other article of the Christian creed, it is an article of faith, and that means a statement based on revelation, the revelation in this case not being the first chapter of Genesis but the Prologue to the Gospel of John. Man meets God in Jesus Christ in personal encounter; but in this meeting he also discovers God the Creator, and this truth comes to man also as a personal summons. It is not the fruit of reflection. What Brunner means by this it is difficult to know. How can I, one element of the creation, experience in so personal a way the God of the electron and the cell and all the other entities in his creation? Rather am I conscious of a limitation to my own experience. Only God can include all these experiences in one person. The best I can do is to infer (by reflection and in faith) that God is Creator; but that is hardly in the same category as the personal revelation of Jesus to man. Brunner denies the witness of the Creation on the grounds that "sinful man is not capable of grasping what God shows him in the work of creation without turning it into something else." But if this argument is valid, then surely it applies with even more force to a man's experience of God as Redeemer; yet this he seems to reject.

[6] Brunner, *op. cit.,* p. 3.
[7] *Ibid.,* p. 19.

Not only does Brunner reject the witness of the Creation, but he goes so far as to say that the evil in nature, nature's meaningless suffering, makes it impossible to equate the world absolutely with the creation of God. There may be valid arguments for postulating demonic influences in the world, but this can hardly be one of them. The modern understanding of evolution is not irrelevant to this problem. Whatever be the inner nature of creativity, it assures us that perfection in any sense is not reached overnight or by any direct path. Nature appears rather to be a huge experiment, and in that experiment, as in all experiments, there is room for accidents to happen. It bears little resemblance to a contrivance, designed and constructed by some sort of infallible cosmic engineer, into which a spanner was later thrown to gum up the works. We know it to have been evolved through painful stages over eons of time by a trial-and-error process. Evolution means nothing unless there is room for accidents to happen; and we know they do happen. Not every living creature that sees the light of day is adapted to survive long or to leave progeny. Natural selection is a selection of random mutations (random in relation to the needs imposed by the environment at the time of the mutation); and many of these mutations do not persist for a single generation. But, despite the seeming waste and the indirect pathways to the adaptation of the living organism to its world, there does emerge a coherence and an integration of the organism which is its life. This is the nature of the creative process in the living world. Dobzhansky gave eloquent expression to this idea in his address to the ninth International Congress of Genetics in Italy when he compared the creative process with the production of a work of art. Both involve the risk of ending in failure. Without the possibility of this risk, there would be no creation. And concerning the creation of living organisms, he said:

The genotypes of living species are the end results on our time level of sequences of historical changes. These changes were such that the carriers of the entire series of ancestral genotypes remained in rapport with their environments. But the congruity with the environment is by no means guaranteed to the future states of the genotype by its present structure. Mutation and gene recombination constantly beget genotypes which never existed before, and which accordingly have not passed the trials of natural selection. Many of the novel genotypes are unfit for survival, most of the phyletic lines which existed in the past led to extinction and not to the now existing life. These phyletic lines were evolutionary blind alleys. This does not make sense to a preformist theory of evolution, but it is understandable if evolution is a natural creative process.[8]

Creation is not possible in a completely preformed or deterministic system. The same point has been well argued by other distinguished biologists, notably Fisher[9] and Thorpe.[10]

Brunner accepts the doctrine of evolution with one hand but rejects it with the other when he denies the possibility of miscreations and accidents in the creative process. Whatever he means by the process of creation is not compatible with what we know to be the way in which the evolutionary process actually happens. It does not make sense with evolution. But the modern understanding of the evolutionary process is not at all incompatible with what might be expected to happen if God is a God of persuasion rather than coercion. We believe this to be true of his relations to persons. Might not the same principle be valid in the rest of nature? Persuasion implies an element of freedom in the creature. Freedom in the sense of rational, moral choice may be confined to man. Among the animals, "spontaneity" in the sense of non-rational, but yet at least in trivial details not predetermined, decision may be essential to all creatures. To be is to act, and an individual creature cannot be constituted by divine action or decisions alone. It must achieve its own creaturely decisions. This may mean that no mechani-

[8] Th. Dobzhansky, "Evolution as a Creative Process," *Proceedings of the Ninth International Congress of Genetics* (*Caryologia* Suppl., 1954), pp. 435–48.

[9] R. A. Fisher, *Creative Aspects of Natural Law* (Fourth Arthur Stanley Eddington Memorial Lecture [Cambridge: The University Press, 1950]).

[10] W. H. Thorpe, *Evolution and Christian Belief* ("Occasional Pamphlets of the British Social Biology Council" [1951]).

cally exact order is possible. A partly chaotic, indetermined, and random element may be unavoidable. This may be the reason that nature is not a contrivance, a sheer mechanism.

There are other respects, too, in which the imperfection and incompleteness of creation might appeal to, rather than appall, the Christian conscience. Paul in the eighth chapter of Romans speaks of the world as incomplete and in travail, with the implication that the creative process is still going on and that it is a struggle. A thoroughgoing acceptance of God as persuasive activity, with the consequent necessity of accepting accident as part of the process of creation, opens up rich fields for understanding, as has been skilfully shown by Hartshorne[11] in *Reality as Social Process* and other works.

To say that God created the world is to say practically nothing. And that is about all that Brunner says about creation. It certainly does not help us to know anything about the nature of creativity. This modern science does help us to see a little more clearly than before. In his rejection of this position,[12] Brunner is not completely 'consistent, for he says that the "mechanical factors" of the evolutionary theory are inadequate as an explanation and that some "non-mechanical" factors are needed. And this, he says, is admitted by scientists of high standing.[13] Both here and elsewhere he appeals to the thought of non-mechanistic scientists as support for his contentions. It would seem that he has gained something from their writings and from his own speculative thought.

The two contrasted viewpoints we have been considering lead to two different inferences concerning the nature of God. If Brunner's view is correct, then he is also correct in concluding that "I, together with the whole of Nature to which I belong, am absolutely dependent upon God; while He on the other hand, is dependent neither upon me nor upon it." Now "dependent" is,

---

[11] Charles Hartshorne, *Reality as Social Process* (Boston: Beacon Press, 1953).

[12] Brunner, *op. cit.*, p. 41.

[13] *Ibid.*, p. 42.

at best, ambiguous. In its stronger meaning it implies inability to exist at all without a certain other thing; in a possible milder meaning it implies only that the dependent thing would exist, but with not entirely the same properties, did the other thing not exist. We depend in the strong sense on God; we require him to exist or be anything at all; but he may depend on us, not for existing or for being himself, but for being the beholder and ruler of just this world rather than some other.[14] To deny even this milder dependence of God can only mean that if evolution had never occurred, it would be the same to God. He gains nothing in richness of experience or from the responsive love of his creatures. Even the love we render him moves him not. But love, if it means anything, is, as Hartshorne has insisted, reciprocal. Love of God for man is an empty form if it means nothing to him, adds nothing to his experience, to his feelings, if we may use such a word. We could not love anything simply incapable of loving or love supremely anything which fails to love supremely. But this is a big field which Hartshorne has developed with adequate insight and in adequate space. I would only add that whatever we feel about this conclusion is for us a judgment of value, and as such I leave it.

This would be a hollow challenge to the viewpoint of so distinguished a theologian as Emil Brunner, were I not, as a biologist, prepared to suggest for the consideration of theologians aspects of evolutionary biology which I believe to be relevant to a theological discussion of creation. Some of these have already been mentioned. We may now list them quite briefly in a more ordered form. A particularly clear elaboration of each of these aspects of evolution with many illustrations can be found in Dobzhansky's book *Genetics, Evolution, and Man*,[15] a book which can be used by biologist and layman alike.

[14] I am indebted to Professor Charles Hartshorne for this analysis of the meaning of "dependent."

[15] Th. Dobzhansky, *Genetics, Evolution, and Man* (New York: John Wiley & Sons, 1955).

THE CONTINUITY OF THE CREATIVE PROCESS

Creation by evolution is a continuous process. It is slow as measured by our usual time standards. But in some living organisms it is fast enough to permit us to measure it over several generations, and for fruit flies this is a matter of a few months. The changes a geneticist observes are usually not sufficient to raise the new forms to the rank of new species. Nevertheless, new species of plants have arisen within a generation of their lives by the process of polyploidy or multiplication of the chromosome set.[16] We can now visualize plants and animals as possessing a rich store of variability and a potentiality for change and so taking advantage of new opportunities as they arise and countering new threats to their existence, such for example as DDT in the case of insects. Nor must we exclude man from this generalization. Mutation and selection have not ceased with the rise of the human species (for examples see Dobzhansky and Allen),[17] though with man the nature of the evolutionary changes has been radically altered by his ability to control his environment and by his "cultural inheritance."

If creation has been and still is a continuous process, we would not expect to find any complete discontinuities in the evolutionary series from first life to man. The evidence, though we must admit its inevitable incompleteness, supports this corollary. This does not, of course, mean that novel characters do not arise. But what we find at the highest level, for example, mental characters in man, have their rudiments in lower forms of life. The ability to learn from experience seemed to begin in the flatworms. It became an important element in the life of

[16] See Dobzhansky's reply to the statement of Pope Pius XII ("A Comment on the Discussion of Genetics by His Holiness, Pius XII," *Science,* CXVIII [1953], 561–63).

[17] Th. Dobzhansky and G. Allen, "Does Natural Selection Continue To Operate in Modern Mankind?" *American Anthropologist,* LVIII (1956), 591–604.

some insects and certainly in birds and mammals, as has been so well demonstrated in recent years by Lorenz and Tinbergen in Europe. The work of the Yerkes Primate Laboratory in Florida shows that chimpanzees can use tools and that they have a rudimentary capacity for abstract thought. Language, without which the development of culture in man would have been impossible, is nevertheless not restricted to man. Bees have a sign language, and by means of this they communicate to one another the distance and direction of food from the hive.

We need not suppose that the aesthetic sense is peculiar to man. Birds sing. Hartshorne has evidence that song is not simply something which serves to keep the flock together or which attracts a mate. The songs of birds are so constructed as to avoid monotony.[18] We need not be so self-centered as to suppose that this is simply for our aesthetic pleasure! Animals enjoy themselves. This is a conclusion corroborated by many students of animal behavior, and we may have to accept it despite the difficulty of conceiving how the aesthetic sense may have evolved. We could go on to list all the characteristics of man which, according to Brunner, constitute his "humanum" and which distinguish him from all other creatures. And for many of these characteristics there are at least rudiments in the lower animals. The line is not so clear cut as Brunner supposes when he claims that the "humanum is characterized by something which is entirely lacking in the animal, subjectively speaking by the mind [*Geist*], and objectively by the creations of culture."[19] And later he writes: "It possesses a dimension which is lacking in biology, the law of norms, the faculty of grasping meaning, freedom, responsibility."[20] Yet mind exists in animals other than man. Culture, although primarily characteristic of man, does have its rudiments in animals, which learn from their parents part of their way of life; some birds learn

[18] Charles Hartshorne, "The Monotony Threshold in Singing Birds," *Auk*, LXXIII (1956), 176–92.
[19] Brunner, *op. cit.*, p. 80.
[20] *Ibid.*, p. 166.

their specific songs from their parents, and the parents also teach them ways of building their nests and, in one species of bird, how to remove tops from milk bottles on front doorsteps! Even the capacity for decorating objects (which Brunner regards as strictly a characteristic of the "humanum") is shared with birds. The Australian bower birds not only decorate their bowers with colored objects but even paint the bower with a mixture of saliva and charcoal which they get from the bark of forest trees which have been burned.

To recognize the kinship of man with the animal kingdom is not to deny that man may also be described as unique in the animal kingdom. This is, in fact, what Dobzhansky does.[21] Man is unique in the extent to which he has developed culture and in the extent to which his evolution is controlled by this. But this is not to deny that rudiments of culture exist in other animals. In so far as rudiments exist and evolve, then we have a continuum. Some of Brunner's statements would seem to lead to this conclusion also, though he stoutly denies this elsewhere. For example, he says: "Whether the Java Ape Man (Pithecanthropus) already possessed the rudiments of the humanum we do not know. Perhaps we might assume that this was true of Peking Man, since he was discovered with the remains of stone implements, and traces of fire."[22] That is to say, the "humanum" had its rudiments in evolutionary history. Yet Brunner goes on to say that the "humanum is, in itself, something that cannot possibly be derived from the animal kingdom, however modest its origin may have been, and therefore very difficult to distinguish from the animal." But there is a very real sense in which the "humanum" as Brunner defines it is "derived from" the animal kingdom. It is that the genetical constitution of man is such as to enable him to develop culture and the qualities of the "humanum" to the extent he has. The genotype of the ape is not one which permits this same development. But the genotype

---

[21] Th. Dobzhansky, *The Biological Basis of Human Freedom* (New York: Columbia University Press, 1957).

[22] Brunner, *op. cit.*, p. 80.

of man is derived from his animal forebears. The purpose of this discussion is certainly not to underemphasize the spiritual uniqueness of man but to suggest that there is still plenty of room for mutual exchange of insights between theologian and biologist before one or the other makes too final a definition of what constitutes the uniqueness of man.

The whole problem of the origin of the higher capacities that we find in man becomes illuminated when we conceive evolution from first life to man as an increase in awareness of the environment. The increase in awareness was made possible by the development of new and vastly complex genotypes. The amoeba is aware of touch, perhaps not much else. A bee is sensitive to several colors and to many scents. But we should not restrict environment to the tangible entities which can be touched and seen. The total environment of man is infinitely richer than that. It includes an intangible aspect which we might call the "qualitative environment" but which is nevertheless just as real as the more tangible environment. For its manifold nature and richness the effective environment of man defies any simple description. Of one thing we may be certain, and that is that the awareness of the qualitative aspects of his environment assumes a vast importance in man. It is this which is the source of his art, religion, and all that we mean by culture. A man's awareness of God is an awareness of his qualitative environment. It would be difficult to circumscribe this part of his environment and to exclude all other creatures from having qualitative experience. Moreover, it is hard to see what is gained by attempting to do this.

The continuity of the creative process means, then, that man has a kinship with the rest of nature and this kinship need not be restricted exclusively to his biological nature. At least, this is the direction in which biological studies seem to be leading us. There are those who, with Whitehead, believe that a thoroughgoing acceptance of the evolutionary hypothesis necessarily leads to a conception of organism as fundamental to the whole of reality. Biology is the study of the larger "organisms," and physics is the study of the smaller "organisms." And every organism, large or small, is a perceiving entity. But the environment perceived has become richer in the evolution from physical particle to man. The organism, whether physical or biological, is not a static machine but a perceiving, responding being. It is very much a "going concern."

CHANCE AND THE ORDER OF NATURE

There is an order in nature which to many of us is a constant source of wonder and inspiration. It does not surprise us that man has so often ascribed this marvelous order to the design of an infallible architect and engineer, who, having designed and built the universe, then left it to its own devices. But the analogy turns out to be a bad one. Modern science is forcing us to abandon it, though, in so doing, it is pointing the way to a new and grander concept of creativity. We must look for a better understanding. The creation of order in nature by evolution is a trial-and-error process. Random events and ordering processes work together. The evidence of biology does not point to an inflexible design or to Paley's old analogy of the watchmaker and the watch or the carpenter and his table. These lost all their force with the rise of Darwin's hypothesis and particularly with its modern elaboration in what is sometimes called "neo-Darwinism." What Darwinism did was not to replace the universe as a divine contrivance with a universe of accident. The process of evolution bears no comparison with the ridiculous analogy of a hundred monkeys knocking at the keys of a hundred typewriters at random and by chance producing the entire plays of Shakespeare. This is an impossibly improbable event, and evolution by any analogous process is just as impossible. Natural selection of random mutations is certainly not like that. The mind is indeed staggered by the effort to conceive so perfect and intricate an organ as the human eye as a product of a trial-and-error process. But the genius of Darwin was to provide the basis of a theory whereby so improbable an event could be conceived to occur. It is the opinion of the statistical geneticist, R. A. Fisher, that "it was Darwin's chief contribution, not only to biology but to the whole of natural science, to have brought to light a process by which contingencies *a priori* impossible, are given, in the process of time, an increasing probability, until it is the non-occurrence rather than their occurrence which becomes highly improbable."[23] The production of an eye by means of random mutations all occurring simultaneously is as improbable or more so than the production of a watch by shaking up its component parts in a vessel. But random mutations, together with selection over countless generations, make the improbable probable. The perfection of the vertebrate eye took at least four hundred million years!

Although new organs and new forms of life are ultimately dependent upon the process of mutation, most mutations that occur are harmful or useless. It is not now difficult to see why this is so. Changes which occur at random are far more likely to be destructive than beneficial. It is easier to destroy a piece of machinery than it is to improve its workings. But a very small proportion of the mutations that occur is useful, and these are saved and perpetuated from generation to generation by the process of natural selection. All kinds of mutations are produced, regardless of whether they are useful or not; they do not occur just once, never to be repeated, but mutations have a rate of occurrence which varies from species to species. There is, then, a deleterious aspect to mutation; but, in spite of this, it is the prime source of constructive variability in the living world. What is useless today may be useful tomorrow. The ability of bacteria to resist streptomycin was perhaps of no advantage to them until men invented this antibiotic. But, once bacteria found themselves in a living body containing streptomycin, the mutation which conferred resistance was immediately beneficial. Random mutation combined with the capacity which organisms

[23] R. A. Fisher, "Retrospect of the Criticisms of the Theory of Natural Selection," in *Evolution as a Process,* ed. Julian Huxley, A. C. Hardy, and E. B. Ford (London: Allen & Unwin, 1954).

possess for the rearrangement of combinations of genes confers upon them their ability to face new situations and to change genetically to meet such exigencies.

In a static environment, mutation might be conceived to be always harmful, once the desired genetical composition was attained. But the world is not static. Environments change constantly. And the only way to meet change is by changing one's self or else changing the environment. The lower organisms tend to depend almost exclusively on the first process. The higher organisms, notably man, depend very largely on the second. Paul exhorts us to "be not conformed to this world but be ye transformed." Or, as Phillips freely translates: "Don't let the world squeeze you into its own mould." That is just what the world has been doing to the lower organisms. But there has been a progressive release from the restrictive aspects of the temporal environment in the evolution of animals. By degrees the animal became more and more independent of environmental vicissitudes. The process reaches a climax in man, who becomes master of, instead of being mastered by, his environment. At least, that is his birthright.

THE TRAVAIL OF CREATION

There are at least two aspects of the cost of creation. One was emphasized in the popularization of the phrase "struggle for existence." In recent years various authors have pointed out the various and common misuses of the phrase. Thorpe, for example, reminds us that natural selection is not essentially a "struggle," nor is it essentially cruel.[24] The essence of the matter is that natural selection depends upon differential reproduction as well as differential survival and favors those individuals with more surviving offspring. "Nature red in tooth and claw" may fit one aspect of the total "struggle for existence," but it is not the whole story or even most of the story. The modern study of evolution brings into focus another cost of creation. That is

[24] Thorpe, *op. cit.,* p. 7.

H

the accumulation of genetically harmful genes in the genetic constitution of the organism.

Not only do mutations occur which are harmful, but many of these are retained in the organism's genetic makeup. Our immense store of genetical variability, handed down to us from our evolutionary ancestry, contains many genes which are lethal to the species in some combinations, others which are semi-lethal, and so on. This is a discovery of modern population genetics. How is it that these genes are retained in the population? In some circumstances and in some combinations these genes are useful. We cannot easily label genes and say this one is harmful and this is useful. That is just the difficulty that eugenics faces. The parable of the tares and the wheat is a parable of modern genetics. Genetics shows how congenital idiots arise, how "accidents" and misfits occur. They seem to be an inevitable part of the creative process. This is just the way we have been made. It is gratuitous to suppose that we have been made in some other sort of way and that what appears bad or harmful has been planted by an alien agent. This does not fit the facts. The misfits are part of the creative process. They are part of the cost of creation. The highest fitness of the population in terms of its ability to procreate and survive is purchased at the price of many genetically unfit individuals. How can this be the way of a Creator whom men also claim to know as a God of love? There is no simple answer to this question. We cannot just look at the crown of creation, man, and ask if the whole process has been worth this. Perhaps no part of the creation is without its value. The whole process should not be conceived as a means to one end, namely, man, but as many ends, each with value in itself. Then, too, the Christian has a special perspective; for he knows that redemptive love was and is costly. It cost the sacrifice of the Son of Man on a cross. Christianity reveals the Cross as central to the meaning of human life. Evolutionary studies are revealing this same cross pattern deeply woven into the very fabric of creation. Perhaps there is a principle here which science and theology can mutually illuminate.

We may believe that creation is continuous, we may believe in the mechanisms of mutation and selection and all they tell us about the cost of creativity. But there remains an inner aspect of reality which is largely hidden from mechanistic analysis, though not necessarily from speculative thought. About this, science may have little to say. Here metaphysics and maybe the theologian can help us to catch a glimpse into the depths. But it will be an unrealistic glimpse unless based on the accurate knowledge of scientific investigation. For does not creativity involve the whole process, mechanical and non-mechanical? They are not two processes but one. The outcome is the order of nature, of organisms intricately and wonderfully made and able to meet what would seem to be an infinity of circumstance, and of man able to meet consciously and in humility the Author of his being.

II

TURMOIL OR GENESIS?

*Pierre Teilhard de Chardin**

THE POSITION OF MAN IN NATURE AND THE
SIGNIFICANCE OF HUMAN SOCIALISATION

Is there in the Universe a Main Axis of Evolution?
(*An attempt to see clearly*)

Introduction

No one can any longer doubt that the Universe, conceived in experimental or phenomenal terms, is a vast temporo-spatial system, corpuscular in nature, from which we cannot sensorially escape (even in thought) in any direction. Viewed in this light everything in the world appears and exists as a function of the whole. This is the broadest, deepest and most unassailable meaning of the idea of Evolution.

* *Pierre Teilhard de Chardin was trained as a Jesuit priest and as a geologist specializing in paleontology. From 1923 to 1946 (except for brief interludes in France and Africa) he worked with scientific groups in China, including the expedition which discovered the skull of Peking Man. He returned to France in 1946, and thence in 1951 to the Wenner*

But it raises a question. How are we to envisage the operation of such a system, which by its nature is both organic and atomic? Is its movement one of disorderly or controlled impulses? Is the world amorphous in structure, or does it on the contrary show signs of containing within itself a favoured axis of evolution?

Following the principle that the greater coherence is an infallible sign of the greater truth, I propose to demonstrate that such an axis does in fact exist, and that it may be defined in terms of the following three (or even four) successive theorems or approximations, each of which clarifies and substantiates the one preceding it on a single line of experience and thought:

a. Life is not an accident in the Material Universe, but the essence of the phenomenon.

b. Reflection (that is to say, Man) is not an incident in the biological world, but a higher form of Life.

c. In the human world the social phenomenon is not a superficial arrangement, but denotes an essential advance of Reflection.

To which may be added, from the Christian point of view:

d. The Christian phylum is not an accessory or divergent shoot in the human social organism, but constitutes the axis itself of socialisation.

Gren Foundation in New York. Since his death in 1955 there has been great interest in his ideas in both Catholic and Protestant circles, as well as among biologists such as Huxley and Dobzhansky; hundreds of articles and dozens of books have appeared dealing with his life and thought (see Chapter 1 above). The article reprinted in its entirety here is dated Paris, 20 December, 1947" and appeared first in L'Anthropologie in September, 1948. It presents a clear summary of his understanding of the directionality of evolution from matter through life and reflection to the "human social organism" (he uses the term "Noosphere," near the end of Theorem III, to refer to mankind as an interacting "thinking layer" covering the earth). In Theorem IV he portrays the Church as the fulfillment of the human social organism, and discusses the synthesis of scientific and religious thought. This translation by Norman Denny is taken from The Future of Man, copyright © 1964 by William Collins Sons & Co., Ltd., London, and Harper & Row, Incorporated, New York, and reprinted by permission.

Let us look in turn at the separate links in this chain o
theorems, each of which, as we shall see, represents a tes
whereby we may better know and measure, in the scale o
spiritual values, the worth and position of others..

*Theorem I. Life is not an Epi-phenomenon in the Materia
Universe, but the Central Phenomenon of Evolution*

Observed within the general framework of Matter as it is now
revealed to science, Life may seem to be of tragically littl
importance in the Universe. In spatial terms we know fo
certain of its existence only on an infinitesimally small body i
the solar system. In terms of Time its whole planetary duratio
is no more than a flash in the huge course of sidereal develop
ment. And structurally its extreme fragility seems to relegate
to the humblest and lowest place among all the substance
engendered during the physico-chemical evolution of cosmi
matter. We can hardly wonder, in the circumstances, tha
agnostics such as Sir James Jeans and Marcel Boll, and eve
convinced believers like Guardini, have uttered expressions o
amazement (tinged with heroic pessimism or triumphant de
tachment) at the apparent insignificance of the phenomenon o
Life in terms of the cosmos—a little mould on a grain of dus
Small wonder, I repeat: but it is no less astonishing tha
minds so outstanding should not have perceived the possibilit
and the advantages of adopting a precisely opposite viewpoin
Life seems to occupy so small a place in Space-Time, that
cannot reasonably be regarded as anything other than incidenta
and accidental. That is the difficulty. But why should we no
reverse the position and say: "The fact that Life is so rarel
encountered in the sidereal immensity is precisely becaus
representing a higher form of cosmic evolution, it can onl
come into existence in privileged circumstances of time an
place." We shall see the full force of this argument (based o
the premise that Life, forever struggling to assert itself, is liabl
to appear at any point in the Universe when the conditions ar
favourable) only when we come to the end of this paper: whe

that is to say, we have perceived the full coherence and fruitfulness of the mental and moral attitudes to which it gives access. But it is important to insist at the outset on the fundamental point that (despite all contrary appearances and prejudices) the best way of scientifically explaining the World is to make up our minds to regard animate beings, not as a fortuitous by-product but as the characteristic and specific higher aim of the universal phenomenon of Evolution.

Let us strip Life of all its anatomical and physiological super-structure, bringing it down to the essentials of its physico-chemical nature. Reduced to its basic mechanism it shows itself to be a straightforward process of increasing complication whereby Matter contrives to arrange itself in corpuscles of ever greater volume, ever more highly organised. But do we not find that at the same time its seeming weaknesses, its fragility and appearance of extreme localisation in time-space, tend to vanish? For underlying these supposedly "exceptional" cellular arrangements we have first the far vaster world of molecules, and underlying this again the immense and decidedly cosmic world of atoms; two worlds displaying, the first by its inter-atomic arrangements and the second by its nuclear groupings, (each in its own way and through different procedures) precisely the same tendency to "fall" into increasingly organised states of complexity.[1] Thus considered, the era of the Organic (living) which may have appeared so exceptional in Nature becomes no more than a further instance, at a particularly high

[1] We may seek to distinguish the phases or pulsations of the cosmic rise into complexity (that is to say, into the Improbable) as follows:
a. The pre-atomic phase: formation of nuclei and electrons;
b. The atomic phase: grouping of nuclei in atoms (fixed and limited number of free "compartments");
c. The molecular phase: grouping of atoms in finite or indefinite chains;
d. The cellular phase: grouping of molecules in centrated clusters.
In all these cases, up to but excluding Man, the arrangement seems to have been brought about mainly by the working of chance and of probing; but in phases *a* to *c* the majority of the groups (except in the case of very large molecules) represent knots of *stability*, whereas in phase *d* the arrangements that survive represent privileged centres of *activity*.

level, of the operation of the same law that governs the whole of the Inorganic. So finally we find the Universe from top to bottom brought within a single, immense coiling movement[2] successively generating nuclei, atoms, molecules, cells and metazoa—the special properties of Life being due solely to the extreme (virtually *infinite*) degree of complexity attained at its level.

Thus the World falls into order, it organises itself, around Life, which is no longer to be regarded as an anomaly but accepted as pointing the direction of its advance (evidence in itself that the axis was well chosen!). Moreover up to a point its progress becomes measurable: for, as observation shows, it is the nature of Matter, when raised corpuscularly to a very high degree of complexity, to become centrated and interiorised— that is to say, to endow itself with Consciousness. This means that the degree of consciousness attained by living creatures (from the moment, naturally, when it becomes discernible) may be used as a parameter to estimate the direction and speed of Evolution (that is to say, of the Cosmic Coiling) in terms of absolute values.

Let us adopt this method and see where it leads us.

Theorem II. Human Reflection is not an Epi-phenomenon of the Organic World, but the Central Phenomenon of Vitalisation

If, as we have agreed, Life is the spearhead of Evolution, does Life in its turn afford us a pointer to the direction of its advance?

[2] It may be as well here to distinguish between the two types of "coiling" or "in-folding" in the evolutionary process:
a. The Coiling of Mass, which sub-divides Matter without organising it (e.g. the stellar masses);
b. The Coiling of Complexity, which organises elementary masses in ever more elaborate structures.
All Mass-Coilings certainly do not result in Coilings of Complexity; but on the other hand all Coilings of Complexity seem to originate or be conditional upon a Mass-Coiling—for example, Life, which could only be achieved on the physical foundation of a planet.

This again is an idea that the latest scientific research does not seem to favour at first glance. Just as Life itself seems to fade into insignificance within the sidereal immensities known to astronomy, so does the happy simplicity which seemed to indicate a steady rise of consciousness from the lower animals to Man lose distinctness in the extraordinary diversity and profusion of living forms now known to biology. Formerly "instinct" could be treated as a sort of homogeneous quantity varying (something like temperature) on a scale running from zero to the point of Reflection representing human thought. Now we have to accustom ourselves to seeing things differently. It is not along a single line that Consciousness has emerged and is increasing on earth, but along an immense fan of nervures, each nervure representing a particular kind of sensory perception and knowledge. There are as many wave-lengths of consciousness as there are living forms.[3] How can we venture to assert that in this spectrum or spreading sheaf of psychisms, any *single* line can exist? Hence the reluctance of many biologists to fix upon a scale of values for use within the animal kingdom. Is Man really more than a protozoan? It has been possible for the question to be seriously asked and left unanswered. But if there were really no answer we should be obliged to conclude that, although the course of Evolution was "directed" up to the emergence of Life, beyond that point all that goes on is a scattering in every direction. We are left with no trail to follow unless we decide, for sufficient reasons, to attribute a unique and privileged value to *reflective* consciousness.

It has become the rather unconsidered fashion, since Bergson, to decry intelligence as compared with other forms or

[3] I.e., in seeking to grasp the interior world and associative faculties of an animal it is not enough to try to diminish or de-centrate our own picture of the world: we have to modify our angle of vision and our way of seeing. Failing this we fall into the anthropomorphic illusions which cause us to be amazed at the phenomena of mimetism, or by mechanical arrangements which we ourselves could only carry out with the full aid of science, whereas the insect or the bat seems to have acquired the skill directly.

aspects of cognition. To the extent that this is simply a reaction against a static and abstract rationalism, it is wholly salutary; but it becomes pernicious if it goes so far as to cause us to overlook what is truly exceptional and essential in the phenomenon of Thought—the power of Consciousness to centrate so perfectly upon itself as to be able to situate itself (itself and the Universe at the same time) in the explicit framework of a present, a past and a *future*—that is to say, in a Space-Time continuum. The more we reflect upon the revolutionary consequences ensuing from this transformation of the laws hitherto governing the world—the growth of powers of *foresight and invention,* prompting and guiding a "planned" rebound of Evolution!—the more must we be persuaded that to regard Intelligence as an anomaly and even a disease of Consciousness is as absurd and sterile as to regard Life as a disease of the earth's surface; and the more do we find ourselves drawn towards another interpretation of the facts, which may be expressed as follows: It is perfectly possible that in the general spectrum of Life the line ending in Man was originally no more than one psychic radiation among countless others. But it happened, for some reason of hazard, position or structure, that this sole ray among the millions contrived to pass the critical barrier separating the Unreflective from the Reflective—that is to say, to enter the sphere of intelligence, foresight and freedom of action. Because it did so (and although in a sense, I must repeat, this ray was only one attempt among many) the whole essential stream of terrestrial biological evolution is now flowing through the breach which has been made. The cosmic tide may at one time have seemed to be immobilised, lost in the vast reservoir of living forms; but through the ages the level of consciousness was steadily rising behind the barrier, until finally, by means of the human brain (the most "centro-complex" organism yet achieved to our knowledge in the universe) there has occurred, at a first ending of time, the breaking of the dykes, followed by what is now in progress, the flooding of Thought over the entire surface of the biosphere.

Thus regarded, everything in the history of the world takes shape, and what is better, everything *goes on.*

Theorem III. Socialisation is not an Epi-phenomenon in the Sphere of Reflective Life but the Essential Phenomenon of Hominisation

I believe that few readers will quarrel with my reasoning in favour of Theorems I and II. Where that part of the argument is concerned, the way through the jungle of facts has been cleared by a century of research and discussion. We may assert today that there is almost complete unanimity among scientists regarding the central position of Life in the Universe, and of Man in Life. It is beyond this point—beyond Man in his anatomical and spiritual individuality—that the path vanishes in the undergrowth and the dispute begins. We have now entered the battle: let us see what the position is.

What hinders and even prevents us from advancing beyond this point is our evident inability to conceive of anything more organically complex or psychically centrated than the human type emerging in Nature as it now is. Hence the instinctive tendency, so widespread even among men of science, to regard the tide of Life on earth as having for practical purposes ceased to flow. According to this view, Life, having reached the reflective stage, must not only disperse in diverging ethno-cultural units, but must finally culminate (and one might say, *evaporate*) in separate individualities, each within the enclosed sphere of its sensibilities and knowledge representing an independent, absolute summit of the Universe.

That is one way of looking at it. But before we acquiesce in a hypothesis which to me seems nothing but the implied admission of a dead-end, we need to be quite sure that the forces of vitalisation really do possess no outlet upon earth, above the level of the human individual. We are told that the way ahead is completely closed. But have those who believe this given any thought to the forces of socialisation?

From habit, and from ignorance, we are inclined to consider the human social phenomenon as no less commonplace and uninteresting than the human phenomenon of reflection. What, we ask in effect, can be more sadly natural than that the human particles, since, unluckily for them, they exist in crowds and masses, should feel the need to organise themselves so as to make existence tolerable? What is this but a process of necessary adjustment, with no mystery about it? That is the view taken by many people as they gaze with melancholy disquiet at the turbulent swell of humanity; and by it the whole edifice of human relationships and social structures is reduced to the level of a regulated epi-phenomenon, having no value or substance of its own, and therefore no future in its own right.

But here, and for the third time, why should we not adopt a position diametrically opposed to the one which is most familiar and, at first sight, most simple? Why not assume instead that, if it is by reason of the cosmic structure, and not by chance, that man has become "legion," by the same token it is not through chance, but through the prolonged effect of "cosmic coiling," that the human layer is weaving and folding-in upon itself in the way we see it to be doing? On this basis the fundamental evolutionary process of the Universe does not stop at the elemental level of the human brain and human reflection. On the contrary, at this stage the "complexity-consciousness" mechanism gains an added impulse, acquiring a new dimension through new procedures. It is no longer simply a matter of cells organised by the hazards of natural selection, but of completed zoological units inventively building themselves into organisms on a planetary scale. Adopting this organic view of the social phenomenon, we find that not only does the structure of our terrestrial society become meaningful both in a general sense (the gradual rise of tension or psychic temperature under technico-social pressure) and in detail (the "anatomy" and "physiology" of the Noosphere) but the whole process takes on a *convergent* aspect: the human phenomenon, seen in its entirety, appears to flow towards a critical point of maturation (and perhaps even of psychic withdrawal)[4] corresponding to the concentration of collective Reflection at a single centre embracing all the individual units of reflection upon Earth.

Further than this we cannot see and our argument must cease—except, as I have now to show, in the case of the Christian, who, drawing upon an added source of knowledge, may advance yet another step.

Theorem IV. The Church is neither an Epi- nor a Para-phenomenon in the growth of the Human Social Organism, but constitutes the very Axis (or Nucleus) about which it Forms

To those accustomed to see in the phenomenon of religion nothing more than a purely conventional association of minds in the sphere of the "imaginary," this fourth and final theorem will seem astonishing and may even come under suspicion as "illuminism." Yet it arises directly out of the juxtaposition of two concepts of the World: the one which practical considerations have just led us to adopt, and the one which every Christian is bound to accept if he is to remain orthodox. As we know, the belief that the human individual cannot perfect himself or fully exist except through the organic unification of all men in God is essential and fundamental to Christian doctrine.[5] To this mystical super-organism, joined in Grace and charity, we have now added a mysterious equivalent organism born of biology: the "Noospheric" human unity gradually achieved by the totalising and centrating effect of Reflection. How can these two super-entities, the one "supernatural," the other natural, fail to come

[4] Necessitated, it would seem, by the requirement of irreversibility developed on the way by the coiling of the Cosmos upon itself.

[5] From the Christian point of view (which in this coincides with the biological viewpoint logically carried to its extreme) the "gathering together" of the Spirit gradually accomplished in the course of the "coiling" of the Universe, occurs in two tempos and by two stages—*a* by slow "evaporation" (individual deaths); and simultaneously *b* by incorporation in the collective human organism ("the mystic body") whose maturation will only be complete at the end of Time, through the Parousia.

together and harmonise in Christian thought; the critical point of maturation envisaged by science being simply the physical condition and experimental aspect of the critical point of the Parousia postulated and awaited in the name of Revelation? Clearly for the conjunction to be effected it is necessary (as is already happening) for it to gain possession of many devout minds. But we must be clear that this change in our vision goes far beyond any purely intellectual and abstract merging of two complementary pictures, one rational, the other religious, of "the end of the world."

For one thing, by this conjunction Christian cosmology, harmonised and effectively articulated at its peak with Human cosmology, shows itself to be fundamentally and in real values homogeneous with the latter. Thus dogma is no mere flowering of the imagination but something authentically born of history; and it is in literal not metaphorical terms that the Christian believer can illumine and further the genesis of the Universe around him in the form of a Christogenesis.

Moreover, by very virtue of the interlocking of the two "geneses" the ascending force of Christianity is directly geared to the propulsive mechanism of human super-evolution. To the Christian, for whom the whole process of hominisation is merely a paving of the way for the ultimate Parousia, it is above all Christ who invests Himself with the whole reality of the Universe; but at the same time it is the Universe which is illumined with all the warmth and immortality of Christ. So that finally (the point cannot be too strongly stressed) a new impulse becomes possible and is now beginning to take shape in human consciousness. Born of the psychic combination of two kinds of faith—in the transcendent action of a personal God and the innate perfectibility of a World in progress—it is an impulse, (or better, a spirit of love) that is truly evolutionary. We can indeed say of it that it is the only kind of spiritual energy capable of causing the formidable human machine, in which, from what we can see, all the future and all the hopes of Evolution must henceforth be concentrated, to function at full power, without danger from egotism or from mechanisation, and to the full extent of its potentialities.

Conclusion

What I set out to show, and hope to have shown, is that, viewed from a certain angle, the internal stir of the Cosmos no longer appears disorderly: it takes a given direction following a major axis of movement at the completion of which the human phenomenon becomes detached as the most advanced form of the largest and most characteristic of cosmic processes, that of in-folding. This axis, as we have seen, may be conveniently determined by means of three succeeding theorems, so closely related that our acceptance or rejection of any one of them must materially affect our attitude to the others.

The coherence of the argument (not a closed one, like a system of logic, but open, like a method or key to progressive research) is such that I believe only solid, positive reasons can lead to its rejection; and for my part I can see none that is adequate. But it is nevertheless true that, above all if they are taken separately, none of the propositions I have formulated is rigidly deductive or, therefore, conclusive: each is more in the nature of an intuition, that is to say, a kind of choice. So it is possible to part company from the sequence at each stage: but only if in doing so we accept the alternative choice. But this, to the logical mind, threatens to have dangerous repercussions in the field of action.

As an instance let us take the particularly crucial and meaningful Third Theorem—or option.

Do we accept the idea, strongly supported by fact, that the individual man cannot achieve his wholeness (that is to say, reflect and personalise himself completely upon himself) except in solidarity with all other men, present, past and future? If we do, the awareness aroused in us of being each a responsible element in a rebounding course of Evolution must, at the same time as it gives rise to a desire and reason for action, inspire us with a fundamental sense of obligation and a precise system of moral tendencies. In matters of love or money or liberty, of politics, economics or society, we not only find our main line of conduct and criteria of choice structurally laid down for us ("ever higher in convergence") but furthermore, our instinct for research and creation ("to consummate the Universe in ourselves") discovers endless justification and sustenance. In short, everything makes sense, everything glows with life; and the flow of human sap rises to the very heart of the Christian faith.

But if, on the other hand, we refuse to regard human socialisation as anything more than a chance arrangement, a *modus vivendi* lacking all power of internal growth, then (excepting, at the most, a few elementary rules safeguarding the living-space of the individual) we find the whole structure of politico-economico-social relations reduced to an arbitrary system of conventional and temporary expedients. Everything in the human world becomes artificial in the worst sense of the word; everything is divested of importance, urgency and interest; Christianity itself becomes no more than a sort of alien proliferation, without analogy or roots in the Phenomenon of Man.

Faced by so wide a divergence of attitudes, can we fail to see that the attempt made in these pages to determine a cosmic axis of evolution, far from being a mere intellectual diversion, is by way of expressing the condition of survival for the human race? And more especially how can we do other than feel that it is about the social phenomenon, according to the degree of central and organic value which we attribute to it, that Mankind is in process of re-assessing and re-grouping itself?

12

PHILOSOPHICAL REFLECTIONS
ON CREATION

Owen R. Jones*

W hat is divine creation? I write, not as a theologian who might be expected to affirm what the doctrine means, but rather as a philosopher for whom the question is "What *could* the doctrine mean?" There are some who feel that recent philosophy has been too much concerned with questions of meaning and too little concerned with questions of truth, but it seems to me that the question of meaning is necessarily prior to the question of truth. Nothing can be true that does not have a meaning, and we would not know how to find out nor decide if a statement or doctrine is true, unless we knew its meaning first. It may perhaps be contended that the truth of Christian Doctrine is not a matter of finding out, deciding, or knowing, but that it is a matter of faith and belief. Even so, the question of

* O. R. Jones is Senior Lecturer in Philosophy at the University College of Wales. Among his writings are articles in philosophical journals and a volume applying the methods of linguistic analysis to biblical theology, The Concept of Holiness (1961). In this unpublished essay he draws a clear distinction between astronomical theories about stellar origins and theological assertions which are "a way of looking at the world as a creation," that is, as a purposeful self-expression; he explores the analogy between creativity in the arts and divine creativity.

meaning is still prior. What is the use of believing that a doctrine is true if one does not know what it means? One is surely putting the cart before the horse if one asks first whether it is reasonable to believe the doctrine, and then starts wondering what the doctrine means.

I should make it clear at the start that I do not intend to go into the *implications* of the doctrine, except incidentally or in so far as that may help us to get at this doctrine's crucial meaning. Much theological discussion of the doctrine has been concerned with what *follows* from it; for example that the creature should worship his creator, or that we should not regard the earth and its treasures as our own. But there is a meaning of the doctrine which is prior to any implications that follow from it, though the word "meaning" is often used in a wide sense to refer to the implications as well. The meaning that I am after is the meaning *from* which the implications follow.

I shall not be concerned with any interpretation of the doctrine which regards the Genesis accounts as literally true in all details. If *that* were what the doctrine meant then it would, in a sense, be *too* clear and simple; at any rate, there would be no philosophical problem then. Divine creation is a fit subject for philosophical discussion precisely because believers have denied the literal interpretation, and have maintained that another account is needed. That is why it becomes proper to ask: What other account *could* there be? Indeed, the reasons which have made people doubt the literal truth of the Genesis accounts are also the reasons which have led them to doubt if there is any room for an alternative account, or even for the notion of creation at all. The reasons for the weakening of the hold of the Genesis accounts are to be found in the advance of scientific cosmology, the theory of evolution, and the discovery of scientific methods of estimating the age of fossils, of the earth, and of the universe. These are also the reasons which have led many to give up any belief in creation. People have come to expect the scientist to tell them everything of importance about the universe, and to believe that when the story is fully told there will be no room for the notion of creation in it. If the theist finds himself falling into the grips of this frame of mind his only hope would seem to be for a breakdown to occur in the scientific enterprise so far as cosmology is concerned. While in this frame of mind one assumes that there *is* a conflict between religion and science; one supposes that the Christian religion upholds belief in creation, and that science excludes any such account. The only hope then is that the scientist may be forced sooner or later to realize the limitations of his method and theory and to concede that in his cosmology in particular he is brought to a dead end where creation has to be admitted after all.

COSMOLOGICAL THEORIES IN ASTRONOMY

As some theists see it, something like this has actually happened in recent years. The story goes as follows. It has been suggested that the "red shift" of the spectral lines of the light received from distant galaxies is to be explained as a Doppler effect. That is to say, it is due to the motion of the galaxies away from the observer. On the assumption that the same physical laws are operative throughout the universe, this leads to the view that all the galaxies are moving away from each other. Other arguments have since been produced to prove the point, and the notion of an expanding universe has by now gained wide acceptance amongst modern cosmologists. It is even claimed that the velocities of the recession of the galaxies can be measured. Dr. E. P. Hubble came out with the result that the distance between any two galaxies is doubling every thirteen hundred million years or so. It follows from this that at some time in the past, between one and ten billion years ago, the galaxies were closely crowded together. If we go far back enough we come to the starting point of the process of expansion, a beginning of the universe, a gigantic explosion perhaps, an event beyond which the scientist cannot possibly penetrate. Sir Edmund Whittaker suggests that "there was an epoch about

10^9 or 10^{10} years ago, on the further side of which this cosmos, if it existed at all, existed in a form totally unlike anything known by us."[1] He goes on to say that "we may perhaps without impropriety refer to it as the creation" and adds, "the creation itself being a unique event, is of course outside science altogether."[2] Isn't this heartening news for the theist? Why shouldn't he welcome this evidence as the proof of the Christian doctrine, since even the scientist *himself,* Whittaker in this case, regards it as pointing conclusively to the existence of a creator God? Whittaker himself regards all this as vindicating the cosmological proof of the existence of God. St Thomas Aquinas, we know, had difficulty in showing that the regress of caused causes cannot be taken back to infinity, but "this difficulty now disappears automatically, since the chain cannot in any case be prolonged backward beyond the creation At this point we escape from the order of the Newtonian cosmos, and, as in St. Thomas' original proof, the sequence of causes terminates in God."[3]

Some prominent theists have welcomed all this with open arms. Pope Pius XII, in his allocution to the Pontifical Academy of Science delivered in 1951, said that modern science "with the same clear and critical look with which it examines and passes judgment on facts, perceives and recognizes the work of creative omnipotence, whose power, set in motion by the mighty *Fiat* pronounced milliards of years ago by the Creating Spirit, spread out over the universe, calling into existence with a gesture of generous love matter bursting forth with energy. In fact, it would seem that present-day science, with one sweeping step back across millions of centuries, has succeeded in bearing witness to that primordial *Fiat lux* uttered at the moment when, along with matter, there burst forth from nothing a sea of light and radiation, while the particles of chemical

[1] E. Whittaker, *Space and Spirit* (London: Nelson, 1946), p. 118.
[2] *Ibid.,* p. 121.
[3] *Ibid.,* p. 125.

elements split and formed into millions of galaxies."[4] How wonderfully well scientific and theological language seem to mix together; matter bursting forth with energy is now to be seen as a gesture of generous love. The Pope went on to say that modern science has "followed the course and direction of cosmic developments and, just as it was able to get a glimpse of the term towards which these developments were inexorably leading, so also has it located too their beginning in time some five milliard years ago. Thus, with that conclusiveness which is characteristic of physical proofs, it has confirmed the contingency of the universe and also the well-founded deduction as to the epoch when the cosmos came from the Hands of the Creator. Hence creation took place in time. Therefore there is a creator. Therefore God exists. Although it is neither explicit nor complete, this is the reply we were awaiting from science. . . ." Here, then, we have one influential theist enthusiastically identifying his own position with that of a modern cosmologist, both agreeing that the Christian doctrine of divine creation has, at last, been *confirmed,* rather than challenged, by modern scientific cosmology. It is clear that they both regard creation as a single once-and-for-all event which happened as a beginning of the universe, and that they assume the cosmology just described, which supposes such an event, to be vindicated.

The vulnerability of such a position is obvious. The cosmology just described has by no means been vindicated. On the contrary, there are prominent modern scientists who have much more faith in a different theory altogether. Herman Bondi, Fred Hoyle, and others have favored what has come to be known as the Steady-State theory. They deny that there is a diminishing of density in the matter occupying the space between the galaxies, and by the same token deny that we would find increasing density if we could go further into the past history of the universe. The implication is that there was no beginning or

---

[4] Reported in *Tablet,* December 1951.

originating event. The Steady-State theory posits that, though the universe is expanding, the density of galaxies and inter-galaxical matter remains constant. It remains constant because new atoms are being produced continually at the appropriate rate. The rate is so small (about one hydrogen atom in a space equal to a living room every few million years) that there is no practical method of finding out if this is in fact happening, but it is claimed that the theory is in principle testable and may there-fore find confirmation at some date in the future. That is not all. The Steady-State theory is but one alternative to the one welcomed so enthusiastically by Pope Pius XII. There are others, too, and in view of this it would seem rather rash to join hands with Whittaker at this stage and take it as certain that his theory is the correct one.

It would be equally rash, for similar reasons, for the theist to stake everything on the success of the Steady-State theory and to modify his position accordingly. His modified claim would, presumably, be that God creates the world continuously by supplying atoms out of nothing as the Steady-State theory seems to require. But this position is just as vulnerable as the first, for the Steady-State theorists themselves would be the first to admit that their theory *may* be shown to be false. Furthermore, it is not inconceivable that a cosmology should be produced which is scientifically acceptable and which does not allow for any dead ends such as the two theories I have already mentioned seem to allow. Such a theory would not leave room for divine creation either by a big bang or in little pops.[5]

In view of all this, what position should theists take? Many who have refrained from joining in exultation with Sir Edmund Whittaker and Pope Pius XII still feel that the Christian doctrine of creation and scientific cosmology have *some* bearing on one another. Many would wish to deny that the doctrine of creation is compatible with the last possible cosmology that I mentioned, for example. Should the theist then live in fear lest

[5] Words used by E. L. Mascall, *Christian Theology and Natural Science* (London: Longman's Green & Co., 1956), p. 162.

the theories which are incompatible with his belief be vindicated? Yet why should he not live in faith rather than fear; faith that the scientific theories that are incompatible with his belief in creation will never be vindicated? This position would seem to be as wise, and to have as much sound sense in it as any.

COSMOLOGY AND CREATION AS
UNRELATED QUESTIONS

However, many theologians, especially Protestants, have taken a more extreme attitude to the whole problem. They have cut the Gordian knot by maintaining that the doctrine of creation has nothing to do with science and scientific cosmology at all. They take the view that it is of no consequence to that doctrine of creation what happens in the field of scientific cosmology. No matter what cosmology wins the day, it makes no difference to the doctrine of creation for that doctrine is compatible with any cosmology, and conflicts with none. This is the attitude that seems to lie behind the words of J. S. Whale: "The Christian doctrine of creation does not arise from our interest in explaining the world or accounting for its "origin" at some approximately datable time in the cosmic past. The doctrine of creation "out of nothing" is not a scientific description of the beginning of the time series. *Here no scientific statements are possible.*"[6] Again, Gustav Aulen says that "faith in God as Creator is not a theory about the origin of the world through a "first cause," etc. It has in reality *nothing in common* with a rational explanation of the universe."[7] A similar view is echoed by Bultmann: "The doctrine of creation is not a speculative cosmology."[8] All these statements contain what seems to me to be an obvious element of truth, namely that the Christian

[6] J. S. Whale, *Christian Doctrine* (Cambridge: Cambridge University Press, 1952), p. 32. Italics added.

[7] G. Aulen, *The Faith of the Christian Church* (Philadelphia: Muhlenberg Press, 1948), p. 181. Italics added.

[8] R. Bultmann, *Primitive Christianity* (New York: Meridian Books, 1956), p. 15.

doctrine of creation is not a theoretical, scientific cosmology; but I think a further assumption is implicit in what these writers say about creation, namely that the doctrine has no implications that can conflict with cosmology. It seems to me that the latter assumption is altogether different from the former and perhaps more dubious. The former denies the *identity* of the doctrine of creation and cosmological theory, whereas the latter denies any *logical relation* whatever between the doctrine and cosmological theory. It seems to me that one should be much more wary of denying the latter.

The theologians who deny that the doctrine of creation is a scientific cosmology seem to deny that there is any logical relation between the two. A. G. N. Flew is not therefore altogether to blame for saying that there are two senses of the word "creation." "In the first, the popular, sense questions about whether the world was or was not created are questions to which the latest news from the science front is relevant. Because if the world was eternal and had no beginning, then there would be no room for creation, in this sense. In the second, *the* theological sense, questions about creation are questions about the absolute ontological dependence to which particular scientific discoveries are *simply irrelevant.*"[9] Flew has to admit in the same context that almost everyone who has believed in creation in the second sense has *also* believed that the world had a beginning. I am not convinced that belief in creation and belief in a beginning of the universe are as distinct and as separate as Flew seems to think, and therefore I am not anything like as sure as he is that scientific discoveries are quite irrelevant to the doctrine of creation. Thus, while I have criticized Whittaker and Pope Pius for assuming the truth of Whittaker's cosmology prematurely, yet I am not altogether out of sympathy with their feeling that this particular type of

[9] A. Flew and A. MacIntyre, eds., *New Essays in Philosophical Theology* (New York: The Macmillan Company, 1955), p. 176. Italics added.

cosmology fits in better with the Christian doctrine of creation than some others.

However, the question which really bothers me, and which I regard as important, remains untouched. That is this question: What does the doctrine of creation *mean?* What does it say? This is obviously a crucial question for those who deny that the doctrine has anything at all to do with cosmology in any way. But it is no less a question for those who think that the Whittaker cosmology supports belief in creation. Even if scientific cosmology tells us that there is a dead end beyond which it cannot go in retrospect—a beginning which defeats scientific description—it does not follow that this *illuminates* the doctrine of creation or tells us *what* creation consists in. These are the questions that need to be tackled.

CREATION NOT A TEMPORAL EVENT

So let us consider some attempts at illuminating the problem as I have raised it. I begin with St. Thomas Aquinas. He made a good point when he denied that creation is a change. Change implies something pre-existent which undergoes the change; it implies something *which* changes, something which was different before the change from what it became after the change. Now, all the events, occurrences, happenings, processes that we are normally acquainted with are changes of one sort or another, and St. Thomas is in effect denying that creation is an event, an occurrence or process comparable with those which we know. To create is not to bring about a change *in* a state of affairs, but to *bring into being* a state of affairs where none existed. Creation did not happen, occur, or take place *in* time. To quote St. Thomas: "God *brought into being* both the creature and time together."[10] He regards this bringing into being as divine *action,* but clearly he cannot mean any ordinary action comparable to most of our actions. Our actions are

[10] *Aquinas, Summa Contra Gentiles* II, xxxv.

normally such as to produce *changes*. Thus the import of St. Thomas' point is on the whole negative. He clears the ground to some degree by telling us what creation is *not*. We still want to know *what* it is.

St. Thomas ties this point up closely with another which I find less acceptable. He maintains that creation is also *preservation*. "This preservation of things by God does not take place by some new action, but by a prolongation of that action by which he gives existence; and this action is without change or time."[11] How can an action be *prolonged* without time? That is the question that defeats me here. Surely it must defeat St. Thomas too! The notion of nontemporal preservation seems to be a self-contradictory one, and what Aquinas says about divine preservation does not help. He says that God does not preserve things "in any other way than by always giving them being."[12] The word "always" again seems to imply time. It is not my business now to pass criticism on the claim that God does preserve the universe, but there does seem to be a difficulty in maintaining that God's creative act is also his act of preserving the universe, precisely because the creative act is said to be outside time while preservation seems only to make sense as a process *in* time. I think it would be more consistent to maintain the two points as separate articles of faith, for there is no open inconsistency in maintaining that God created the world outside time *and* preserves the world in time, or better still, *for* a time.

Perhaps a more favorable interpretation of Aquinas would be possible if we could restrict ourselves to his notion of dependency. He says that "as it *depends* on the will of God that he produces things into being, so it *depends* on his will that he preserves them in being."[13] That the world *depends* on God *need* not imply that an active *process* of preserving is involved. The world could be said to *depend* on the will of God without it being implied that God *carries on* doing something for some

[11] *Aquinas, Summa Theologia* I, civ, 1.
[12] *Ibid.*, ix, 2c.
[13] *Ibid.*, ix, 2c.

length of time. However, this interpretation does not seem to be open to Aquinas for he says that preservation is a *prolongation* of the creative act, and that God is *always giving* things being. If this is really what he wants to say, then it seems to me that he should distinguish more sharply between creation and preservation, allowing that, while creation is *not* a process or event in time, preservation *is*.

If we put aside Aquinas' stress on preservation, the valuable, though negative, point that remains is his insistence that creation is not a temporal event or process. But if it is *not* this, then *what* is it? That is the question we should pursue. In pursuing it, let us turn to views of others who have grappled with the problem. What positive suggestions have Flew and MacKinnon to make in their discussion after agreeing that creation has nothing to do with cosmology? MacKinnon suggests that "it belongs rather to an imaginative vision of the world,"[14] and Flew, taking his cue from the word "vision" says "it seems to me that what is involved is more like a *model,* an *image,* or a *picture.*"[15] A little later, MacKinnon puts it like this, "To believe in creation is to see the world in a certain way,"[16] and he points out that Brunner, too, emphasizes that this is at least a part of the context of the doctrine. MacKinnon has the edge on Flew in his way of making the point here. Flew quotes St. Paul's words "in him were all things created in the heavens and upon the earth, things visible and invisible, all things have been created through him and unto him." Flew thinks St. Paul is "offering us a *picture* in terms of which to think of the universe around us."[17] I see no *picture* here, but one could see the words as expressing what MacKinnon calls a *vision* of the world, a certain way of looking at the world.

Others have put forward a similar view. I will mention but one—T. R. Miles in his book, *Religion and the Scientific*

14 Flew and MacIntyre, *op. cit.,* p. 175.
15 *Ibid.,* p. 177.
16 *Ibid.,* p. 179.
17 *Ibid.,* p. 177.

Outlook. He thinks the creation doctrine could be regarded as a parable whose point is to give us a new slant on the world, a new orientation. It is a matter of looking at the world differently. The point is obviously the same as MacKinnon's. It is also worthy of notice that both Miles and MacKinnon hint at a close relationship between the doctrine of creation and the Redemption in Christ, "the riddle of a life lived and a death died," as MacKinnon puts it, and this is of course a point which some prominent theologians have stressed, notably L. S. Thornton in his volumes subtitled *The Form of a Servant*. None of the writers I have just mentioned, Flew, MacKinnon, nor Miles, take the point raised much further, nor explicate it more fully. It seems to me that it can be taken further, and be more fully explained. Furthermore, I think that a view of creation is possible which shows the "vision interpretation of creation" as fitting in tidily with the point which St. Thomas emphasized. The view I have in mind can be brought out by considering an analogy, namely, that of creativity in the arts. I now would like to consider fairly carefully this analogy.

THE ANALOGY OF CREATIVITY IN THE ARTS

The first point I want to establish is that creating in the arts is *not an observable spatio-temporal process. Making,* by contrast, *does* often take the form of an observable spatio-temporal event or process, and since creating a work of art often involves making something too (as in the sculptor's art, for example) it is easy to be misled into thinking that the creating simply is the making, and that the creating is therefore a spatio-temporal process. Making in this sense is, however, very different from creating. For one thing, this kind of making involves the use of tools, possibly machinery, or at least the bare hands. The question "What did you make it with?" makes good sense, but the question, "What did you create it *with?*" sounds very odd. One simply does not create *with* anything. "What did the poet create his poem with?" There is no answer, any more than there is sense in the question, "Did Handel create his 'Messiah' with anything?" Of course not.

Again, the observable spatio-temporal process of making something presupposes *pre-existent material*. Things are made *out of* wood, clay, iron, and so on. But *out of* what did Beethoven create his Seventh Symphony? What did Robert Frost create his poems *out of?* Words? One might *metaphorically* speak of a poem as built up of words, and the words might *metaphorically* be spoken of as the bricks out of which the structure called a poem was built. But one cannot say that a poem is literally made out of words, precisely because words do not constitute spatio-temporal pre-existent material. It is equally wrong to say that the sculptor created his masterpiece out of marble. This would be all right if "created out of" could be equated with "chiseled out of" but, of course, these words are *not* equivalent. One could chisel out of marble and lamentably fail to create. Little wonder then that God is said to have created the world out of nothing, for the fact is that creation, in the relevant sense, is never *out of* anything.

The difference between spatio-temporal processes on the one hand, and creating on the other, can be further brought out by noting that the former can be timed, whereas creation *cannot be timed*. How would you time the creativity of the painter? When does it begin? Does the application of the first daub of paint mark the starting point? Or does creativity set in when the process of applying daubs of paint is a quarter of the way through? There is no answer, for the question is not in order. Furthermore, spatio-temporal processes that can be timed can also be interrupted, abandoned halfway through, speeded up, slowed down, and so forth. It is odd to ask "How much of the creating was completed when it was abandoned?" or "At what stage was your creating interrupted?" Do we say of some people that they create very fast and of others that they are slow creators? We do not talk of creating in that way, and the implication is that creating is not a spatio-temporal process for such processes can be speeded up, slowed down, interrupted, and so forth.

The point that I am trying to establish could be expressed by saying that there is all the difference in the world between the *creation* of a work of art and the *executing* of it. The latter is a process that can be timed and observed, but that is not the creation. Indeed the sculptor sometimes delegates the work of *executing* a work to other craftsmen. The difference between creating and executing a work of art may be blurred because producers of creative works of art do not always conceive their work *before* executing it. The sculptor may find that his conception of the work comes *as* he chisels and hammers away. But it is important to realize that conceiving a work of art and executing it do *not necessarily* run together in this way. Chopin claimed that some of his musical compositions came to him as it were in a flash, and it was as much as he could do to write out the score as fast as he could. And the sculptor, no doubt, sometimes "sees" the finished work in the unhewn stone.

What I have just said may have suggested that to create a work of art is to conceive it. And some may jump to the conclusion that creation is therefore an *inward* process of thought, a process that sometimes precedes, and sometimes accompanies, the execution of the work. However, I think that this is a suggestion that must be resisted. What is a process of thought? Not a series of cerebral events certainly. It must be, if anything, something that could be expressed in spoken or written words, and it is no doubt true that such a process often precedes the producing of a great creative piece of poetry. Suppose a poet writes out all that he thinks in producing a great poem. It is not probable that he will write out the complete, finished, perfect poem at one go. It is much more likely that he will start writing and then cross out and restart, that he will make many corrections, alterations, improvements, and so on. It is thus that a process of thought *may* precede the finished work. But all this is not necessary except as a matter of fact. Mortals do not as a matter of fact write out great poems without a hitch at the first attempt, but it is not *inconceivable* that they should. That is to say, the concept of creation as such does not *necessarily* imply a process of thought at all. It is not contained in the very *meaning* of the word "creation" that a process of thought such as I have described should *precede* the complete work.

How do you decide if a poet has really succeeded in *creating* something? Do you look for some spatio-temporal process—the movement of his hand and fingers in writing the poem—or the brain processes involved? Surely not. Do you look for some thought process then, an inner process which the poet might have, but did not actually write down? But I have just argued that there might conceivably be none. So my conclusion at this stage is that creation is neither an outward spatio-temporal process *nor* an inward temporal process. So what does creativity in the arts amount to?

AN ARTISTIC CREATION BESPEAKS A PERSON

If you want to find out if a poet has succeeded in creating something, that his poem is a *creation,* then you can only get the answer by *reading* the poem, *re*reading it, reading it aloud, reading it silently, *evaluating* it. That is to say, you do not discover if a poem is a creation by looking for some process or other, but rather by attending to the poem. If it is a creation, then that fact is *written on its face* as it were. This is not simply to reduce creation to a category of evaluation, for one is not simply saying that a poem is good, that it is economical in expression, and so forth. One implies more than this when one says that a poem is a creation, namely, that it is *original,* that it *bespeaks* an individual person. I think there are two points here that we should not confuse. Firstly, it is true that much original, creative work of art constitutes a self-expression of the artist himself; the artist's work, the poet's poem, the novelist's novel, often tell you something about the creator of the work in question, and perhaps give you an insight into his nature and personality that you would not otherwise have. Secondly, a work of art may bespeak a person without necessarily being expressive of that person's character or personality. By this I mean that a work can produce an immediate conviction on the part of the beholder that it is intentional and purposive even though we have no idea as to *how* the work was produced, or as to what its spatio-temporal history is.

Let me try to bring this point out more clearly by reference to two very different situations in the following way. Suppose you see a brittle dead twig lying on the ground near some trees. Here there is no inclination, let alone a compulsion, to think of the situation as personal, to think that a person is responsible for the twig's being where it is. One thinks of the brittleness of the twig and of the effects of gusts of wind and we are quite happy to regard the situation as explicable in those terms. Now, consider a very different situation. You hear the sound as of a harp coming in the form of a beautiful melody. Let us suppose you know something about music and can recognize what is great and original, and that the melody you hear strikes you as being such. You now feel compelled to regard it as something for which a person is responsible; you simply *cannot help* feeling that those notes were *intended* to follow each other as they do. Here is a situation such that no explanation in terms of natural events could remove your conviction that a person is involved in it. Suppose that you discover, upon investigation, that the harp was lying horizontally out in the open, and that it was raining hailstones, and that the hailstones were producing the notes by striking the strings of the harp. What would one say then? I am not sure what one would say, but I find it difficult to imagine that anyone could cease completely to regard the situation as bespeaking a person. *Given* that what we see strikes us as being an original creation, then we *inevitably* regard the situation as bespeaking a person, no matter what other explanations turn out to be appropriate.

I have tried to argue that any work of art that is an original creation is such that its origin is manifest on its face as it were.

But this does not mean that the characteristics which mark it out as a creation are easily describable. Quite the contrary. When critics try to bring out such characteristics, they find themselves using language in an unusual manner. What they want to express is so difficult to express that they have to put words to strange, if not strained, uses. Consider, as an example, Lockspeiser's description of the work called *Narmouna* by Lalo. He speaks of *"unrelenting,* persistent rhythms, *wild* fanfare on trumpets . . . *powerful* work . . . much *bolder* in *colour* . . human, vibrant, alive."[18]

Furthermore, if one is to appreciate what the critic is saying when he uses language like this, one must already know something about music. Indeed, if one is to appreciate *fully* what he is saying, and to *recognize* the characteristics he describes in the music, then one must have taken a serious interest in music, one must have *lived* for the art, one must have committed oneself. Dabbling is no use. Thus when I say that a work which can be truly called a creation carries its authenticity on its face as it were, it is not implied that the originality of the work is obvious to anyone. We have to learn the language of the art and that is far from being a simple matter.

SEEING THE WORLD AS A CREATION

Now it is time to return to the doctrine of divine creation. My first point is that trying to account for divine creativity in terms of scientific cosmology is like identifying the creation of the artist with what happens on the face of the canvas, what happens in his muscular and nervous systems and so on. To do this is to go off on the wrong track altogether, and to miss the point completely in both cases. Divine creativity is no more a *spatio-temporal process* than is the creativity of the artist, poet, or musician. That is why St. Thomas was so right to insist that divine creation is not a change; it is also why recent Protestant theologians are right in denying that the doctrine of creation is

[18] *The Listener,* Vol. LIV, No. 1399, p. 1101.

I

modern cosmology. It is not a description of a spatio-temporal process at all, and therefore cannot be an alternative account of the origin of the universe which is in competition with scientific cosmology either. It is sometimes said that the Genesis account is correct in asserting *that* God created the world, but wrong in its description of *how* God created the world; it is then asserted that modern science gives us a better account of *how* God created. This however is to commit the fallacy I have tried to expose; it is to assume that creation is a spatio-temporal process after all. If the development of my argument is sound, then the Genesis account gives *better* insight into the nature of creation than does modern cosmology, for the Genesis account does at least depict the creative situation as a situation of *personal* activity, whereas modern cosmology does not.

This brings me to the second point I wish to derive from my analogy, namely, that to claim that the universe is a divine creation is to claim at least that it *bespeaks a person*. This is not to take the Genesis account literally; it is not to claim that God made man with his hands or that He uttered the words attributed to the Creator in Genesis. It is, however, to assert that the world is such that once it is seen in the right light, once we have a proper vision of it, then we just cannot get away from the conviction that a *person* is responsible for it, that it betrays intention and purpose. To see the world thus is to see it *differently,* to have a new slant on it, to have a new vision of it as Flew, MacKinnon, and Miles suggested. It is to see the universe as bespeaking a person. Berkeley also expressed a point of view very similar to the one I am advocating when he claimed that the world is a divine visual language.

This brings me to my third point, for Berkeley was mistaken in thinking that this divine visual language is obvious to everyone. My analogy provides a safeguard against making such a mistake, for it is clear that the originality and creative nature of a work of art is *not obvious to anyone*. It can only be appreciated through discernment acquired after living for the art and taking a serious interest in it. Similarly, we should not be in the position of maintaining that the world can be seen as a creation no matter how you look at it. To see it *as* a creation calls for insight and discernment, and just as one might well begin to try and appreciate works of art by listening to what those who have acquired discernment in this matter have to say about it, so we might begin to see the world as a creation by listening to what the theologians have to say.

A further point, our analogy warns us not to expect their story to be told in simple language. Just as the critic of art finds himself using language in *a strained and paradoxical way,* so also we might well expect the theologian's account to be no less difficult, strained, and paradoxical. Perhaps we should even forgive him for sometimes evolving such monstrous jargon as, for example, the word "Christocentric." At any rate, we should try to follow his theme in his attempt to show how creation and redemption are inextricably bound together.

Following the intricacies of such an account is almost like trying to acquire *a new language.* I suggested that one cannot be in a position to appreciate the art critics' comments unless we have done more than dabble in the form of art in question. Similarly, one cannot expect to get any hold of what the theologian is trying to say unless one takes a serious interest in religion. If grasping the point of the doctrine of creation is like acquiring a new language, perhaps we would do well to remember that Wittgenstein held that a language is *a way of life.* Thus, to acquire this one, a person would have to become religious.

Not only this, but one should also remember that the world is not like a work of art which can be seen as already completed. Any view of the world which neglects the historical, and also the future, perspective can only be a slice, a cross-section, rather like a frozen, photographic still, taken in the middle of a play. One could perhaps express the point by saying that the world which has been created is not a created *thing,* but a created *history.* Yet, we should not conclude from this that the creation, or creating, itself is a historical process. To say that the world is created is, on the view I have expounded so far, to say that as a stretch of historical development it bespeaks a person when seen in the correct light.

SEEING THE WORLD AS GOD'S SELF-EXPRESSION

I have, so far, only argued that the doctrine of creation can be interpreted as the claim that the world bespeaks a person: but does it not involve a greater claim than this, namely, that the world bespeaks a certain *kind* of person, of which there is and could be, only one? The doctrine says that *God* created the world and our interpretation should therefore be not simply that the world bespeaks a person—any person or some person—but that *it bespeaks God*. In view of this, perhaps we should develop an aspect of our analogy that I have rather neglected hitherto. I did mention, without then enlarging upon the fact, that a work of art sometimes tells us something about its author. It not only bespeaks a personal author, but is also a self-expression of the author. Indeed, the word "creation" carries the implication of *self-expression* in many contexts. For example, children are sometimes given periods in the school curriculum during which they can do what they like with the materials at their disposal, and this activity is often called "creative activity" or "self-expression activity." That is to say the words "creative activity" and "self-expression" are sometimes, in some contexts at least, used interchangeably. May we not say that great works of art, too, are self-expressions, and that to recognize a creative masterpiece for what it is, is also *one* way of knowing a person? It will be granted on all sides that a person becomes known through his facial expressions through his talk, through his letters, and so forth. Is there any reason why he should *not*, if he happen to be a poet, make himself known in his poetry, too?

At any rate, it is by no means outrageously implausible to suggest that the world is a creation of this kind, a creation that is also, to some degree at least, *a self-expression of its author.*

imagine many believers would want to argue that the doctrine of creation does indeed assert this, not simply that the world bespeaks a person, but that it bespeaks a certain *kind* of person, and that it is a self-expression of that person. But the argument does run into difficulties. The difficulty would arise in trying to *show* that the world bespeaks *such a person* as God is believed to be. There would seem to be some ground for saying that if the world bespeaks a person, and is a self-expression of that person, then he is far from being free of malevolence. The problem is, of course, the old *problem of evil*.

However, I do not think this problem need bother us too much so far as the business at hand goes, for the task before us is that of explicating the *meaning* of the doctrine of creation. It is well to remember that the believer is in the position of exercising *faith,* and the problem for us is to find *what* is the expression of faith which the doctrine of creation formulates. My suggestion so far is that it expresses the faith that the world bespeaks a person such as God is believed to be. It is not irrational to believe as a matter of faith *that* the world *does* bespeak such a person even though *we* cannot as yet clearly see it *as* bespeaking such a person. The claim expressed in the doctrine is not that the world bespeaks God no matter *how* you look at it, but rather that it bespeaks God only if seen in a certain light. It is always open to the believer to concede that he has not as yet had the appropriate vision of the world in anything like its fullness.

It is now time to remind you of the promise I held out earlier on in this paper, namely, to develop a view of creation that would show the *vision* view of it as fitting in tidily with the Thomist view. I think our analogy does bring out very well, and much more fully than did MacKinnon, Flew, or Miles, what could be meant by saying that "to believe in creation is *to see the world in a certain way*" (MacKinnon), or as I would prefer to say, "to believe that the world can be seen in a certain way." Since it also shows how creation is *not* a spatio-temporal process, it explicates the point St. Thomas emphasized, namely, that creation is not a change. Thus the two views come together in a conspectus which amplifies and enriches both.

THE PROBLEM OF DIVINE ACTIVITY

Our analogy has served us well, but still not well enough as yet, for there is a residual but crucial aspect of our problem which remains to be discussed: it is an aspect of which we should be especially reminded by St. Thomas' account. You will remember that he spoke of creation *as divine activity*. He did indeed make clear that the activity in question was not a change, not a spatio-temporal process, and our analogy has done justice to that point. But hasn't our development of the analogy overlooked completely something St. Thomas wants to convey by his use of the word "activity"? While agreeing that creation is not a spatio-temporal process, St. Thomas would still want to insist that there was *activity* of *some* kind. God *did* something in creating the world. This emphasis upon the *activity* of God in creation, on the fact that he *did* something in creating the world, has been preserved through the traditional habit of expressing our faith in the creator by calling him "the *Maker* of heaven and earth." Yet if this making is not a spatio-temporal process, then what kind of making is it? The Thomist answer to this question is the doctrine of analogy according to which the word "make" does not mean quite the same thing when applied to what God did as contrasted with what man does, though the meanings are not altogether different either.

Peter Geach, an astute interpreter of St. Thomas, suggests that we get nearer to the meaning of the word as applied to God if we consider what it means in a sentence like *"the minstrel made music"*—as contrasted with what it means if we say, for example, "the blacksmith makes a shoe."[19] Geach points out that the blacksmith makes the shoe out of pre-existing matter,

[19] G. E. M. Anscombe and P. T. Geach, *Three Philosophers* (Oxford: Basil Blackwell, 1961), p. 110.

and also that the shoe has independent existence once it is made. The minstrel's music, on the other hand, is not made out of anything, and stops as soon as the minstrel stops making it. Geach is presumably thinking, not of the minstrel as a composer of music, but as a performer, and in choosing this example he is keeping very close to the intentions of St. Thomas; that is to say, he has chosen an example that will show how God's creative activity is the same as his activity in preserving the world. Yet one has doubts about this example too. Making music in this sense would seem to be a spatio-temporal process involving the use of instruments, but God's creating the world is not a spatio-temporal process and, presumably, did not involve the use of anything like instruments. Suppose however the performing minstrel *creates his music as he goes along* (and this may be what Geach had in mind), then we have the clearest case of doing something which is not reducible to the sequence of events involved in moving the bow across the string. What explanatory analysis could one give of such an act of creation?

The task of giving such an analysis would take me far beyond the limits of the present essay. It would involve, among other things, a close consideration of the notion of *intention* and of the question: What is it to behave *rationally* and with knowledge of what one is doing?[20] Thus it is tempting for me to end on a rather complacent note, simply pointing out that whatever difficulties there may be in the claim that God created the world, we already have analogous difficulties in accounting for *creation* at the human level. Since we are still convinced that it does make sense to talk of human creation despite the difficulty of explaining what such an human act of creation could be, why should we be any less convinced that it makes sense to talk of divine creation, for the crucial difficulties are located at this point in both cases. The two analogous cases are not, however,

[20] For a discussion of such questions see, for example, G. E. M. Anscombe, *Intention* (Oxford: Basil Blackwell, 1957); A. I. Melden, *Free Action* (London: Routledge & Kegan Paul, 1961); Jonathan Bennett, *Rationality* (London: Routledge & Kegan Paul, 1964).

entirely comparable all the way through, and I must bring this essay to a close by highlighting a crucial difference between the two cases, thereby bringing into focus a difficulty which does beset belief in divine creation and which does *not* beset belief in human creation.

I have already sufficiently laboured the point that creation is not an observable spatio-temporal change, but this does not mean that such changes are totally irrelevant. On the contrary, it seems clear to me that in cases of human creation there is always *a unique relation between the creator and the created work* such that one particular person, and no one else, may be said to be the creator of that particular work. Such a relation involves observable spatio-temporal changes in that the artist has *painted* the picture using his brush with his hand, foot, or mouth as the case may be; the poet has *written* his poem, or *typed* it, or *dictated* it; the composer has *written* his score; the sculptor has done his own *chiseling* or else he was responsible for *giving the directions* to the craftsmen who executed the work. The point may be put more generally as follows. When a person (*P*) is said to have created a certain work (*W*) it is implied that there is a description of what *P* did, and a description of what happened when *W* came into being, which dovetail into one another in such a way that no one other than *P* could be said to have created *W*.

The importance of the unique relationship can be brought out in the following way by referring again to the example I brought up a short while ago of the harp producing a melody by hailstones dropping on its strings. I argued then that one could not but regard such a situation as bespeaking a person. Now imagine someone making the objection that we should not speak of an actual creation by a person in such a situation, and that the most we would have a right to say would be "It is *as if* there were a person at work here." What reply could we make to such an objection? Surely, it is a strong objection, for there is something missing in this situation which is present in ordinary situations of creation by a person. What is missing is the unique relationship I have spoken of. Since this element is missing perhaps we should *not* say that the melody is created by a person, whatever the melody is like; perhaps the most we should say is that "It is *as if* the melody were created by a person."

DIVINE CREATION AND SCIENTIFIC COSMOLOGY

To return now to the problem of divine creation, the point I have just raised has at least two important implications with regard to this problem. The first takes us back to the question of scientific cosmology. If God created the world, then, following the latest stage in the development of our analogy, there must be an account of what happened when the world came into existence, and an account of what God did, which dovetail into one another in such a way that no one other than God could properly be said to be the author of our universe. It seems to me that this condition places a restriction on what the believer in divine creation can accept by way of an answer to the question: *What happened when the world came into existence?* And since scientific cosmology does deal with this question, there would seem to be a restriction on what the believer in divine creation can accept from the cosmologist. He can only accept an account which will dovetail into his account of what God has done in such a way that no one other than God may properly be said to be the author of the universe.

Indeed there seem to be *some* explanations which *rule out personal activity altogether* in situations which might otherwise be taken to bespeak a person. Suppose you are in a house where you suddenly hear a sequence of taps which sound as though a person were lightly hammering a piece of metal. Your first impulse might be to think that there was a man somewhere around tapping a piece of metal; but if it is explained to you that the central heating system switched itself off and the tapping noise is due to the lowering of the temperature and the subsequent regular contraction of metal parts and so forth, then you lose your conviction that a person was at work in the house. Under different circumstances there might have been a scientific explanation which did *not* interfere with your conviction that a person was at work. Suppose, for example, you are told about the movements of certain atoms, the changes in certain molecules and cells, the contraction of certain muscles, the movement of a certain arm such that a hammer tapped a piece of metal, then you have an explanation which in no way conflicts with your original conviction that a person was at work. Thus we should distinguish between explanations that do, and explanations that do not, conflict with convictions about the existence of personal activity; and similarly there may be a case for distinguishing between cosmologies that do and those that do not conflict with the belief that God created the world.

Thus the believer in divine creation should not be too happy about maintaining that *any* cosmology will do, or that it does not matter what the cosmologists say. That would be too much like maintaining that Leonardo da Vinci was the creator of the masterpiece "Mona Lisa" no matter how the paint got on the canvas. It should be obvious enough in the latter case that it is only if the paint came onto the canvas in one way and not another that Leonardo da Vinci, rather than someone else or no one at all, could properly be said to be the creator of the masterpiece. And if our analogy is to apply, then there would seem to be a comparable restriction as to what cosmology can be right if belief in divine creation is to be vindicated. So it seems that some philosophers and theologians have been much too cavalier in their dismissal of scientific cosmology as having no bearing whatsoever on the problem of divine creation.

NO CAUSAL RELATIONSHIP BETWEEN GOD AND WORLD

The second implication which the last development of our analogy has for the doctrine of creation is that before we can properly say that God created the world there must be *something that God did* which is comparable to the artist's handling of his brush, the poet's writing of his poem, or the musician's writing of his score. But this is the point at which we seem to have a radical disparity between human creation and divine creation, for it seems to be out of the question that God could conceivably have done anything comparable to what human creators do along the lines just indicated. The reason for this is that *God does not have a body.* Not only this, but he could not have a body without becoming a part of the universe of which he is supposed to be the creator; and even if it is conceivable that he should become incarnate in the universe *after* it has been created, it is quite inconceivable that he should become incarnate in the universe *before* he created it. We may suppose that God has a nonmaterial body, but there is nothing to choose between supposing this and supposing that God has no body at all, and in neither case does the analogy with the creative artist hold any longer. So this appears to be the point at which the attempt to carry our analogy through comes to a grinding halt.

How serious is this difficulty? It will be remembered that the question I have raised about creation is the question as to its *meaning,* and the analogy with the creative artist was invoked to answer this question. Since the application of the analogy is limited in the way I have just indicated the illumination available as to the meaning of the claim that God created the world is limited to that extent. The seriousness of the limitation could be brought out by appeal to an example once more. Suppose you have a creative minstrel who composes as he plays his piano. This involves manipulating his fingers on the keys, and that in turn causes the hammers to strike the chords in such a way as to produce the music. The bulk of my discussion has gone to show that the musician's creativity in a case like this could not consist simply in the movements of his fingers, or any physical changes involved in the manipulation. Nevertheless the movements of his fingers are related to his creative activity in an important way. The relation is such that if he had not done anything that was *causally related* to the hammers striking the chords, then he would not be said to have created the music.

Suppose you have a piano producing wonderful music with no one manipulating the keys. What could we say then? One might still say that the music is created by someone, someone who has quite unusual causal links with the hammers which strike the chords, and we can understand what such a contention amounts to, for much is possible in a situation like this in this day and age. It would be good entertainment to think up and suggest possible bizarre causal links that might be set up to do the trick. But suppose it is contended that the music is created by someone who does not even have a body at all. This gives rise to a different puzzlement altogether, and it is not a puzzlement as to what causal links there could be this time, for we are convinced at the outset that there could be none. We would be puzzled rather as to the meaning of the contention. It seems to me that a similar puzzlement exists with regard to the contention that God created the world, and for a similar reason, since God has no body.

As a last-ditch defense of the analogy one might try arguing that even though God had no body *his decisions are causally related* to cosmological events in the same way as the artistic creator's decisions are related to the movements of his hands as he paints, plays the piano, or whatever else. I am not at all convinced that this will do, for there are strong arguments for saying that the artist (or any other performer) *does not cause* his hands to move at all.[21] Certainly there is a dilemma here so far as the application of our analogy is concerned. Suppose we say that the artist moves his hand by willing his hand to move, then we seem to be confined to a choice between two alternatives neither of which enables us to benefit from our analogy. On the one hand, if we say that the willing in question is a bodily change of some kind then we are simply back to the previous problem, for there could be no bodily change in a God who does not have a body. On the other hand if we say that the willing is not a bodily event then it is every bit as difficult to see

[21] See, e. g., Melden, *op. cit.,* especially chap. 5. Cf. G. N. A. Vesey, "Volition" in *Philosophy,* Vol. XXXVI, No. 138 (1961).

how such willing could *conceivably* be causally related to a body movement as it is to see how a nonembodied God could be causally related to any material event. In neither case does the analogy help.

To conclude, I have not of course shown, or tried to show, that the doctrine of creation is meaningless. On the contrary, I have tried to find out what meaning it could have by exploiting one particular analogy, seeing how far it will take us, and finally bringing out its shortcomings. The earlier development of the analogy brought out the affinity between the "vision" theory of creation and the Thomist doctrine, but I think that my discussion of the difficulties of the analogy highlight the difference between the two views. The "vision" interpretation especially as we have it from Flew, Miles, and MacKinnon does not run into the difficulties I have raised, for it does not claim that God *did* anything to create the world. This view of the doctrine makes it a matter of seeing the world in a certain way, taking a certain view of it, having a certain slant on it. This lends itself easily to an "as if" interpretation—the world is as though it were created by a personal agent—but it shuns the question as to what it could mean to say that God did create the world. Hence the lack of worry about cosmology and of any attempt to tackle the question as to how God created the world. This interpretation seems to me to fall short of orthodox theistic demands. The Thomist doctrine, by giving such prominence to the idea of God *acting* and *doing* something in creation measures up more satisfactorily to the theist's requirements, but it does run headlong into the difficulties I have raised as to how God's activity relates to what happened when the world came into being. The Thomist still needs a philosophical account of God's creative act and needs to show how that would fit in with scientific cosmology. The "vision" theory hardly asks as much as our analogy gives, while the Thomist doctrine asks more than it can give. The former view is philosophically easy but theologically inadequate, whereas the latter is theologically adequate but philosophically difficult.

PART FOUR:
TECHNOLOGY AND MAN

13

THE CHRISTIAN IN
A WORLD OF TECHNOLOGY

*Harvey Cox**

I t is doubtful whether technology in its modern form would ever have been possible without the biblical faith. The impact of the biblical faith culminating in the gospel of Jesus Christ constitutes an indispensable precondition without which contemporary scientific technology is unthinkable. Even though the church has very frequently opposed scientific and technological advances—Galileo is the best example—when it does so it is always acting against its own presuppositions and is betraying the very gospel it is called to defend. Technology means "tool," but modern scientific technology is not simply a tool that can be used for good or for evil. It is also a culturally formative power that defines the shape of the world we live in and conditions our

* *Harvey Cox is Associate Professor of Church and Society at Harvard Divinity School. His writings have combined theological and sociological analyses of modern society. The affirmative attitude toward technology and urbanization expressed in* The Secular City *(1965) has received widespread discussion. The following chapter was one of the preparatory papers for the World Council of Churches' Conference on Church and Society held in Geneva in July, 1966. It was printed in Denys Munby, ed.,* Economic Growth in World Perspective *(London: SCM Press, 1966) and is included here through the kindness of the World Council of Churches.*

way of perceiving that world. It has been contended by some that a technological civilization does not permit the possibility of Christian faith, that it is inherently and essentially anti-Christian. This is not true. The Christian gospel is not the "culture religion" of pretechnological society. Nor is it a particular expression of some general religious spirit that will necessarily vanish when scientific technology has done its work. The Christian gospel, rather, is the Word of God calling men in every age and within any social or cultural ethos to take responsibility for himself and his neighbor in history before the Living God. Far from making Christian faith impossible, in many ways the technologization of our world makes the call of the gospel more unavoidable than ever. It sharpens the issue of obedience or disobedience, maturity or immaturity, response or refusal. It presses the issues of Christian faith more urgently and presents the alternatives more sharply.

We shall begin by showing how the cultural impact of the biblical faith provides a necessary precondition for technology. Three main motifs will be discussed: (1) the "disenchantment" of the natural world, (2) the worth of human work, and (3) the possibility of change.

THE BIBLICAL BASIS OF MODERN TECHNOLOGY

1. *The Disenchantment of the World of Nature.* The disenchantment of the world of nature is a cultural prerequisite of technology. No technology can operate where the world is still seen to be holy, where nature is conceived of as the habitat of benign or demonic forces to be wooed or placated. A sharp break between the object of faith and the natural world is a necessary prelude to technological change. The result of the lack of such a break can be seen in some nonwestern countries today, where the mere introduction of modern scientific equipment cannot effect changes so long as forests and streams, fields and rocks are experienced as the locus of deity.

The biblical doctrine of creation de-mythologizes the world

of nature. It subjects natural phenomena—sun, moon, stars—to a radical de-divinization. They are no longer to be seen as the objects of religious awe and reverence, but as creations of God placed in the world to serve God's purposes and therefore man's well-being. When we compare the Genesis version of creation with the Babylonian myths from which the motifs and figures were borrowed, it becomes even clearer that the Bible makes a distinctive contribution. The world of nature is de-divinized, made available to man for his projects and purposes.

2. *The Worth of Human Work in the Bible*. Aristotle believed that only the slaves should work. He taught that the really mature man, *ho spoudiaos,* should spend his hours in meditation. Work was a lesser activity, directed toward a lower end. Therefore, those who wished to engage in the highest kind of activity should shun work. Aristotle also believed that everything really significant had already appeared and been invented. Man's job involved only the classification and cataloguing of what already was. Invention and the fashioning of the new did not play any role in his world-view.

The Bible, quite to the contrary, viewed man as a being with responsibility for work and achievement in history. No disparaging distinction was possible between the "higher activity" of mental cerebration and the "lower" activity of toil with the hands. Such a distinction could grow only out of a basically dualistic view of man as essentially a spirit more or less imprisoned within a body. But such a dichotomous view is not possible for the Bible. Man was seen as a psychosomatic unity and no disparagement of the body, of work, or of earthly activities was possible.

The biblical view of work is important because it provides one of the key elements in the intellectual structure of modern technology. When science consists of mere speculation and deduction, as it did with most of the Greeks and with the early Renaissance scientists, "modern science" has not yet appeared. Only with the utilization of equipment, with measurement, observation, experiment and laboratory work do modern science and technology appear on the scene. Modern scientific technology is the result of a confluence of unsystematic "tinkering," on the one hand, and untested intellectual hypothesizing, on the other. So long as these two were kept separate by stations in life, by class structure, by separations of "will" and "intellect," no breakthrough to modern technical civilization was possible. But when this basically nonbiblical separation began to be healed toward the end of the Renaissance, when scientists began using equipment and technicians began utilizing scientific theory, the new age had come. An acceptance and respect for human work is an essential element of technology. Without the biblical vision, it might never have been possible.

3. *The Possibility of Changing Things.* Another prerequisite for technological society is that man must believe change is both possible and desirable. He must have some reason for changing things, for initiating projects, for using tools to accomplish some purpose. This desire for change seems natural enough for us, but it would in no way appeal to a man trapped within a fatalistic or cyclic view of history. Only when history is seen as the theater of human response, as the scene of God's call and man's responsibility, does it make sense to try to alter what has been.

A "closed universe" in which everything is already finished, simply waiting to be discovered by man, does not encourage technology. It may encourage speculation or even exploration, but the real animus of the scientific enterprise is an inventive and creative one, that is, to do something new.

In vivid contrast to the deities of the ancient Near East, whose existence was closely associated with the changing of the seasons, the revolution of astral bodies or the annual flooding of the great river, Yahweh disclosed himself in events of social change, principally the Exodus. While the nature gods were thus locked in a circle of cosmic recurrence, Yahweh did things that were utterly new and unprecedented. ("Behold, I am doing a new thing!") Thus an "open universe" was disclosed, one in which both God and man fashion new things, make innovations, change and alter existing practices.

But toward what end should man do these things? Again the Bible provided an important clue. Man was commissioned by God to name the animals and to tend the garden. Gerhard von Rad reminds us in his famous Genesis commentary that naming was for the Hebrews a kind of command, and that God himself had begun the creation by calling (that is, naming) the light "day" and the darkness "night." Thus, man and God are both involved in the naming and controlling which constitute the creative process. The creation is not finished once and for all, as it is with Aristotle. God does not "rest" until he has created man and enlisted him in the creating process. Thus, for the Bible, creation is "open-ended." It is not finished once and for all, but goes on wherever order is wrestled out of chaos. Man is made responsible for his world.

Naturally we must take the fall of man into consideration. Man is not only God's partner; he is also a rebel and betrayer. But, as Karl Barth has reminded us so clearly in his exegesis of Romans 5, the most basic thing about man is not his sin but his restoration. In Christ man *is* responsible and free; the old Adam has been defeated and displaced. The reality of our existence is our new being as the new Adam, commissioned to care for our brothers, share the world with our fellowman (here especially the woman), tend the garden of the universe and name its phenomena by drawing them into the web of human purpose.

This restoration of man to a position of responsibility for the world, an indispensable prerequisite for technology, is emphasized, as Gogarten has pointed out, in the Galatians figure of sonship replacing tutelage to a schoolmaster. It is again reinforced by the parables of Jesus in which the image of the master who leaves the estate in the care of stewards is constantly repeated. It is made abundantly clear that we are the stewards not only of money, but also of power and responsibility. Thus, the wicked steward who beats and mistreats the servant is judged as harshly as the one who buries his money rather than using it imaginatively.

These then are the basic theological motifs which lie behind and make possible the appearance of technology: man, placed in a natural world that is at his disposal, sensing the value of human work and charged with the responsibility of using the material universe to fashion artifices that will accomplish human purposes. Now let us go on to ask: What are the distorted views of technology that have crept into the theological conversation, some of them under the cloak of religious appeals?

RELIGIOUS DISTORTIONS OF TECHNOLOGY

There are many religiously tinged evaluations of technology abroad, most of them false and misleading. We shall touch here only on the three most frequent and most insidious ones: (1) romanticism, (2) utopianism, and (3) conservatism.

1. *Romanticism*. Where men have forgotten, or never adequately known the transcendent God who reveals himself in human events, a pagan reverence for nature may still obtain. It is a residual form of animism or nature worship, structurally comparable in some cases to the Baal worship which the children of Israel met when they arrived in Canaan.

The religious romantic is horrified to see nature used or altered by man. Though he is certainly right in questioning the thoughtless and arbitrary misutilization of nature, the decimation of forests, the pollution of rivers, the destruction of green areas, still he is wrong if he objects in principle to the drawing of nature into the orbit of human responsibility and control. The creation of the world is an expression of God's love for man; so the natural world exists, in a sense, *for* man. But it exists for him not to be bullied and bruised; it exists to be cultivated, enjoyed and shared. There is evidence in the New Testament that the natural world shares in the fall of man and that it too waits for the redemption. This means that nature, as such, is not a source of healing and salvation, but that it shares in both the weal and the woe of man. It means also that its redemption is not prior to man's but takes place only as man is redeemed. The redemption of nature, in short, takes place as nature shares in what God has done for man in Jesus Christ. Nature is redeemed when it becomes an instrument by which man expresses his love for his neighbor. Man loves his neighbor by taking responsibility with him for the shaping and guiding of history.

Biblical faith rejects romanticism as a distortion of the gospel. It therefore rejects any religio-romantic suspicion of technology with its arcadian longing for a more idyllic and elemental life.

2. *Utopianism*. At the opposite extreme is the opinion that through the application of scientific technology all the ills of man can be solved. The machine takes the place of Jesus Christ as the Savior of man. This mistaken notion sometimes takes the form of technocratism, the belief that if technically trained people could be put at the centers of decision making, all political problems would be solved. Such a view is based on a tragically naïve assumption that vastly underestimates the depth and complexity of the political and social issues confronting the modern world. Political decisions have to do with many imponderable factors that are still resistant to the application of the refined measurement demanded by the technological method. Since man is free, human behavior can never be totally predicted. Political leadership is more of an "art" than science, though certain elements of science can help. The political leader must develop the gifts of intuition and even of instinct; he must be able to weigh probabilities and come to a compromise solution in which neither side gets everything it asks for. All this must frequently take place within such a short span of time that the possibility of measuring all factors carefully must often be foregone. The idea of a technocracy is a false and dangerous utopian scheme, and it constitutes a heretical distortion of the Christian hope for the kingdom of God.

But this is not to say that technologists can make no contribution to the political process. They can and do. The valuable suggestions on monitoring and inspecting the testing of nuclear weapons made by American and Soviet scientists without a doubt made a contribution to the achievement of a test-ban treaty. But the point is that after the scientists and technologists had done their work, the political leaders still had to make a decision.

Technologists can both help and mislead political leaders as they forge national policies. One good illustration of both is the use of a "games theory" and computers in policy making. Using the data fed into them by analysts, automatic computers can weigh any number of factors and produce information on the probable result of a particular course of action. The difficulty and danger of this process, however, is the assumption that those who "feed" the machines are always a part of the data fed to them. The selection and weighing of factors finally determines what kinds of answers will be given by the computers. This does not mean that computers should not be used in helping decision makers, whether in agriculture, industry or anywhere else. Computers can be used to explore the *probable* results of the various policies the decision makers are considering. But the computers must not be allowed to *make* the decisions, and the frame of reference within which their thinking and "programing" goes on must always be subject to further criticism and revision. Otherwise the horrible possibility of an atomic disaster touched off by a mistaken bit of programing with an automatic computer moves out of the realm of science fiction and into the realm of possibility.

Technocratism is a kind of gnosticism. It implies that only those with a certain esoteric "know-how" are fit to rule. In democratic societies, however, all the people should share in the decision-making process to the extent that this is possible given the technical problems involved. Technologists have their role to play along with everyone else. They contribute part, indeed an essential part, to the process, but their role should not be determinative.

Technology does not in itself solve any problem. It merely gives to man the means of solving problems he has not been able to solve before; and at the same time it "increases the stakes." It makes it necessary, indeed inescapable, that man accept the maturity and responsibility entailed in tackling these problen.s. Nuclear energy is merely the most dramatic example of the promise and demand inherent in technology. Now man *can* do constructive and compassionate things for his fellowman that were never possible before; but at the same time man now *must* find ways to settle the differences between different societies without resorting to war since war can no longer result in anything but catastrophic destruction and could not in any sense of the word be "won" by either side.

We can be grateful to technology not only for the tools it has given us to do a better job in caring for the garden of the earth, feeding the hungry, clothing the naked and bringing the entire cosmos into the web of human purpose: we can also thank technology that it has presented us with the challenge to "put away childish things," to leave behind the petty nationalism, jealousy and saber rattling of an earlier period and to accept the fact that the whole world is now one neighborhood. I can now travel from New York to Paris in less time than it took my grandfather to travel from New York to Boston[1]—technology has made us neighbors. The question now is, will we *live* as neighbors?

3. *Conservatism.* Those who wish to see the status quo stay the way it is always oppose technology. They are consistent in doing so. Social change, the setting aside of old ways and the adoption of new ways, often comes on the heels of technological change. The so-called "underdeveloped areas" are the best examples of this fact today. But we all see this in our own countries no matter where we come from. When improved

---

[1] It is lamentable that despite the astonishing speed and availability of travel, many people cannot utilize them because of restrictions placed on travel by many governments based wholly on political or ideological considerations.

travel binds one nation to another, ideas travel along those roads and the social stagnation which comes from ignorance and isolation is challenged. New inventions threaten the power of those whose money and interest is invested in the existing ways of doing things. Thus, those who are dedicated to maintaining things the way they are will frequently find reasons to oppose technological change.

Unfortunately the church has often been on the side of those who were resisting social change rather than on the side of those who were leading it. Since the social basis for this change sometimes rested in new technological, industrial and scientific advances, the church has developed in many instances an antitechnological bias. But the gospel of Jesus Christ is too strong and too incisive to be enveloped forever in spurious religious arguments against science or technology. Galileo, Copernicus and Darwin were attacked by the church or its leaders. But in our time the balance may be righting itself. The call of the gospel is heard and obeyed by people deeply involved in producing social change and in designing the apparatus, equipment and techniques which make previous social arrangements no longer viable. Still a residue of antitechnological conservatism remains.

The chief religious weapon of conservatism is a doctrine of God which draws a straight line from God to the existing political or economic institutions of a society. God becomes the cosmic policeman, sanctifying the existing distribution of power. But the eschatological dimension is lost in this schema; hence, it must be questioned from a theological perspective. Jesus Christ comes as the one who calls us into a new life, into change and movement, into joyous responsibility for the future more than stubborn defense of the past or the present. Likewise the scientific imagination demands flights of fancy and disciplined phantasy. It requires a mentality in which one must envisage something which *is not yet,* something that might be or could be. This the conservative mentality cannot do; hence it is condemned to stagnation.

We conserve what is good in the world not by impounding or

"pickling" it but by constantly reappropriating it in the light of what today brings and tomorrow promises. The willingness to let go of what "worked" yesterday in order to find something that will work tomorrow is essential in our world today. It is at this point that Christian faith parts company with conservatism and casts its lot with the coming one.

We have rejected romanticism, utopianism and conservatism as valid Christian responses to technology. Now we must ask: What are the real problems and possibilities of a technical civilization and how do we address ourselves to them?

PROBLEMS AND POSSIBILITIES OF TECHNICAL CIVILIZATION

Four specific areas suggest themselves as those in which technology presents modern man with inescapable choices, in which God seems to be saying, "This day, I set before you life or death." The first is modern weaponry; second, food production; third, automation; and fourth, the mass media. We shall touch on each one very briefly, noting the peril and promise it carries with it.

1. *Modern Weaponry*. We have already mentioned nuclear weapons. We are thankful as Christians that a test-ban treaty has been accomplished, but we remain uneasy so long as stockpiles of hydrogen weapons and rocket delivery systems exist. We hope that the test-ban treaty represents only a first step toward the goal of complete disarmament.

But all the attention on nuclear weapons has sometimes distracted our attention from equally perilous developments in weaponry. What about biological and chemical weapons, the possibility of using disease germs, death rays and new types of gases? All these innovations dramatize the fact that effecting a cessation of nuclear weapons testing has in no sense solved the anguishing problem we face. Modern weaponry calls us to a level of maturity heretofore unknown in human history, one in which reason, patience, restraint and compromise must replace bellicosity. The dangers of what military thinkers call "escalation"—beginning with small weapons and moving to larger ones—is possible even in the smallest altercation between global powers. For this reason, provisional solutions to the political tensions and a general improvement in the climate of the international scene are forced on us by modern weaponry.

To choose immaturity and childish brashness in the days of the longbow, the machine gun or the flamethrower was dangerous, but not always self-destructive. Today it can be only catastrophic. This represents a wholly new stage in human history, and it has been brought about largely by technology.

2. *Modern Methods of Food Production*. Our times have witnessed startling discoveries in agronomy and in the scientific management of agriculture and food production. It is possible that the use of atomic radiation on seeds and soil, and the reconstruction of the genetic structure of food animals may produce unprecedented advances in food production in the very near future. Through technology man is about to harvest the teeming food supply of the sea and fashion nutritive substances out of formerly useless material. The construction of synthetic protein, for example, will be accomplished shortly.

But the *availability* of abundance in no way guarantees its distribution. Despite these uncanny technological advances, UNESCO reported last year that the number of starving and undernourished people had increased rather than diminished. The chasm that exists between the rich, highly industrialized nations and the poor, developing nations is widening rather than narrowing. The advances of modern medicine and the consequent decline in infant mortality has accelerated the world's population growth so that many nations, despite a rapid economic growth rate, can barely keep abreast of burgeoning baby statistics.

In short, technology challenges the rich nations to take responsibility, along with the poor nations, to fashion methods of *distribution* that are commensurate with the abundance available. The world has been compared to a cellar in which there are twenty men, and four of them have half the food. This situation is inherently unstable and explosive. It is even more disheartening to see that although some nations must take measures to limit the production of food so that farm prices may be secured, other nations are faced recurrently with famine conditions.

For the first time in human history it is now possible to abolish hunger. Never before was this within the realm of imagination, let alone a possibility. The reason hunger and want have not been abolished is not that the technology is lacking. It is available. The reason is that the economic and political systems of distribution we now have cannot do the job they are supposed to do. Once again, technology calls man to maturity. He could not be blamed for hungry children when the tools for feeding them were not yet invented. But now that these tools have been invented, he is without excuse. It is possible for him to bring clothing, food and housing to "the least of these my brethren," but he has not yet done so.

3. *Automation.* The newest technological breakthrough is the harnessing of electronic computers to automated production equipment, eliminating the need for all but the smallest human role in large segments of the productive process. There are now oil, chemical and even steel plants in which the work force has been reduced to one-tenth or one-twentieth of its previous size by this so-called "cybernation." Automation is the "second industrial revolution," and it comes before we had really adjusted to the first. It brings with it all sorts of new problems and opportunities. Some of them are as follows:

a. "Unskilled work" is disappearing, the kind usually done by uneducated or undereducated persons. Mining, for example, is becoming a technological specialty for university graduates, not a job for untrained workers. The need for a longer period of formal education and for the constant retraining of workers whose skills become obsolescent will become ever more pressing.

b. A shorter work-week, longer vacations and earlier retirement will very soon become the rule. The electrical repair workers of New York City already have a standard work week of thirty hours only. Now what will people do in this increasing leisure time? What will happen to ethics of assiduity and ambition that have become part of a way of life often associated with Christianity?

c. On the positive side, can we so interpret the gospel that it will enable people to live with joy and meaning in a world in which work plays a less and less central role? Aristole once said that until the harp could play itself societies would always need slaves. His statement was intended as a defense of slavery. However, we now have a society in which the harp *can* play itself, in which a new race of mechanical slaves may take over the toil and drudgery that has often darkened human life. Can we develop a Christian ethic of leisure?

d. We live in a world of nearly instantaneous communication. Through communications satellites it is now possible to watch events happening thousands of miles away. Through television with synchronized translations, Americans will soon be able to sit in on party congresses, and Europeans on congressional committees, all without leaving home. I shall watch the Bolshoi Ballet from my Boston living room. Already we share our films; and it is evident to anyone who has traveled widely in the world that young people of all nations often feel closely drawn together because of a shared familiarity with entertainment, sports and mass media events and personalities. Here again technology has broken down walls between peoples and enabled us to know each other better. What American, for example, who saw "Ballad of a Soldier" or "When the Cranes Are Flying" could avoid having a deeper understanding of the hopes and aspirations of the people of the U.S.S.R.? And millions have seen these films. We should not underestimate the film. It is the first art form produced by the technological era, and it has untold power to mold attitudes and shape opinions. Those who appreciate the film should remember that it is a characteristically modern, technological form of art, that it could not be enjoyed by pretechnological societies.

But how can we be sure that the mass media will be used to strengthen the forces of reason and restraint rather than to stoke the fires of hatred and contempt? How can we know that these new techniques will be used for beauty rather than ugliness, for truth rather than falsehood? Sadly enough, for every true and beautiful film, for every truthful newspaper article, for every balanced and reasonable radio program, we are subjected to many others that are misleading, distorted and propagandistic. Technology provides us with the means by which all men may know and understand each other better. But the same tools can be used to spread falsehood and misinformation.

Again the stakes are now higher. A malevolent newspaper in the nineteenth century could do some damage; today it can do much more damage. The demand for maturity is more pressing. The airways of the world, the ether through which the images of the mass media travel, belong to God. They are made available to us to use responsibly, to tend and care for, not to waste or misuse. Like the stewards of the vineyard in the parable, we should be utilizing these airways in a manner pleasing to the One whose real property they are, to build the basis for world understanding and human community. The TV camera, the communications satellite, the printing press—all these are just as much a part of God's created order as the animals and birds; and it is our task and responsibility to name them, to give them value and significance.

We have now mentioned weaponry, food production, automation and mass media as the areas in which the challenge of the power and peril of technology is most evident, in which the necessity to "put away childish things" is clearest. But all these technical advances tend merely to exacerbate problems we already had. Let us turn now to two main dangers technology brings with it, problems which we did not have, at least in this form, before technology. They are the impersonality of power and the appearance of a utilitarian spirit. These problems might be attributed to what has been called "the technological mentality."

PROBLEMS OF THE TECHNOLOGICAL MENTALITY

Technology not only transforms our exterior world. It also greatly modifies the way we think. Man thinks differently in the age of the supersonic plane than he did in the age of the horse and carriage. Technology has influenced our ways of organizing work, of structuring society, of fashioning goals. Two relatively new problems produced by technology are (1) the impersonality of power and (2) the utilitarian spirit.

1. *The Impersonality of Power.* Bureaucracy is the social expression of technology. Bureaucracy organizes people on the basis of rational, logical analysis. It sees them only for what they contribute to the goal for which the bureaucracy functions. Advancement tends to be given to those people who function smoothly within their niche, who enable the program to flow uninterruptedly. Just as the parts of a machine are expected to serve a particular, partial function, so the people in a bureaucracy tend to view their own relationship to the whole in a mechanical, segmented way. The danger of this technological logic is that responsibility tends to be diffused so that no one feels personally responsible for what is happening. There is no one to blame or praise. Everyone has had the unpleasant experience of being confronted with a bureaucracy, personified by a particular bureaucrat, in a situation in which the unique aspects of one's "case" seemed to be overlooked and one was treated as a cipher or a statistic. The problem of how one discovers where decisions are *really* made, where power is *actually* wielded, is a difficult one.

This diffusion of power results in an impersonality of decision which in turn leads to a drift toward inertia-in-motion. A bureaucracy seems to develop a "mind of its own" which drags along those who fill its niches and cancels out human freedom in a very disconcerting way. Acts of destruction on a terrible scale (one thinks of the "final solution" during the Third

Reich) become parceled out to thousands of people, each doing one tiny particle of the work, while the responsibility for the whole mechanism is obscured, or lost sight of. Thus Adolf Eichmann could claim that his job was simply "arranging train schedules."

How, in organized, bureaucratic society, does one regain the sense of personal involvement and individual responsibility that is indispensable if the giant structures of modern industrial societies are not to become "principalities and powers" that once again hold man in thrall? Here it is necessary to devise points of conversation and reflection, places and periods in which those involved in bureaucratic organization can become critically aware of the whole complex of which they are a small part, and recognize that what it is doing *is* their responsibility.

2. *The Utilitarian Logic.* The utilitarian logic is another cultural by-product of technology. It teaches people to ask of any person or thing, "What use is it?" Of course there is nothing wrong with subjecting things to this question. To be related to human purpose is, after all, what lends meaning and worth to the phenomena of history. However, the danger of the question of utility is that it is asked from within a narrow frame of reference. It tends to be asked by people who want to know what purpose this thing will serve within *my* purposes and goals.

It is a common failing of technologically trained people that they do not see the "usefulness" of, for example, art and humanistic studies. They tend to believe that any ideas or skills that cannot be applied rather directly to the productive enterprise are not useful and hence are worthless.

This judgment, however, is based on a narrowly provincial view of the meaning of human life. Man is involved in the productive process, but he has often other involvements that transcend this one. Man asks inevitably about the good and the true and the beautiful. He needs poetry and art to be fully human. He has a family and friends and he is part of a cultural heritage that includes music and literature by which his life can

K

be broadened and enriched. It is true that many humanistically oriented people also become stubbornly antitechnological and some even take pride in knowing nothing about modern science. This too is inexcusable; but so too is the antihumanistic bent of some technicians, who reduce the whole world to what fits or does not fit into the immediate technological enterprise. What is needed of course is a reconciliation of what the English writer C. P. Snow once called "the two cultures." The wall between them, like the wall between nations, races, and groups in the modern world, is one of the barriers the gospel of Jesus Christ abolishes. Consequently Christians should constantly be looking for ways to witness to the oneness of the world despite the emergence of two cultures. Just as Jesus Christ breaks down the barrier between Jews and Greeks, today he breaks down the barrier between technicians and humanists, and calls them both to a joyful celebration of what God has done for man and what man can do in response.

The impersonality of power and the utilitarian spirit are two of the distinctive problems of technological civilization. They are problems our grandfathers did not have to face, at least in the way we must face them. But they are not insurmountable problems. They can be solved, and the gospel of Jesus Christ both calls us to find answers to them and provides us with sources of strength and stamina to grapple with them intelligently.

CONCLUSION

Technology is not just a new tool kit with which to tackle old problems. It has utterly transfigured the world in which we live. It has changed our ways of living, of working, of thinking and imagining. It has placed before us in the most urgent way, problems we might not have had to deal with in the past. Many would prefer to return to the simpler, less formidable difficulties of the pretechnological era. But that is impossible. History is not reversible. It goes forward toward a fulfillment, and within the historical process we can discern, with the eyes of faith, the presence and power of the Living God. He no longer allows us to remain adolescent, tampering and trifling with human life. He now creates for us a civilization in which the only alternatives are maturity or death, responsibility or destruction. Perhaps those who long for the coziness of the nineteenth century or the medieval period are really refusing to grow up, are lingering too long in childhood, are unwilling to shoulder the terrible responsibilities which adulthood always thrusts upon us.

These are serious problems. How can we overcome provincialism in a shrunken world where neighbors whose views are different from ours can no longer be avoided? How do we decide, given the infinite possibilities of technology, what to make and what not to make, what to do first and what to postpone for later? How do we elaborate institutions by which the largest number of people possible can be drawn into the responsibility of making decisions affecting their own destiny? What are the appropriate goals of our shiny technological apparatus? Is it more important to reach the moon than to provide a minimum diet and decent housing for every child in the world?

The once terrifying forces of nature, the thunder clap and the lightning flash, no longer frighten modern man. He has tamed the wild panthers of the natural world and harnessed their energies for his own uses. But now man himself is the cause of terror. His machines and his machine-like organizations can do more damage, or bring more health, than all the thunder and lightning of the aeons put together. But we know that the God and father of Jesus Christ is not just the God of nature. He is also the Lord of history, the supreme sovereign of political and economic life. He is now de-mythologizing the structures of corporate human existence and bringing them under human control, just as he once conquered the natural forces. He continues to dethrone the principalities and powers, making them available to man as his captives, as instrumentalities for the building of human community. The God of Abraham, Isaac and Jacob, is also the Lord of technological man. He holds in his hand a future for this technological man far richer and more brilliant than anything we have yet imagined.

14

TECHNOLOGY AND MAN:
A CHRISTIAN VISION

W. Norris Clarke, S.J.*

M y particular task is to present in brief outline a basic Christian vision of the meaning and place of technology in the total life of man. I say *a* rather than *the* Christian vision, because outside of certain fundamental general principles there is no fixed and obligatory position on technology that all Christians —or even all Catholics—must hold in order to be good Christians. We are dealing here rather with a case of "applied theology," i.e., the creative application of the basic principles of Christian thought to a new concrete problem in the life of man outside of the immediately religious sphere. In such cases there are often several different attitudes it is possible to take toward the same problem, each inspired by some authentic

* W. Norris Clarke is Professor of Philosophy at Fordham University and Editor-in-Chief of the International Philosophical Quarterly. In addition to articles in both philosophical and theological journals, he has written extensively on the implications of technology and automation. We include here the major portion of a chapter he contributed to The Technological Order, edited by C. F. Stover. We omit from the footnotes several quotations in French. Reprinted from The Technological Order, pp. 38–47, 53–58, by permission of the Wayne State University Press. Copyright © 1963 by Wayne State University Press, Detroit, Michigan.

aspect of the total Christian message, hence each with a legitimate claim to be *an* authentic Christian attitude on the point in
question. There is far more pluralism of opinion in the Church,
especially on matters of applied theology like this, than is
generally realized by those outside of it.

In the present question there are two main perspectives
among Roman Catholic thinkers. One is predominantly pessi-
mistic, looking on technology primarily as a dehumanizing
force, radically if not incurably materialistic and secularist in its
roots and fruits, and calculated of its nature, unless severely
reined in, to corrupt the humanistic, spiritualist, and religious
development of future man. Some have even spoken of it as a
"demonic force," which, though not intrinsically evil in itself, is
such an apt instrument for the devil's purpose of turning man
away from his true spiritual destiny that it is in fact too
dangerous a power for sinful man to handle with safety.

Those who hold this view, at least among Catholics, are
found principally, it seems, among humanists of a literary and
artistic temperament who have never quite accepted modern
experimental science as a truly humane enterprise, due mainly
to its preoccupation with matter and the quantitative aspects of
the world. This group has been slowly dwindling in size, voice,
and influence, it seems to me, since the last war, though some of
its attitudes still command wide allegiance among sincere religious-minded people.[1]

---

[1] Cf., for example, E. Mounier's exposition of this attitude among
French Catholics especially and his vigorous answer: "The Case against
the Machine," in *Be Not Afraid* (London: Rockcliff, 1951); also G.
Bernanos, *La France contra les robots* (Paris,, 1938); N. Berdiaeff,
"L'homme dans la civilisation technique," in *Progrès technique et progrès
moral*, Rencontres internationales de Genève Neuchâtel: La Baconnière,
1947), esp. p. 84. Gabriel Marcel has also frequently linked technology
with depersonalization. See also D. von Hildebrand in *Technology and
Christian Culture*, ed. R. Mohan (Cath. Univ. of America Press, 1960).
For the whole problem of the place of science in a Christian humanism,
my own article might help, "Christian Humanism for Today," Special
Symposium on Christian Humanism in *Social Order*, 3 (1963), 269–88,

The second main perspective among Catholic thinkers places a much more positive value on technology as an element in the total development of man as an image of God. A steadily increasing weight of Catholic thought, it seems to me, has been swinging to this position, and it is undeniably in this direction that the teaching of the last three Popes has been tending. It is this view which I intend to present in this paper. Yet even within this general orientation there is a wide spectrum running from strong optimism to deep uncertainty and anxiety as to whether we actually will make use of technology for our fulfillment rather than our destruction, or at least whether we are moving in that direction at present.[2]

I might add one further word in clarification of the term "Christian." I do not restrict myself to the "Catholic" view because, although I am drawing chiefly on Catholic sources, the same general evaluation would seem to me in accord with the spirit of any Christian vision of man that is not professedly anti-humanistic or exclusively eschatological in its outlook. Furthermore, I would like to state very explicitly that most of the fundamental principles in this Christian vision can be subscribed to also by a religious-minded Jew or by anyone, in fact, who believes in a theistic humanism, that is, in the value of the self-development of man in this life as a means of fulfilling his destiny of ultimate union with God in another and immortal life.

---

and my debate with Fred. Wilhelmsen "End of the Modern World?" *America* 99 (April 19 and June 7, 1958), 108, 310; and "Christians Confront Technology," *America,* 101 (Sept. 26, 1959), 761.

[2] In addition to references in note 1, see J. Mouroux, *Meaning of Man* (New York: Sheed and Ward, 1948), and G. Thils, *Théologie des réalités terrestres* and *Théologie de l'histoire* (Bruges: Desclée de Brouwer, 1949) for general expositions of this point of view. The whole debate on the meaning and value of history, i.e., the theology of history, between incarnationalists and eschatologists, underlies this question. One of the best overall philosophical (only to a limited extent theological) discussions by a Christian is A. J. van Melsen's *Science and Technology* (Pittsburgh: Duquesne Univ. Press, 1961).

I. SUBORDINATION TO THE TOTAL
GOOD OF MAN

I shall now set myself to sketching the broad outlines of the view of technology identified above. The clearest way of doing this would undoubtedly be to move down from above, that is, from God and His plan for man and the universe down to technology as an element in this plan. But in fact I am going to follow the opposite path, that is, to advance in a series of ascending spirals beginning from what is closer to us, from what is more immediately determinable and more widely agreed upon about the relation of technology to man, then rising to the analysis of man as a hierarchy of spirit over matter, next to the theistic vision of the origin and meaning of human life, and finally up to the full Christian vision of man's present and ultimate destiny, a vision accessible only to those who believe in the Christian Revelation given by God to His Church. The purpose of following this ascending path is that, in an audience like this, including as it does persons of all shades of religion or lack of it, I may be able to keep as many of you with me on the ascent for as long a time as your own principles can stand it. Thus our area of agreement can be the largest possible.

The first and very general principle is one which should be fundamental in any serious reflection on man and technology. It is that technology, being a partial activity of man, can be properly evaluated only if it is set in the context of the total reality and good of man and not judged as a self-sufficient whole exclusively in terms of its own inner laws and dynamism. The same is true of any partial human activity, such as, for example, athletics, or recreation, or business, etc. Thus it would be a dangerous distortion of perspective to say that whatever is good for the advance of athletics is good for man, just as it would be to say that whatever is good for General Motors is good for the country. The overall balanced fulfillment of man must always be the center of focus and all particular activities and functions, whether of individuals or of social groups, subordinated to this primary goal.

This principle may seem, perhaps, so elementary that it should be taken for granted. It is, indeed, elementary, and I feel reasonably sure that no one here would be in doubt about it. Yet it would be a great mistake to believe that in proportion as a basic truth is basic and elementary so much the more widely is it realized and practiced. It is the great simple truths that are often the first ones forgotten in the hectic demands of immediate living governed by short range vision. It is thus all too easy for those immediately engaged in the exciting work of technology itself so to narrow their horizons that the mere glimpse of the possibility of some new technical advance can immediately trigger the decision to introduce it into the living organism of human society without any inhibiting second thought about its overall repercussions on the social body as a whole. Hence a first essential principle for the wise use of technology in any culture is the conviction that it cannot (without profoundly disruptive effects) be made an end in itself, allowed to develop and be applied, throttle wide open, with no other guiding principle than the unfolding of its own intrinsic potentialities at the fastest possible tempo. This conviction must be firmly held and acted on by the leaders of our society, from the government down, and impressed by appropriate control from above, if necessary, on the decision-makers within technology itself, if they are not able or willing to see its necessity under their own initiative. As a matter of fact, many of the latter already do see it quite as clearly as anyone else. This vision may not always be equally shared, however, on the lower echelons of technological planning and execution.[3]

---

[3] Cf. Guido de Ruggiero, "La fin et les moyens," in *Progrès technique et progrès moral,* cited in n. 1; and Van Melsen, *Science and Technology,* Ch. 13, sect. 31: "The Technological Order as a Culture of Means." See also the very strong remarks of George Kennan at the *Colloques de Rheinfelden,* last section on "La société industrielle et la bonne vie," on the need of strict control by governments of new exploitations of technology.

II. SUBORDINATION OF BODY TO SPIRIT

This general regulative principle laid down, let us now see how it is to be filled out with more definite content. The first level of analysis establishes a hierarchy or graded order of activities and powers in man. The basic principle of ordering is the superiority of the spiritual dimension in man over the material, and the corresponding prerogative and obligation of the spirit to dominate its corporeal substratum so that the latter becomes the prompt, docile, and efficacious instrument of the higher life of the spirit in man. We might add here in parenthesis that it is still possible to go along with many of the elements in this analysis of the nature of man even if one does not understand or accept the technical philosophical interpretation of the human soul as strictly spiritual or immaterial, i.e., on a level radically different in kind from the material order. The minimum essential is to recognize that the intellectual and moral level of life in man (including freedom, love, art and all their corresponding values) is his highest and most specifically human level of activity, to which all lower psychic as well as biological activities should be subordinated according to a natural hierarchy of values and goals.

According to this analysis of man, the fundamental role of the whole material universe is to serve as a theater and instrument for the gradual evolution of man, both individual and race, to full self-consciousness, self-mastery, self-development, and self-expression of his free, conscious spirit in and through matter. Accordingly, the role of technology is twofold. Its first aim is *liberation* of man from servitude to matter. That is to say, its role is to free man's energies more and more from their primitive state of almost total absorption in sheer brute physical labor as an essential condition for physical survival. By inventing more and more effective techniques for getting nature to work for him instead of against him, man frees himself progressively from absorption in fulfilling his elementary animal needs, in fact from exhausting physical labor in achieving any of his goals, lower or higher. The energy thus liberated can be diverted upwards into his various higher and more characteristically human levels of activity, i.e., more and more penetrated by spirit. The fundamental principle of technology at work here is that in proportion as any activity of man depends more predominantly on sheer physical effort, especially of a routine repetitive kind, so much the more apt is it to be handled by machines, releasing the person himself for other activities requiring skills of a more intellectual and creative order. Thus technology is an indispensable instrument in man's progressive self-realization of his nature and dignity as a man, that is, as superior to all the lower levels of non-rational material beings.[4]

The second function of technology looks in the opposite direction from the first. The first was to liberate or elevate man above servitude to matter. The second looks back again toward matter. It becomes the instrument whereby the liberated spirit of man can turn again toward the material world and dominate it in a new active way, making it a medium for the spirit's creative *self-expression* and *self-realization*.

This involves a distinctively new attitude of man toward nature. The latter now appears no longer as it did to ancient man, as a great sacrosanct force, moving along its own age-old immutable course inviolable by man, who merely lives off its natural or cultivated by-products. It appears rather as a great plastic network of forces open to its very depths to the creative molding power of the human mind and will, and inviting by its very malleability the recreative touch of man.[5]

This profound shift in attitude towards nature opens up a new and almost limitless perspective in man's relation to the cosmos in which he lives. Man's relation to material nature now appears as a dynamically evolving dialogue between himself and

[4] See the strong and unequivocal statement of this principle by Eric Voegelin in the *Colloques de Rheinfelden* on technology and man (Paris: Collman-Levy, 1960), p. 60.

[5] Cf. Van Melsen, *Science and Technology,* ch. 9: "Changes in the Conception of Nature and World View."

matter, in the course of which he first discovers his own self as superior to, and hence destined to become master of, nature, and then learns to use it more and more efficaciously as the medium for his own creative self-expression.

One important philosophical as well as psychological by-product of this new attitude to the world of nature is a new understanding of the relation between matter and spirit. In the traditional spiritualist vision of man, at least in the West,[6] the tendency was all too frequently to look on matter primarily as the negation, the opposite of spirit, weighing it down, imprisoning it. The most effective remedy was to turn away from matter towards a world of pure uncontaminated spirit. Now matter appears rather as a kind of complement or correlative to spirit, not radically opposed to it and closed to it, but mysteriously open and apt, if properly handled, to receive the impression of spirit and to serve as medium for the spirit's own self-expression and self-development. The Thomistic doctrine of the natural union of soul and body, not as a punishment but for the good of the soul, and of the soul as the natural "form" or informing principle of the body, here takes on a depth and richness of meaning which might have startled, as it would also have delighted, I am sure, even St. Thomas Aquinas himself. For now the whole material universe becomes, as it were, an extension of man's own body, and thus becomes informed by his soul in an indirect and instrumental way.[7]

The fundamental moral principle relevant here is that man's newfound power over matter should be used according to the proper order of values, that is, for the expression and fulfillment of his higher and more spiritual capacities, and not merely for his greater material and sensual self-indulgence and catering to the body. It would be a monstrous perversion indeed of the

[6] I understand that in certain of the traditional Indian views of man matter is also looked upon as profoundly open and receptive to spirit, rather than as opposed to it, though the notion of self-realization or self-expression *through* matter still does not seem to me to have been given the strong value I am giving it here.

[7] Van Melsen, *Science and Technology*, p. 257.

whole meaning of man's liberation from matter by technology if, once liberated, he now freely and deliberately enslaved himself to it again in a new servitude more debasing than the original indeliberate subservience forced upon him from without.

III. MAN THE IMAGE OF GOD

Let us now mount one rung higher in our ascending spiral. The previous level established the order of subordination between matter and spirit and therefore oriented the aim of technology upwards as an instrument for the life of spirit. But it left undetermined just what was the deeper significance and ultimate goal of man's self-development through the mighty power of technology which he has now made his servant.

Here the theistic vision of man and the universe opens up new horizons. Man's own origin and destiny now emerge not as a mere accident of landing on top of the heap of the world of matter by some lucky turn of the blind wheel of chance. They are the result rather of God's own creative activity, first bringing into being the material universe as a matrix and instrument for the development of the spirit of man, and then infusing each human soul into this evolving system at its appropriate time and place.

The fundamental perspective here is of man created, as the Book of Genesis puts it, "to the image and likeness of God," with a divinely given destiny to unfold and develop this image to the fullest possible extent in this life, in order to be united in eternal beatific union with Him in the next.

Man's self-development and self-expression through matter, with technology as his instrument, now appear not just as the satisfaction of some egotistic drive for power and self-affirmation, but as the fulfilling of a much higher and more sacred vocation, the God-given vocation to authentic self-realization as the image of God his Creator. The material world which is to be the object of man's technological domination is now seen not as some hostile or indifferent power that man has tamed by his own prowess and can exploit ruthlessly at his own will with no further responsibility save to himself. It is rather both a loving gift and a sacred trust to be used well as its Giver intended, with a sense of responsibility and stewardship to be accounted for.

The notion of a dynamic image of God to be developed lends here a much deeper significance and dignity to man's cultivation both of science and technology. For man to imitate God, his Creator and—in the full Christian perspective—his Father, he must act like his Father, do what He is doing so far as he can. Now God is at once contemplative and active. He has not only thought up the material universe, with all its intricate network of laws, but He has actively brought it into existence and supports and guides its vast pulsating network of forces. God is both a thinker and a worker, so to speak. So too man should imitate God his Father by both thinking and working in the world. By understanding the nature and laws of action of the cosmos and himself in it he is rethinking, rediscovering the creative plan of the universe first thought up by God Himself.[8] But this contemplative outlook alone would not be enough if he wishes to reflect the full image of God. He must also try his hand as a worker, not to create some totally new world out of nothing, which only God can do, but to recreate the world that has been given him, malleable and plastic under his fingers, to be transformed by his own initiative and artistic inventiveness, so that it will express in a new way both the divine image of its Creator and the human image of its recreator.[9]

I think it should be evident enough that this notion of man as

[8] One might recall the words of the astronomer Kepler as he began to understand the workings of the planets: "I am thinking God's thoughts after him."

[9] Cf. J.-L. Kahn, "La valeur culturelle de la technique," in *La Technique et l'homme*, p. 85 ff. In addition to the references in note 10, esp. the last one, see Mouroux, *Meaning of Man*, p. 28: "God has confided it [the earth] to his care that he may put his stamp upon it, give it a human face and figure, integrate it with his own life and so fulfill it." Also see the fine book of a Protestant scientist, C. A. Coulson, *Science, Technology and the Christian* (New York: Abingdon, 1960), ch. 3, 5.

dynamic image of God, with the vocation to develop this image by an evolving dialogue with the material cosmos, sets technology in a wider framework which provides strong religious, moral, and humanistic controls on its exploitation. Judaism, together with most theistic thought in the West not dominated by the Platonic tradition, can go along, it seems to me, with most of what I have said so far. As for the East, I understand that even certain recent Hindu currents of thought are departing from their more traditional outlook of complete otherworldliness and renouncement of matter to allow a more positive role in human development to an evolving material cosmos, and hence to man's mastery of it by technology.

IV. THE CHRISTIAN DIMENSION: SIN AND REDEMPTION

Let us advance now to the last and (to a Christian, at least) highest rung of our ascending spiral, the specifically Christian perspective. This adds on, first, the notion of a primordial sinfulness of the human race, or Fall of man, and secondly, redemption from this state of alienation from God by the incarnation, death, and resurrection of the Son of God, the Second Person of the Blessed Trinity, become man.

The first of these two factors is the state of sinfulness of man stemming from a primordial aberration of the race from God, called Original Sin, and compounded further by the individual sinfulness of each human being down the ages. As a result there is a fundamental duality or ambivalence in man's will. Instead of being drawn spontaneously toward God and his authentic good in a properly ordered manner, man tends also spontaneously toward self-centered egotism, sensuality, self-indulgence, lust for power, wealth, pride, and self-aggrandizement. In fact, unless enlightened and strengthened by divine grace, man tends more immediately and spontaneously to satisfy his lower, more material, and more selfish desires than his higher, more spiritual, and more altruistic or self-transcending desires.

Thus technology must now be set in the framework of a radical ambivalence in man toward both good and evil at once, with the resulting very real possibility of grave misuse of this powerful instrument, itself morally neutral and capable of being put to either good or evil use. The danger is especially great in the case of technology, since by its fundamental orientation toward matter it puts in man's hands the power to gratify almost without limit his material and sensual appetites, if he wishes to turn technology primarily toward these ends. There is also the fact that technology has a peculiar power to absorb the attention of those engaged in it, by virtue of its exciting challenge and spectacularly visible results, whereas the fruits of the spiritual activities of man are less immediate, tangible, and easy to assess.[10]

Hence the alert Christian, alive to the full implications of the Christian vision of man, will look on technology with a restrained and carefully qualified optimism, seeing it as at once a great potential good for man by nature and yet in the hands of fallen and selfish human nature an almost equally potent instrument for evil. He will have none of the naïve starry-eyed optimism of those who believe that man if left to himself is really a sweet, innocent, woolly white little creature who will be good as gold except for an occasional rare excursion into naughtiness, or of the *a priori* optimism of those who believe in the religion of automatic constant forward progress, that things are necessarily getting better and better all the time and that any progress in any field at any time is automatically good and for the benefit of man.

The second element in the Christian vision is the redemption through the Son of God made man. This brings along with it several new implications or more strongly highlights implications already present in Hebraic theism. One is the intrinsic

[10] Cf. Coulson, *op. cit.* (n. 9), p. 60: "This is probably the gravest danger in all our considerations of technology and the machine—that we get so busy with it that we forget the spiritual background without which all our expertise will become positively harmful."

goodness and dignity of matter itself, which has been sanctified and elevated by the descent into it of God Himself and His assumption of it into personal union with Himself by means of a human body formed from the basic stuff of the material universe just like any other man's. Here we see the God-man Himself using matter as an efficacious instrument or medium both for expressing His own divinity to man in a privileged, we might say, guaranteed, human image, and also for channeling the salvific effects of His divine grace to men through the seven sacraments, each a synthesis of a visible material sign informed by an efficacious spiritual power. In other words, the Incarnation and Redemption through the God-man gives Christians the perfect archetype and model of the openness of matter to spirit we spoke of earlier and its intrinsic aptness to serve as the medium of the spirit's self-expression and creative power. This is, as it were, a confirmation from above, by God's own example, of what man could already have discovered, at least in theory, by reflection on his own nature and the experience of working with matter, even though historically the lesson had not yet at that time become clear to him. Thus the labor of the young Jesus as a carpenter in Nazareth already lends in principle a divine sanction to the whole technological activity of man through history. And the doctrine of the ultimate resurrection of all human bodies in a new, more "spiritualized" mode of existence, i.e., totally open and docile to the workings of spirit within it, delivers a final *coup de grâce* to the "angelism" of the Platonic and Manichean traditions by presaging the final "deliverance from bondage" and transformation by spirit of the material cosmos itself, mysteriously hinted at by St. Peter when he speaks of "a new heaven and a new earth" to come (II Pet. 3:13; cf. Apoc. 21:1).

There is another and equally important facet, however, to the doctrine of the redemption that acts as a foil to the above highly positive and optimistic perspective. This is the doctrine of redemption through suffering, self-denial, and detachment from this world, symbolized by the death of the Redeemer on the

L

Cross as a sacrifice of atonement to His Father for the sins of men. Thus "No man can be my disciple," in the words of Christ, "unless he deny himself, take up his cross, and follow me." (Mt. 16:24.)

Now this central doctrine of life through death, self-fulfillment through self-denial, paradoxical as it may seem, does not by any means cancel out the strongly positive evaluation of technology outlined above, i.e., as an instrument for the self-expression and self-development of man's spirit. For the aim of authentic Christian self-denial, especially of the body, is not simply to repress or crush out the life of the body as something evil in itself or intrinsically alien and hostile to the soul (as the Platonic tradition tended to do). It is rather to discipline and curb its primitive tendencies to rebellion and insubordination against spirit, to blind irrational absorption in immediate satisfaction of its own appetites, either in conflict with, or indifferent to, the higher goals and values of the spirit. In a word, it is precisely to establish in man the proper docility of matter to spirit and, at a deeper level, the dominance of unselfish outgoing love over self-centered egotism.

But as we saw earlier, technology itself, if properly controlled and oriented, should have as its primary objective precisely this same liberation and unfolding of the life of spirit. Hence the spirit of Christian mortification can actually operate as a powerful controlling factor for directing the use of our technological power along the proper lines for the authentic enrichment of man on the highest levels of his human capacities, instead of allowing it to be diverted toward the mere gratification of man's inferior appetites and desires and thus enslave him further to matter rather than liberate and elevate him above it. One might well say, in fact, that only men with something like the Christian virtue of self-denial, whether applied to sensuality or to egotism, would really be safe enough to entrust with the responsibility of deciding in which directions to follow up the almost limitless potentialities made available to us by technology. The wider the range of possibilities open to a man's free choice, as we all know, the greater his need for self-discipline and selectivity, lest he destroy himself.[11]

Nonetheless, there is no doubt that this aspect of Christianity, this spirit of the Cross, cannot help but exercise a powerful moderating effect, not only on the orientation of technology towards serving the life of spirit, but also on too eager and exclusive an absorption of one's energies in the enterprise of technology. If the primary goals of man are held to be spiritual rather than the mastery of matter, then the pursuit of technology will naturally take its place as *one* legitimate and necessary activity of man in an integrated hierarchy of human activities, all subordinated to the total good and ultimate destiny of man.

It seems hardly necessary to point out that, in this perspective of Christ as a divine-human mediator between man and God, the basic theistic notion of man as unfolding image of God on earth receives an immense deepening, elevation, and more efficacious implementation. The goal of natural self-realization as spirit in matter now becomes that of supernatural self-transformation through union with the God-man as adopted sons of God, destined to share ultimately in the infinite richness of the divine life itself.

.   .   .   .   .   .

We might now sum up as follows the general message of the contemporary teaching of the Church on technology, as reflected especially in recent papal documents.

1. It expresses a firm approval in principle of the technological enterprise of modern man. It evaluates it as an activity rooted in the very nature of man as a spirit-matter composite and as a necessary instrument for the adequate fulfillment of his

---

[11] In addition to most of the above references, see E. Mascall, *The Importance of Being Human* (New York: Columbia Univ. Press, 1958), p. 101: "It is only in so far as man's natural powers are taken up into the supernatural order that the venom which has infected them can be drawn from them and that they can become fully instrumental to the true welfare of the human race."

vocation of self-development and self-expression in and through the material universe.

2. It affirms equally, however, that technology by its nature is ordered to be an instrument towards a higher end of full personal and spiritual development, not a self-justifying end in itself. Hence its execution in practice should be clearly kept subordinate to its higher aim. It should be treated as an instrument, not as an end in itself, as a servant, not an idol.

3. Because of the moral weakness of man and his strong propensity toward indulging his lower nature and self-centered egotism at the expense of his higher goals and faculties, the cultivation of technology for its own immediate rewards as ends in themselves presents a strong temptation for modern man, perhaps the central temptation for human society in the present and coming chapters of human history. Clear-cut realization of the hierarchy of human values and firm moral self-discipline, both on the part of individuals and of social groups at all levels, are therefore essential if man is to handle safely the powerful but ambiguous instrument of technology. To train the young properly for wielding this responsibility should be one of the primary aims of moral, religious, and humanistic education today, and should be explicitly recognized as such by the teaching community itself. It is not clear, we might add, that this awareness is at all sufficiently recognized and widespread as yet.

4. Even when the development of technology is carried out in the proper spirit and intention, it tends, like all human activities, to produce its own dangerous side-effects. These fall principally under the head of depersonalizing and dehumanizing effects on the individuals engaged in the enterprise or those affected by it, such as the families of workers, etc. They arise from various tendencies, such as subordination of human life excessively to the rhythms and needs of a machine economy, suppression of human freedom and initiative by social regimentation or submergence in the organization for its own sake, etc. Hence constant vigilance over the system in practice must be

exercised by responsible business, political, moral, religious, and educational leaders. In other words, to use the language of cybernation, there must be built into the system what we might call humanistic and moral self-regulating devices or feedback controls. Perhaps one peculiarly apt organ for such a function would be foundations specially oriented in this direction. The brochure on *Cybernation* by Donald Michael recently put out by the Center for the Study of Democratic Institutions is itself a significant contribution along these lines.

In the light of the latter, plus my own reflections and those of many others, I think it is worth adding to the previous sketch of the dangers accompanying technological progress the following. In accordance with the general principles we have laid down, technological progress will be in order and beneficent only if it develops always in subordination to, and at the service of, the general common good of the nation or culture using it. But one of the most vexing problems of our civilization as it is evolving today is that we are far more skillful at technological advance than at solving the social, economic, and human problems it raises. Thus our ability to control and order material nature races ahead, whereas our ability to order and control social, economic, and cultural and moral forces, i.e., human nature, is fumbling, uncertain, and lagging far behind. Hence there is grave danger that if the tempo of technological change is allowed to go on accelerating as fast as its own internal rhythm will permit, it can create an atmosphere of constant rapid flux that can be seriously disruptive of the psychological and social stability of a culture. Where external cultural landmarks disappear too rapidly, the effect can be demoralizing and disorienting to all save strongly principled and "inner-directed" people.[12]

How to handle this gap between the different rhythms of technological as compared with cultural development is a difficult challenge to meet. It will need the concerted theoretical and

---

[12] Cf. Coulson, *Science, Technology and the Christian,* last chapter, and Thomas O'Dea, "Technology and Social Change: East and West," *Western Humanities Rev.* 13 (1959), pp. 151–62.

practical wisdom of many thinkers and specialists. I have no easy solutions to offer, myself, only the urgent call to awareness and reflection. One thing, however, is clear to me. In a world of ever more rapidly changing external environment, where deliberately stimulated change is part of the very "biological rhythm" of modern industrial society, it is essential to educate the young more consciously than ever before in the basic human skill of how to remain psychologically and morally stable in a world of external flux. Otherwise a restless, shallow, rootless, and anxious people will be incapable of making any truly fruitful use of the ever increasing cornucopia of means poured out by our technological genius. Like the overspecialized dinosaurs of prehistory, we may suddenly find ourselves ripe for extinction. Or like so many civilizations in history, we may decay from within, like rotten fruit, and be swept into the dustbin of history.

The essential principle of education involved here, it seems to me, is a shift of emphasis from means to ends, from teaching customs or *ways* of doing things—so quickly obsolete or irrelevant today—to teaching basic values or *goals* to be aimed at steadily through the flux of changing ways and means. For it is the unique property of ends or goals, as any good philosopher can tell you, to unify and confer intelligibility on action and motion. A single stable goal can give fixed sense and meaning to a vast interweaving flux of otherwise chaotic actions. The stability of goal-oriented action derives from its single direction and point of arrival, not from its particular *path* of getting there. It is the stability of the compass for the ship, rather than that of the railroad track for the train, that must be the ideal of education for the future.

In conclusion, the phenomenon of modern technology, of man's sudden coming into his natural inheritance as master of material nature, poses a staggering challenge to our whole race as we scan the horizons ahead. The stakes are higher than they have ever been in human history before. And the risks are proportionately great. But the passage to maturity is always a risk, a striking out into the unknown, whether for an individual, a society, or the race as a whole. In the light of the Christian vision of man there should be no hesitation either that we should be willing to rise with courage and hope to the challenge, rather than turn back in fear, or that we can meet it success-fully, with the humbly implored aid of the Master of History. For it is God Himself, our Father, who is calling us on, through the pull of our own unfolding powers, to assume the full stature of our vocation to become sons of God and images of the Creator in this world, and hence to become wise masters of the material universe that God has given us in stewardship as the theater and instrument of our own self-discovery and self-development.

But the condition of any durable long-range success—possibly even of short-range survival—is that man recognize at least the general lines of his authentic nature and destiny. We can bear the responsibility, with God's help, of trying to be sons of God and stewards under Him of the cosmos that He planned and made for us. We cannot bear the burden of trying to be lonely gods of a purposeless universe we did not make, with no other place to go, and no strength or wisdom but our own to rely upon.[13]

---

[13] H. de Lubac, S.J. *The Discovery of God* (New York: Kenedy, 1960), p. 179.

MINDS AND MACHINES

John Habgood*

I want you to meet Horace," said the engineer, "there is virtually no difference between him and a human being."

I looked at Horace, a formidable array of panels and
switches stretching the whole length of the room. Outwardly it
was only too obvious that Horace was not a human being and,
however complex the maze of wires and cells behind those
panels, I could not believe that it could even begin to behave
like one. I knew, of course, that Horace could play chess or
compose a tune; computers had been able to do that sort of
thing even back in the early 1960's. But there are many types of
human behaviour which we label "mechanical" anyway, and I
remember how early machine-made music had been dismissed
with just that adjective; it was hack stuff, hardly worthy to be
called music at all. I put some of my doubts into words.

"Horace can do much better than that," came the reply.

* John Habgood was awarded his doctorate for research in physiology,
and taught pharmacology at Cambridge until he resigned in 1952 to
study theology. From 1956 to 1962 he was vice-principal of Westcott
House, Cambridge; currently he is Rector of Jedburgh. He contributed
a chapter on science and religion to Soundings (1962), edited by Alec
Vidler. The selection here is Chapter 12 from his own book, Truths in
Tension. Copyright © 1964 by John Habgood and reprinted by permission of Holt, Rinehart and Winston, Inc.

"Modern computers go through a long process of programming. We feed them on the best music and literature, in much the same way as you educate a child. And then with their built-in randomisers we find them throwing up genuinely new ideas, which their programming enables them to recognise and select. I doubt whether a critic nowadays could tell the difference between the music Horace produces and the stuff churned out by living composers."

"Very interesting," I said. "You mean to say that Horace can make real decisions about what is good or bad musically?"

"No difficulty about that," said the engineer. "It's all a question of learning from experience, and a machine can do that as well as a human—in fact better, because it has a far more reliable memory."

"But surely it doesn't understand what it's doing?"

"It depends on what you mean by understanding. If you mean the ability to relate the things you have learnt to other things, then Horace can do that as well as you can."

I was getting desperate by this time, and I gave one of the panels in front of me a kick. "Well, anyway it's got no feelings."

"Not that sort of feeling, certainly," went on the engineer in his maddeningly superior way, "but the funny thing is that the other day we asked him to make a very difficult decision, and lots of contradictory answers came out, almost as if he was agitated and couldn't make up his mind. Whereas other sorts of work he just laps up."

A little green light gleamed balefully, and I was almost certain Horace winked. I began to wish it would lap up the engineer. He was still talking.

"Horace has quite a personality, you know. The other day he said to me 'Anything you can do, I can do better,' but that was only pride." The green light glowed even brighter, and for the first time the engineer noticed it. "I am sorry, sir," he added quickly to Horace, "I was only joking."

And then I realised for the first time who was master.

.   .   .   .

Was that a fantasy, or a real glimpse of the future? There seems little doubt that in principle Horace's claim "anything you can do I can do better" has a good deal of truth in it. Already computers are able to make calculations and predictions which are far too difficult or laborious for human mathematicians. Machines which could mimic the whole vast range of human activity would have to be so inconceivably complex and costly that they may never be built; but many engineers believe that in principle there is no reason why they should not. They believe that the human brain works in essentially the same way as a computer; and therefore it can have no fundamental properties which cannot be reduced to the terms of electrical engineering.

For some Christians these claims have seemed as alarming as the claims made about the physico-chemical basis of life. But I believe their fears are unnecessary. Just as the living cell is undoubtedly a highly complex chemical system in which it is foolish to look for some extra "vital principle," so the human brain seems to behave very much like a highly complex computer; and as long as we are considering its performance as an analyser, calculator, predictor or decision maker, there is no need to look any further for some extra "mental factor." In the study of brain function the most useful terms, at the moment, are those drawn from this particular branch of engineering.

But the study of brain function is not the same as the study of the mind, just as the study of life processes is not the same as the experience of being alive. The words "brain" and "mind" are not simply interchangeable, though I know one physiologist who thought he was making a useful contribution to knowledge by using the word "brain" where anyone else would have used "mind"; in fact he was simply spreading confusion. No doubt, what is going on in our brain is directly related to what is going on in our mind, and vice versa; but we know about them in quite different ways, one from the outside and the other from the inside. Both types of knowing give us a partial picture of the whole, but they must not be confused. We talk about "thought" and "consciousness" because we think and are conscious; the words describe part of our direct experience. We talk about "electrical changes in nervous tissue" because we have learnt to interpret, say, the patterns on an oscillograph screen, in a certain way; the words are part of our interpreted sense experience. We must not simply transfer words used to describe one kind of experience to contexts where we are discussing the other kind, without being very careful about what we are doing; otherwise we might find ourselves talking about monstrosities like "thoughts three feet square" or "cheerful electrons."

The confusions which people actually fall into, of course, are much more subtle than these. Some words are particularly tempting because they are so easy to transfer; for example, words like "predict" and "analyse." We know what it is to predict, by predicting. We can also arrive at a fairly objective definition of prediction, say, in mechanical terms; and for most purposes we can ignore the different origins of the two uses.

Now along comes an electrical engineer who builds a predicting machine and compares its performance with ours. We admit that it predicts. And similarly with analysis, calculation, decision making, etc. The engineer then builds a machine which can do all these things, and plays his trump card. "What is thinking but a combination of prediction, analysis, calculation, decision making, etc.? Aren't you forced to admit that my machine can think?"

Our instinctive reaction is probably to feel that the question is absurd, and I believe that that reaction is right. But many people fail to see how the trick has been played. By breaking down the notion of "thought" into a large number of components, and each time glossing over the difference between, say, prediction as experienced and prediction as described in a machine, it is eventually possible to arrive at a description of "thinking" which leaves out the subjective element altogether. We *seem* to be asking a queer question about the inner life of a computer, whereas the engineer is in fact answering a different question about the number of different kinds of operation which the computer can perform.

Yet it is not simply a confusion of terms which underlies questions like "Do machines think?" or "Are computers conscious?" Granted that there is a big difference between our inner and outer experience, between what we know as true within ourselves, and what we investigate in the world around us, the fact is that we do not use this language of inner experience only about ourselves. We use it of other people. We say not only "I think" but "John and Mary think." So why shouldn't we say "Horace the computer thinks"?

This brings us to the edge of one of the stickiest problems of philosophy. How do we know that other people think and feel as we do? To avoid turning this chapter into a long philosophical discourse I am simply going to expound what I believe to be the most convincing answer to the problem, without arguing it in any detail. It is a fairly common answer nowadays, so perhaps argument is not necessary anyway.

We know that other people think, partly by deducing it from their behaviour. When we ask an attendant in Madame Tussaud's to show us the exit, and receive only a waxy stare in reply, a very simple deduction shows us our mistake. In much the same way in fairy stories the prince was sometimes able to deduce, by studying behaviour, that a particularly loathsome-looking frog was in fact a princess going through an awkward spell. In both cases behaviour gives the clue to what, if anything, is going on inside.

But this is only part of the answer. In particular cases, when we feel we may have been deceived or mistaken, we go through a process of deduction. This is not what happens, though, in our general relationships with other people. We do not first become aware of our own experience of thinking, and then by observing our behaviour and comparing it with that of others, go on to deduce that they think as we do. I believe it is much nearer the truth to say that our knowledge of ourselves is completely bound up with our knowledge of others. We grow up and become what we are in relationship with other people; without that relationship we should not become human beings at all. When, as has sometimes happened, children have been brought up by wolves, completely cut off from human society, they seem to be lacking in any sort of human self-awareness. It is human society which makes us human; and human society presupposes a recognition of one another as basically alike.

The important word in that last sentence is "presupposes." In talking about our knowledge of other people through our general relationships with them, I am not talking about some mysterious sixth sense which enables us to know what is going on in their minds. I am talking about a *presupposition* of social life, and one that is so basic that without it we could not even have an individual human consciousness in ourselves. In other words, we know that other people in general have minds, as directly and certainly as we know it of ourselves.

But how do we have this relationship with other people? One of its great instruments is language. In particular cases we judge what people are thinking by what they say. And this has led some people to question the claim to direct knowledge of other people's minds by asserting that we do, after all, only know what is going on in them through their behaviour. Isn't talking a sort of behaviour?

True. And it is true also that language is almost our only clue to the *contents* of people's minds. But the point is that it is a kind of behaviour which, if it is to be significant for us, already presupposes that our minds are to some extent alike—that we mean roughly the same things by the same words. Language presupposes society and a realm of shared experience. Insofar as we ourselves do a great deal of our thinking in words, or concepts closely related to language, even our own private thoughts presuppose the society in which our minds have been formed, and carry with them the built-in assumption that other people can share the same kind of experience.

There is a sense, then, in which the question "How do we

know that other people think and feel as we do?" is an unreal one. We know it directly, and if we did not know it we should not know that we thought or felt ourselves.

When we ask the same question of Horace, the engineer, as we have seen, is tempted to answer in terms of Horace's behaviour. But this is not the only test. We may admit that Horace behaves like us in many respects, but deny that we can enter the same kind of relationship with him that we have with another human being. "He's very clever," we say disparagingly, "but he's only a machine. He isn't one of us." In other words, we don't value him as a human person; we don't recognise a kinship with him; he doesn't belong to that world of personal relationships which has made us what we are. Our puzzlement about him brings out into the open an element in human relationships which so far has not been mentioned—the element of respect.

We understand a machine best by a rigidly objective analysis of its mode of operation. We also need to know something about the intentions of its designer. We cannot say that we fully understand it until we know what it is meant to do. Such respect as we have for a machine is generally respect for the skill and ingenuity of the men who designed and constructed it.

We come to understand human beings in many different ways and on many different levels. For some purposes it is quite sufficient merely to analyse their mode of operation. But there are certain levels of understanding which are only possible to those who are prepared to approach other people with respect and sympathy, even with a touch of awe. There is a knowledge which comes, not by rigidly objective analysis, but by opening up to another person and allowing oneself to be changed. This is not scientific knowledge. But it is just as real and fundamental a part of our experience as the more humdrum data which are the ordinary stuff of scientific analysis.

Why do we respect human beings, and learn things through our respect, while we refuse the same kind of respect to machines? I believe the answer is ultimately religious. For

Christians every human being is "made in the image of God" and is a person "for whom Christ died." Therefore Christians are committed to a way of life which emphasises as much as possible the unique value of each individual. There is no way of proving that everyone is worthy of respect, except by seeing how this attitude fits into a general religious outlook. Similarly there may be no way of proving that certain computers ought not to be called human, and vice versa, except by seeing that human beings, whether they work like computers or not, have a unique status given them by God. To act on this belief, and to treat others with this kind of godly respect, is, as I have already said, to open up new depths of personal knowledge which carry their own conviction of truth. But the initial step is an act of religious faith. Note, however, that this is not faith in a mysterious something inside the human brain, which an engineer can never manufacture to put inside one of his machines. It is faith in the rightness of an attitude to adopt towards human beings, based on the belief that God values those human beings in a certain way. We may respect the performance of computers, and value them very highly indeed in terms of cash, but unless I am very much mistaken most people would regard godly respect as dangerous idolatry.

I have said nothing in this chapter about Christian belief in the soul. A discussion on the level of "Do computers and/or human beings have souls?" would have focused attention on the existence or otherwise of "the mysterious something in the human brain," which is just the sort of thing I have tried to avoid. My aim has been to show how by talking about minds and machines, and by investigating the roots of our uneasiness at extravagant claims made on behalf of the machine, we eventually find ourselves back at religion. But the religious questions which have emerged are genuinely religious ones: "Why do we value human beings?": not quasi-scientific questions about "mysterious somethings." And it is this first kind of question which Christian language about the soul is trying to answer, even though it is often treated as if it were an example

of the latter. Belief in the soul, in other words, expresses a
Christian's awareness that he can enter into relationship with
God, and his intention to treat himself and all men as uniquely
valued by God. It is an object of faith, not of scientific
knowledge, because it concerns our personal relationships and
our intentions; and these are spheres in which faith is not a
second-best road to knowledge; it is the only road there is.

If we choose to treat human beings like computers and
computers like human beings, it is difficult to think of any
watertight arguments which could dissuade us. There is the
practical objection that we might find the computers very much
more efficient at their jobs than we are at ours—and then the
question of who was master might cease to be merely whimsi-
cal. But presumably if we really believed that there was no
essential difference between men and machines, this is a conclusion we might welcome.

To say that the only defence against this sort of view is to
have faith in the value and possibilities of men, is not to be
obscurantist or escapist. It is to state the only conditions under
which it is possible to get close enough to men for their value
and the depths of their personal lives to become apparent. It is
to choose *not* to treat human beings like computers, and to
discover that experience vindicates the choice.

16

GENETIC CONTROL
AND THE FUTURE OF MAN

Theodosius Dobzhansky*

D oes natural selection continue to operate in modern mankind? Some scientists and popular writers have contended
that it does not. Warnings and prophesies of dire calamities have
been issued on this basis—mankind is headed for biological
decadence and even extinction. Indeed, suspension of natural
selection would be a serious matter. In the long run it would be
disastrous, if natural selection were not replaced by some other
agency, such as an artificial selection, capable of performing
some of the same functions as did natural selection. Here, then,
is a problem of utmost importance, surely one of the most serious ones that mankind has to face. It must be examined carefully, with a firm resolve to avoid hasty conclusions not warranted by the evidence available.

* Theodosius Dobzhansky, professor at the Rockefeller Institute in
New York, is one of the world's most distinguished biologists. He received the 1964 National Medal of Science for his work in human
genetics. Among his many scientific articles and books is Mankind
Evolving (1962). He contributed a chapter to Harlow Shapley, ed.,
Science Ponders Religion (1960). The selection below constitutes the
concluding pages of Heredity and the Nature of Man, copyright © 1964,
by Theodosius Dobzhansky. Reprinted by permission of Harcourt, Brace
& World, Inc.

ARE CULTURE AND NATURAL
SELECTION COMPATIBLE?

It is simply not true that natural selection has ceased to operate in the human species. To make this clear, let us ask ourselves how one could possibly do away with natural selection, if that were desirable. One theoretically possible, but not practically realizable, method would be to have every pair of parents produce the same number of children, all these children without exception to survive, to marry, and again to produce the same number of progeny. Another, and equally fantastic, way to abolish natural selection would be to have the number of children that a couple may produce determined by drawing lots, so that the fertility of the parents would in no way depend on their genes, to have all children survive to maturity, and then either all to marry, or some, chosen by lot, to remain unmarried. Surely nothing like this ever happened anywhere in recorded history.

Genes for amaurotic idiocy are still being eliminated by death, and those for achondroplasia by failure of some dwarfs to find mates. The problem is not whether natural selection still operates, for surely it does. In a way, the problem is a more serious one—whether or not the selection is now doing what we, men, consider good and desirable. Natural selection certainly does not work at present as it did in the man of the Stone Age or in precivilized societies. This is both inevitable and beneficial. Civilized environments present challenges utterly different from those of the environments of the past, and we wish to be fit to live in our present environments, not in those of the Middle Ages or of the Stone Age.

It is certainly true that normalizing selection has become relaxed in human populations with respect to some undesirable mutant genes. Some hereditary diseases can be "cured" by medical or surgical treatment. An infant with retinoblastoma may have his life saved by surgical removal of the afflicted eye;

galactosemia is not fatal if the galactose is removed from the diet; acrodermatitis enteropatica is cured by a special drug; diabetes mellitus by insulin; myopia by wearing properly made glasses. In short, medicine, hygiene, and civilized conditions save many lives that would otherwise be cut short. This situation is here to stay, or to develop further when the medical sciences learn to control many now "incurable" genetically conditioned defects. Nobody in his right mind would want it to be otherwise.

Unless persons who know that they are carriers of genetic defects refrain from having children, they pass the defective genes to their progenies. The lives saved will thus engender new lives which will stand in need of being saved in the generations to come. The numbers of genetically more or less gravely incapacitated persons will then grow from generation to generation. This is so because the mutation process will continue to add defective genes at the same rate it always did, or even at still higher rates if the mutagenic radiations and other mutagens are not controlled. It is a depressing thought that we are helping the ailing, the lame, and the deformed only to make our descendants more ailing, more lame, and more deformed. Here, then, is a dilemma—if we enable the weak and the deformed to live and to propagate their kind, we face the prospect of a genetic twilight; but if we let them die or suffer when we can save or help them, we face the certainty of a moral twilight.

There is no easy escape from this dilemma. The problem of controlling and guiding human evolution has no single or simple solution. But neither is it hopelessly insoluble. Each genetic condition will have to be considered on its own merits, since it is certain that the measures taken for different conditions will not be the same. A few examples will make clear why this is so. The surgical treatment of retinoblastoma involves removal of the afflicted eyes, which leaves the person blind. Having retinoblastoma more widespread than it is, no doubt, is undesirable. Education that would make people familiar with elementary genetics and biology may be a real help here; it is perhaps not excessively optimistic to hope that a person who is blind because of retinoblastoma, and who knows that his progeny is liable to inherit his defect, may draw the proper conclusion from this knowledge and refrain from having children. Genetic counseling, when individual persons or couples seek and receive advice from competent physicians or specialists in human genetics, can also play an important role. Apart from being informed about the risks and the odds of the appearance of undesirable genetic traits in the progeny, people often stand in need of psychological support. They must be made to realize that being carriers of undesirable genes need not lead to feelings of guilt or of shame. Genetic counseling in so-called heredity clinics is becoming more and more widespread in civilized countries.

To be sure, different persons will not always reach the same decision on the basis of the same facts. Is it, for example, such hard luck to be an achondroplastic dwarf that the risk of having an achondroplastic child must always be avoided? And what about diabetes mellitus, a condition already so widespread, especially if the manifestations of this genetic defect can be reasonably well kept under control by insulin treatment? Finally, with respect to myopia, only fanatics would urge that all myopics should be sterilized or otherwise prevented from having children. Our society can probably stand having myopia become somewhat more widespread than it is now; the remedy is not sterilization, but provisions for more pairs of glasses to be manufactured.

The relaxation of normalizing natural selection with respect to some traits has been so much written and talked about that one should be reminded that there is also the reverse side of this coin. With respect to other traits, normalizing selection is not less, but more rigid in civilized than in primitive man. A dominant gene, which is not rare in the white population of South Africa, produces so-called porphyria, a condition that used to have little effect on the survival or fertility of its carriers. The porphyrics are, however, highly sensitive to the effects of barbiturates, and may be paralyzed and die as a result of medical treatments beneficial to nonporphyrics. Another gene, causing a deficiency of a certain enzyme in the blood (glucose-6-phosphate dehydrogenase, abbreviated G6PD), is rather widespread in some populations living in malarial countries. There is good reason to suppose that it was useful, because it conferred some resistance to malaria. Certain drugs, such as primaquine and sulfonamides, induce, however, a dangerous anemia in persons with this gene. These persons also suffer a serious illness, called favism, after a meal of fresh fava beans, which are eaten by persons free of this gene without any unpleasant consequences. Favism has long been known, but its dependence on the gene for the enzyme deficiency has been discovered only recently.

Considering mankind as a whole, the above genetic traits are not very common and therefore not very important. It may be otherwise with genes that confer resistance to, or predispose toward, nervous breakdown and nervous disorders. It is at least possible that the selection for such resistance has become more rigorous in technologically advanced societies than it was under more primitive, or, if you wish, more "natural" conditions. The life of Stone Age man, or, for that matter, of a peasant tilling the soil, was not free of stresses and worries. These stresses were, however, of kinds different from those to which we are exposed, and it is at least possible that the genes that confer resistance to them are not the same.

I do not wish to be understood as maintaining that the genetic future of mankind is safe and need not cause any concern. Above all, it should be realized that not enough is known about this tremendous problem. Genetics in general, and genetics of man in particular, are in urgent need of more research. For if natural selection does not function as man wishes that it would, then remedial measures must be taken. Natural selection must be replaced by eugenical artificial selection. This idea constitutes the sound core of eugenics, the applied science of human betterment.

Negative and positive eugenics can be distinguished. The

former seeks methods to discourage the spread of undesirable genes, and the latter to encourage the spread of desirable ones. Unfortunately, the idea of eugenics suffered grievous harm at the hands of its overenthusiastic supporters. Especially between 1900 and 1930, some partisans of eugenics were making rash promises, such as that all social ills would disappear within a few generations if their pet programs were to be adopted. Eugenics was compromised even more badly when for a period of about a third of a century it was captured by people who wanted it to become a pseudo-scientific basis of a reactionary political philosophy. It is to be hoped that a more scientific eugenics will overcome this reputation.

The eugenical programs advanced in recent years by some eminent scientists may also be questioned. It has been proposed, for example, that the seminal fluid of superior men be collected and preserved in a frozen condition, so that it can be used, possibly for many years to come, for artificial insemination of women who will supposedly be happy to become mothers of children of superior sires. The proposal, in fact, goes far beyond this "modest" beginning. Techniques should be developed to obtain not only superior spermatozoa of males, but also egg cells of superior females. The finest egg cells will be combined with the choicest spermatozoa; the fertilized eggs will then be implanted to develop in the uteri of women who are not good enough to propagate their own genes, but nevertheless qualified to nurture the superior fetuses and the resulting infants and children. Further, techniques are to be invented to obtain fetuses from a tissue culture of body cells of superior individuals; this would guarantee the finest genetic endowment in the progeny.

Such programs remind one of the *Brave New World* utopia devised by Aldous Huxley as a warning against treating human beings as though they were mere automata. The objection against these programs is not only that they attempt to flout some of the emotions dearest to human beings. They also presume that we know far more than we actually do about what kinds of genetic endowments would be best for man to have, not only at present, but also in the remote future. It can show no lack of respect for the greatness of men like Darwin, Galileo, and Beethoven, to name only a few, to say that a world with many millions of Darwins, Galileos, or Beethovens may not be the best possible world.

OUTLOOK FOR THE FUTURE

It is an error to think that the progress of mankind would be safe and irresistible if only natural selection were permitted to operate unobstructed by civilization. Natural selection does not guarantee even the survival of the species, let alone its improvement. Dinosaurs became extinct despite their evolution having been piloted by natural selection quite unhampered by culture. Natural selection is automatic, mechanical, blind. It brings about genetic changes that often, though not always, appear to be purposeful, furthering the survival and opposing the extinction of the species. And yet, natural selection has no purpose. Only man can have purposes.

Man, if he so chooses, may introduce his purposes into his evolution. Man's biological predicament is not that natural selection has ceased to act; it is that the selection may not be doing what we wish it to do. Man is the sole product of evolution who has achieved the knowledge that he came into this universe out of animality by means of evolution. He may choose to direct his evolution toward the attainment of the purposes he regards as good, or which he believes to represent the will of the Creator.

The crux of the matter is evidently what purposes, aims, or goals we should choose to strive for. Let us not delude ourselves with easy answers. One such answer is that a superior knowledge of human biology would make it unmistakable which plan is the best and should be followed. Another is that biological evolution has itself implanted in man ethical ideas and inclinations favorable for this evolution's continued progress. Now, I would be among the last to doubt that biology sheds some light on human nature; but for planning even the biological evolution of mankind, let alone its cultural evolution, biology is palpably insufficient.

Some biologists, among whom Julian Huxley is probably the most famous modern representative, thought that man's discrimination between good and evil is a product of biological evolution. Our ethics are built by past natural selection as a part of our biological nature. This is too much to claim for evolution. As C. H. Waddington neatly puts it, what evolution has done is to make us "ethicizing beings" and "authority acceptors," especially in childhood. Just as our genes determine our ability to speak but not what we shall say, so the ethical principles we accept come not from our biological, but from our cultural inheritance. Man's biological evolution has produced an organic basis for his cultural evolution. It is in order to serve as the foundation for man's cultural advancement that man's biological nature must be not only maintained but, if possible, improved and ennobled. In planning human evolution, including biological evolution, biology must be guided by man's spiritual and cultural heritage. Religion, philosophy, art, man's entire accumulated wisdom and experience are here indispensable.

Human evolution has forced mankind to a crossroad from which there is no turning back and no escape. Our animal past is irretrievably lost—we could not go back to it even if we wished to. The choice is between a twilight, cultural as well as biological, or a progressive adaptation of man's genes to his culture, and of man's culture to his genes. I am optimistic enough to hope that the right choices will be achieved before it is too late. Some people call our age the Age of Anxiety, and this puts optimism in need of justification. I am an optimist because I know that mankind, the living world, and the whole universe have evolved and are evolving. Look into yourself and look at the world around you. Everywhere there is a tremendous amount of ugliness as well as of beauty, much that is good and admirable and a lot that is evil and horrible. My point is that the knowledge that we are evolving bestows hope. Whether one feels that beauty and good or that ugliness and evil predominate in the world, one knows that this world was not created all at once, fixed and unchangeable forever. Creation is not an event, but a process, not complete but continuing. Progress and betterment are by no means guaranteed or vouchsafed in evolution. However, man may strive to bring them about, and this striving is what gives meaning and dignity to human life, individually and collectively. So, let me repeat, evolution bestows hope.

17

LIFE ON OTHER PLANETS

W. Burnet Easton, Jr.*

A few years ago *The New Yorker* magazine carried a cartoon in which a group of clergymen was lined up on one side of a huge table. On the other side was a group of Air Force officers, obviously very high brass. A general was speaking to the clergymen, and the caption underneath read, "We have just received a message from one of our spaceships which we think will interest you gentlemen." In its humorous way that cartoon points up perhaps the most far-reaching and profound revolution of the twentieth century: the possibility—many would say the probability —that there is intelligent life on other worlds in the universe.

It is not exactly a new idea. Science fiction has been making hay of such speculations for a long time. In 1940, Spencer Jones, British Astronomer Royal, published a book, *Life on Other Worlds,* which cautiously suggested the possibility. More recently there have been scores of articles in both scientific and

---

* W. B. Easton has taught at Lawrence College and Park College, and is currently Professor of Theology at Bloomfield College in New Jersey. Among his articles and books are The Faith of a Protestant *(1946) and* Basic Christian Beliefs *(1958). He describes himself as "a Christian existentialist of more or less neo-orthodox persuasion." In the following article he discusses the theological significance of recent speculations about intelligent life on other worlds.*

popular journals, debating and mostly supporting the idea.[1] Assuming that the laws of the universe are uniform, the conditions which could produce life as we know it are indeed exceedingly limited. But the stars are so numerous that astronomers estimate that if only one star in a million has a planetary system, and if in turn only one planet in a million fulfills the necessary conditions for life, there would still be 100,000,000 planets suitable for life. Several theories have been proposed as to how life might arise from nonliving molecules on such planets. Evolutionary history elsewhere perhaps did not even remotely resemble that on planet earth, but many biologists argue that various kinds of organisms would have been produced. A space flight to Mars will yield evidence on this question, though probably only lower forms of life could survive its extremes of temperature. The majority of experts now say that the most plausible assumptions—though admittedly speculative—favor the hypothesis that there are sentient and conscious organisms on other solar systems. Scientists have been taking this possibility seriously enough to experiment with devices for receiving any messages sent out by intelligent beings who might be on planets around certain of the nearer stars. Under the direction of Dr. Otto Struve, the National Radio-Astronomy Observatory at Green Bank, West Virginia, has already set up such a listening post.

All of this is fairly common knowledge, but only recently have some people awakened to the revolutionary implications involved. Dr. Struve has stated the matter succinctly. In one of the Karl Taylor Compton lectures at M.I.T. in 1959, after speaking of the Copernican revolution (which proved that the earth is not the center of the universe) and the Trumpler revolution (which proved that the sun is not the center of the Milky Way), he went on, "The third [revolution] is occurring now, and whether we want it or not, we must be part of it. It is the revolution embodied in the question, 'Are we alone in the

[1] See, for example, Harlow Shapley, *Of Stars and Men* (Boston: Beacon Press, 1958).

universe?' Instinctively we think of mankind as something unique, something that exists only on earth; and all the wonders of the universe are intended for *our* benefit and enjoyment." But now it appears likely that we are not alone.

Intellectually we accept this as we do so many new scientific developments we hear about; yet emotionally, psychologically, and religiously, if we think about it, it can be quite a shock. None of the previous revolutions, radical though they seemed at the time, seriously challenged man's unique and special position in the universe. In spite of the new knowledge they brought, man was still the only knower, he was still the unique child of God, different from and superior to everything else in creation. Now astronomers are suggesting, with strong theoretical cogency, that man on this earth may not be particularly unique —in fact he may be a rather inferior specimen of intelligent being; in the total cosmos there may be other intelligent beings far superior to us intellectually, culturally, and spiritually.

In strictly immediate practical terms this is not an important issue. The nearest star is about four and one-half light years away. Assuming that there is a planet around it supporting life (a very remote chance) it would take nine or ten years to get one signal back and forth at the speed of light. To establish meaningful communication would take generations. However, the possibility that there may be intelligent life on other worlds does raise questions for Christian faith.

It does not raise questions for the theist about a God of *some sort*. If God is the ultimate Creator, "the Ground of Existence or Being" (Tillich), or "the Holy Being, prior to all being who lets being be" (Macquarrie), then, as the astronomer Herschel once observed, "If one world glorifies God, more worlds glorify him all the more." Our understanding of God as Creator may be greatly expanded, but the new astronomy does not in principle change the one given in the Bible. The possibility, however, of more highly developed creatures than ourselves in the universe, if confirmed, does raise questions about man's relationship to